The Future of the Past

THE FUTURE
OF
THE PAST

C. VANN WOODWARD

New York   Oxford
OXFORD UNIVERSITY PRESS
1989

OXFORD UNIVERSITY PRESS

Oxford   New York   Toronto
Delhi   Bombay   Calcutta   Madras   Karachi
Petaling Jaya   Singapore   Hong Kong   Tokyo
Nairobi   Dar es Salaam   Cape Town
Melbourne   Auckland

and associated companies in
Berlin   Ibadan

Published by Oxford University Press, Inc.,
200 Madison Avenue, New York, New York 10016

Oxford is a registered trademark of Oxford University Press

Library of Congress Cataloging-in-Publication Data
Woodward, C. Vann (Comer Vann), 1908–
The future of the past : historical writings / C. Vann Woodward.
p.   cm.   ISBN 0–19–505744–9
1. United States—History.   2. Southern States—History.
3. United States—Race relations.   I. Title.
E175.5.W66A2   1989   973–dc20   89–9341   CIP

2 4 6 8 9 7 5 3 1
Printed in the United States of America
on acid-free paper

Contents

Introduction

Keeping the present in reasonable touch with the past is one of the tasks historians feel obliged to take on, but one they can never hope to keep up with. For one thing the passage of time is forever putting distance between past and present and increasing the obscurity of the past. Another thing complicating this task of the historian is the eagerness of so many volunteers who would not only assist him but perhaps take over entirely. These include writers of fiction and drama and the makers of film and television programs. It is from them more than from historians that the public mainly receives whatever conceptions, impressions, fantasies, and delusions it may entertain about the past.

Historians as well as novelists, playwrights, film makers, and television producers keep very much in mind the public and its needs, expectations, and tastes—even its biases, vanities, and nostalgias. In accommodating these demands and weaknesses of the public, however, historians as compared with their competitors are at some considerable disadvantage. Not that historians are above such considerations, nor that they do not at times make concessions to them. But beyond certain fairly well-defined limits they venture at peril to their reputations and in defiance of basic rules of their craft. One of the rules inhibits out-and-out invention of past events and persons. But neither by this nor by numerous other rules of the craft do competing purveyors of the past feel strictly bound.

The restraints that prevent historians from entering this competition should not lead them to dismiss the foibles, fantasies,

and expectations of the laity as being of no concern to them. I
have suggested that they should be well aware of the demands
they disappoint, whether those of a naive laity or a designing
politician, while pursuing the ends they can legitimately meet.
Among the laity's manipulations of history are efforts to improve,
sanitize, gentrify, idealize, or sanctify the past; or, on the other
hand, to discredit, defame, denigrate, or even to blot out portions
of it. The more positive motives behind manipulations of the
past include desires to enhance lineage, pedigree, national pride,
or status by means of ennobling the past. Or the purpose might
be to lend the past a pedagogical role and employ it to teach
"lessons" to the present, shame modern evil-doers, provide a
heritage to live up to, or furnish solace for shortcomings. Deni-
gration of the past, on the other hand, can serve to expunge or
dismiss a shameful heritage, discredit an opponent or rival, or
stress the depravity of ruling or subordinate classes. Some manipulations of the past have no more sinister purpose than to
confer glamor, elegance, picturesqueness, "quaintness" upon objects of nostalgia, to enhance the enchantments of decay. Once
a monopoly of the privileged few, nostalgia has been democra-
tized, so that millions now seek roots and ancestors and antiques,
and throng historic houses and sites in quest of "heritage."

The author of the most thoughtful study of this neglected
field, David Lowenthal, to whom I acknowledge indebtedness,
takes issue with the thesis of J. H. Plumb in *The Death of the
Past* that industrial society "does not need the past," and requires
"no sanctions in the past and no roots in it." Granting that the
yearning for a past creates all sorts of mischief, Lowenthal nevertheless maintains that, "Far from being of less consequence, the
past seems to matter more and more. . . ." In his view the past
not only enjoys a thriving if unruly and nondescript present but
a future as well. As he puts it, "To be is to have been, and to
project our messy, malleable past into our unknown future."
The consequences, in his opinion, are by no means all deplorable: "To know that we are simply the ephemeral lessees of agelong hopes and dreams that have animated generations of en-

deavour helps us to secure, if not to rejoice in, our place in the scheme of things."*

In the pages that follow I have tried to alert the craft of history, its servants and their public, to expectations, opportunities, and problems of the present and to the influences of the present and future upon the past, relationships that are not normally or consciously acknowledged. Even more than they once did, historians confine their services very largely to the work of producing authentic accounts of segments of the past based on evidence that passes rigorous tests for reliability. Granted that this is and should remain their basic obligation and that nothing should divert them from it or be given place over it, that is not enough. Limited to that, historians wind up talking to each other or to themselves. They forget, in their absorption with the past, that it is the quick and not the dead they are addressing. The dead, of course, could not care less, and the quick tend to lose interest if they are not themselves addressed.

Adequate awareness of a public that is addressed requires some degree of sensitivity to its interests and expectations, even some of its more irrational ones. And this not with the purpose of pandering to absurd or impossible demands, but with the need of knowing what wishes are being disappointed and how best to gain and hold attention. At an elementary level, it would be well to be alerted if very large numbers of one's audience began picking up hat and coat and silently departing. That is precisely what has been happening during the last twenty years in that presumably captive audience of academic historians, the students. They have been dropping history in droves and are not coming back, except in a few elite institutions and there only in the last few years, though in impressive numbers.

At another level it is worth pondering what might explain the low esteem to which historians and their current work fell for

---

* David Lowenthal, *The Past Is a Foreign Country* (Cambridge, England, 1985), xxv, 331–40, 364–65; C. Vann Woodward, essay review of the Lowenthal book, *History and Theory*, XXXVI (1987), 346–52; J. H. Plumb, *The Death of the Past* (Boston, 1970), 14.

some years in the intellectual community at large, a community in which they had once enjoyed high place and appreciation. Related to that is the question of how it was that those who currently practice this ancient craft fell so far out of touch with the deeper concerns and temper of their time that they seemed unable to contribute much of worth to the ongoing intellectual dialogue. That was left largely to philosophers, theologians, and scientists, some of whom came to regard the work of contemporary historians as irrelevant, if not worse. With these sister disciplines history once enjoyed stimulating and regular exchange of ideas, relations that should be restored, with history's full participation in the dialogue.

Another traditional affiliation of history that has of late been neglected, broken off, or mutually alienated is that with creative literature and literary criticism. The very concept of historians as men of letters has come to evoke disdain on the one side and derision on the other. That alienation would seem especially unnecessary, not to say unfortunate, in view of the large range of concerns the two kinds of writers share in their human subject matter and their problems of craftsmanship. Reconciliation should not, and need not, come at the cost of unacceptable concessions to the handful of novelists who would blur or deny any real distinction between history and fiction. Or any concession to another handful who claim that fiction can do history better. Plenty of common ground remains without these concessions. Henry Adams was not merely a contemporary and friend of Henry James, but a fellow craftsman who treated in history a theme James returned to repeatedly in fiction—encounters of American innocence with Old World wiles. Adams also shared more than contemporaneity with Count Leo Tolstoy, for he treated the same period of Napoleonic wars in his history that Tolstoy treated in his fiction—and with a very similar philosophy of history and view of the role of heroes and leaders in the shaping of historical events. Both kinds of writers stand to gain by a restoration of relations.

One cause of confusion about history in the intellectual community—even among historians themselves—is the question of whether it is an art or a science. The assumption behind the question is that it has to be the one thing or the other and cannot pretend to be both—or some *tertium quid* that is neither. Many modern historians share this assumption. I do not. I lean rather to the *tertium quid* idea and think of history as a "third something." That goes without denying, however, that good history may, and often must, contain both science and art. Any craft devoted to the analysis and understanding of human behavior, whether in the past or the present, without seeking what help it can get from the modern social and behavioral sciences deserves to be ignored. But on the other hand, any craft that normally sets forth its conclusions in prose under the assumption that this can be done wholly without resort to art is proceeding with an innocence that handicaps the whole enterprise.

The popular conception of history, too often shared by historians themselves, is that it is a record and historians are the keepers. This assigns the keepers an essentially passive role and assumes that there is nothing to be done about what they record since it has already happened anyway, that it therefore neither affects nor is affected by the present or the future. History thus conceived is a sort of verbal museum to preserve and display worthy relics of the past. A moment's reflection on the place history presently occupies in the politics and prospects of current regimes in Russia, China, Austria, and West Germany will dispel all thought of history confined to a passive role. The fate of ideologies, empires, and rulers hangs on historical revelations and revisions. Figures regarded as non-persons and long expunged from history books suddenly reappear. Heroes become villains and villains heroes. Examinations are postponed in the schools while textbooks are rewritten. Only West Germany has had the clear-eyed leadership in coping with the past that its President Richard von Weizsäcker provided. When they sought to see President Reagan's gesture at Bitburg as an act of absolution, Weizsäcker told his fellow citizens, "Anyone who closes his eyes to the past is blind to the present. Whoever refuses to remember the inhumanity is prone to new risks of infection."

To illustrate the impact of past upon present and present

upon past, the constant interaction between them, and their combined influence upon the future I have turned to world events since the Second World War. These events brought to a simultaneous end an age of free security in America, an age of weaponry and warfare, and a period of European domination in world affairs. All these changes profoundly affect the way we read our past and view our future. To illustrate the active role historians can play in widening our historical horizons I have offered several examples of comparative history. These serve to lift understanding of past experiences out of national confines and broaden perspective by placing it in wider context.

The reader will doubtless note the frequency with which the American South serves in the discussions that follow as a point of departure or reference or a source of illustration and comparison. The reason for this is that the history of the South has been the author's major field of study and writing throughout a long career. I am the less disposed to apologize for the use I make of this parochial field of interest the more I have talked with colleagues about the historical themes treated here. They too have their special fields, some of them broader, some narrower in geographic area or scope of time than my own. These differences diminish in importance the broader the historical themes under discussion become. The concentration of my colleague Donald Kagan on the history of Athens in the fifth century B.C. has not impaired our exchange of views on these matters; nor has George W. Pierson's special interest in Alexis de Toqueville and in the history of Yale; nor have Peter Gay's preoccupations with the Enlightenment and with Sigmund Freud. I mention them all with gratitude, and especially Peter Gay for reading and criticizing much of the book in manuscript.

Time present and time past
Are both perhaps present in time future,
And time future contained in time past.

T. S. ELIOT, "Burnt Norton"

I

THINKING
AHEAD

The papers in this section all bear marks of the time in which they were written, the troubled times of the so-called sixties, the decade that actually overlapped the seventies. That these pieces should be grouped under a title suggesting prophecy and the future may seem paradoxical. Yet when they were written the future was a major concern of each and all, although a very cloudy future, dimly perceived. Misperceptions were inevitable, and the future, in any case, is not an entirely legitimate field for historical generalization. By now, however, enough time time should have passed, and enough of the future come to pass, to test the worth of these efforts.

The profession of history—particularly American history, the field of Southern history, and the special subject of Afro-American history—were all then passing through a critical period of change. Crises among historians coincided with crises in national politics, national culture, national race relations, and crises in the universities. In all of these areas a generational disjuncture set youth at odds with their elders, a rupture experienced most keenly in academic life. The young had persuaded themselves there was no precedent for their generation, no "relevance" for them in history, and no need for a past. Black youth were determined to have an entirely new history, one that challenged not only white authority but parental authority as well. Generational as well as ideological and regional ruptures also occurred in views of the South's past.

The jarring disjunctures between old and new, between tradition and innovation in affairs cultural, political, and racial were bound to be reflected in the way we viewed, wrote, taught, and interpreted history and thought about the past. The three papers that follow were efforts to find ways of accommodating innovation to tradition, of reconciling youth to precedent, of locating in the present valid connections with the past, and of mapping the future with paths that the past can project and possibly illuminate.

1

The Future
of the Past

The occasion for this paper was an annual convention of the American Historical Association, and the paper was the presidential address to its members convened at Washington on December 29, 1969. Circumstances of the hour and place were hardly ideal for the purpose at hand. Instead of the handful that normally attended the business meeting of the Association, which this time was to be held immediately after my address, some sixteen hundred turned out—not to hear my words but to assure themselves of seats (and votes) in the business (and politics) that was to follow—eventually to continue with unscheduled extensions of the session into the small hours of the next morning. On the agenda were issues not of the remote past but of the explosive present. They included motions that would commit historians to resolutions concerning war and peace, national policies (domestic and foreign) dealing mainly with Vietnam and black rights—actions that if taken would thoroughly politicize the learned body.

The general proceedings were enlivened by unanticipated events and interventions. My speech was delayed by an unceremonious possession of the podium by three members to announce a "black caucus" then in session. Other caucuses convened and disbanded in preparation for the business meeting

*to follow, during the long hours of which verbal assaults were
to give way to physical struggles for microphones stationed on
the floor. While my remarks were received with relative patience before the political struggle began, they are best read
now with the background noises in mind. Commenting on the
"bitterly contentious meeting," The New Republic observed
that "C. Vann Woodward . . . presided over the cacophony
with the puzzled air of a kindly Southern judge at a hearing
for psychiatric commitment."*

THE FORTUNES AND VITALITIES of the learned disciplines, history as well as the others, vary considerably from period to period.
Decades of confidence and fulfillment are followed by eras of
hesitation and marking time. The relative status and prestige of
the disciplines change accordingly. Without attempting to explain the phenomenon, I would contend that the profession of
history in America enjoyed a period of exceptional felicity, in
fact, something of a boom period, during the two decades following the Second World War.

This estimate is not based on an assessment of the quality
and distinction of the scholarship of that period, though they are
surely not inconsiderable. It is based, rather, on evidence indicat-
ing a sense of corporate well-being, justified or not, that pervaded
the guild in those years. Among the components of felicity were
some that were widely shared in the academic world: the rising
status of college professors in general, for example, and a revived
prestige of the humanities. But apart from these shared advantages were others peculiar to the professional historian. They included emancipation from some old feelings of inferiority. One
sense of inferiority derived from doubts about the validity of
historical knowledge, another from relations between history and
other disciplines, and a third from relations between the historian
and his public, both academic and nonacademic. Insecurities in
each of these areas had haunted historians for years. But after the
Second World War, a rough consensus on the validity of historical knowledge restored confidence in the integrity of the craft.

Relations with sister disciplines, as well as status and prestige among them, improved and strengthened the position of history in American academic life. Beyond the academic walls professional historians began for the first time to capture a reading public to rival that of the amateurs. The substance of things hoped for materialized in the form of larger enrollments, higher salaries, and more substantial royalty checks. But before these tangible rewards, and more important, came the apparent solution of a series of intellectual problems within the guild.[1]

"Solution" is perhaps too strong a word. American historians in the postwar years were more disposed to shrug off than to solve abstruse problems of theory. Unaccustomed to theoretical argument and lagging a generation behind European thought on such problems, they were impatient with these subtleties. More than anything else they wanted to break out of the defensive and subservient position in which they had been cornered. The relativists of the profession in the prewar years had disputed the historians' claim to objectivity. Social scientists, with whom historians had eagerly sought alliance in earlier years, had become patronizing and sometimes contemptuous toward historical scholarship. Historical relativism combined with social science to imprison the historian in the contemporary world and to shift his allegiance and his attention from the past to the present. A powerful school of progressive historians demanded that history be written in accordance with some vision of the future. Critics not only called the integrity of the past in question and subordinated the past to concern for the pressent and the future, but they impugned the validity of historical knowledge itself and relegated the profession devoted to its study to an inferior status among the disciplines. It was no wonder that a leading historian could complain in 1947 of "the confusions in which most historical students have been tossing."[2] The morale of the guild and the self-esteem and confidence of its members were in disarray,

---

[1] The best history of the profession in America during this period is John Higham *et al.*, *History: The Development of Historical Studies in the United States* (Englewood Cliffs, N.J., 1965).
[2] Frederic C. Lane, in *Journal of Economic History*, VII (May 1947), 83.

and some despaired of the beleaguered and defenseless plight of
the craft.

A spirited and somewhat combative reaction soon emerged
among historians. Putting aside niceties of consistency, they began to assert that if physicists could live with relativity, historians
could live with relativism. If relativism was unavoidable, they
would opt for something they imperiously called "objective relativism." Granting the impossibility of certainty, they maintained
that history was "a quest for wisdom instead of a quest for certainty."[3] If the alliance with social sciences were to continue, it
must be on terms of equality and not subservience. Roy F.
Nichols caught the new mood in "a declaration of intellectual
independence" published in the fall of 1948. "History is not art,
science, or literature," he insisted,

> it is *sui generis*. It is a division of knowledge with its own char-
> acter and methods. . . . It is time for historians to be more
> positive about their functions, their objectives, and their meth-
> ods. It is time to stop living by other people's wits, by franti-
> cally seeking to adopt other people's jargon, by humbly seeking
> to be recognized as faithful and reasonably satisfactory hand-
> maids worthy of Thursday afternoons and alternate Sundays
> on which to do what they really wish.

Nichols wanted to release history from both "the clutches of
heedless optimism" and "the slavery of present-mindedness," the
myth of the future as well as imprisonment in the present.[4]

The call for autonomy struck a responsive chord among historians. Just as the founding fathers of the scientific school had
felt it necessary to assert their independence from literature and
philosophy, and their successors from nineteenth-century science,
so a declaration of independence from the social sciences was
now in order. Thus, as John Higham observes, "the outlook of
the professional historian had come full circle," and in the pro-

---

[3] Social Science Research Council, *The Social Sciences in Historical
Study* (New York, 1954), 1–17.
     [4] Roy F. Nichols, "Postwar Reorientation of Historical Thinking," *Ameri-
can Historical Review*, LIV (Oct. 1948), 78–89.

cess "reconstituted the historian's autonomous identity."[5] Autonomy did not preclude alliances on more equal terms, however, and those with the social sciences became more cordial. There were many who wished to keep a foot in both camps. H. Stuart Hughes, for one, took "pride in the mediating character" of history, its "half-scientific, half-artistic nature," and thought that "the historian's supreme technical virtuosity lies in fusing the new method of social and psychological analysis with his traditional storytelling function."[6] Historians thus claimed the best of both worlds. They revived romantic notions such as intuition, insight, empathy, and imagination and proposed at the same time to use them as freely as they did scientific concepts of analysis. They staked out neutral territory and posed not only as mediators between past and present but as conciliators between the "two cultures" and friendly patrons of the third, the social sciences. It was, all things considered, rather high ground that they took and withal a rather privileged position that they claimed.

For a time the historian was fortunate in attracting philosophers and logicians (to whose dialogues about history he was normally deaf) willing to support the claim of historical autonomy and to defend the craft from the philosophical attack on historical explanation.[7] It was also gratifying to find theologians (another group to whom historians were usually deaf) of the stature of Reinhold Niebuhr who took historians seriously and employed their findings respectfully.[8] There were even social scientists who complained of the "a-historical character" of behavioral studies and conceived of lessons to be learned from the historian.[9] Historians assured each other that Western culture

[5] Higham *et al.*, *History*, 135.

[6] H. Stuart Hughes, *History as Art and as Science: Twin Vistas on the Past* (New York, 1964), 3, 77; see also Henry Steele Commager, *The Nature and Study of History* (Columbus, Ohio, 1965).

[7] William H. Dray, *Laws and Explanation in History* (London, 1957), and *Philosophical Analysis and History*, ed. *id.* (New York, 1961), esp. the essays by Sir Isaiah Berlin, W. H. Walsh, J. A. Passmore, Alan Donagan, and Louis O. Mink.

[8] Reinhold Niebuhr, *The Irony of American History* (New York, 1952).

[9] Robert A. Dahl, "The Behavioral Approach," *American Political Science Review*, LV (Dec. 1961), 771.

was "the historical culture par excellence," that the present was "the most historically minded of all ages," that historical consciousness was its distinguishing characteristic. They quoted Friedrich Meinecke as calling this "the greatest spiritual revolution which Western thought has undergone" in modern times, and Johan Huizinga as saying that "historical thinking has entered our very blood."[10] By 1965 Higham could note in his admirable history of the profession a shedding of old inferiority feelings, a quickening of vitality, a revival of confidence, and a "restoration of intellectual self-respect that has taken place since 1945."[11]

In addition to the new confidence in their calling, American historians whose subject was American history discovered among themselves as well as their public a gratifying shift in attitude toward their field of study. In his presidential address to the American Historical Association in 1950, Samuel Eliot Morison noted with satisfaction "a decided change of attitude toward our past, a friendly, almost affectionate attitude, as contrasted with the cynical, almost hateful one of young intellectuals" in earlier years.[12] The new friendliness and affection toward the American past found confirmation in other presidential addresses and in autobiographies by historians prominent in the period. "For the student of United States history," wrote the late Arthur M. Schlesinger, "there is in addition the special joy of discovery and understanding how one's own people have reached their present condition; why . . . we have come to behave like Americans," and how we have "held up a lamp to Europe and, more recently, to Asia and Africa."[13] Recent autobiographies of other American historians similarly reflect nostalgic affection for the American

[10] E. H. Carr, *What Is History?* (London, 1961), 129; John Luckacs, *Historical Consciousness, or the Remembered Past* (New York, 1968), 18, 23.
[11] Higham *et al.*, *History*, 132–37.
[12] Samuel Eliot Morison, "Faith of a Historian," *American Historical Review*, LVI (Jan. 1951), 272; see also Richard Hofstadter, *The Progressive Historians: Turner, Beard, and Parrington* (New York, 1968), 92.
[13] Arthur M. Schlesinger, *In Retrospect: The History of a Historian* (New York, 1963), 203.

past, reconciliation with the present, and optimism about the future.[14]

A "special joy" in discovering how Americans reached their present condition and came to behave like Americans would seem to imply a special satisfaction in the condition of Americans and the way Americans behave. And a friendly and affectionate identification of the present with the past suggests a genial compatibility between the two that bridges the gulf between generations, implies a vitality and relevance of traditional ways, and assumes a fundamentally benign continuity of institutions and ideas. It was essentially a conservative view of the past. The school of interpretation that renounced and succeeded the progressive school usually, though not invariably, found the friendly attitude toward the past congenial to its views.[15] These historians stressed consensus rather than conflict and emphasized stability and homogeneity rather than change and contrast. They dwelt rather nostalgically upon what was appealing or virtuous in the American past, and rarely on the darker, more violent, and tragic aspects of the national experience.

Whether the new attitude toward the American past or the rejuvenated confidence of the American history profession explains it or not, the fact is that history has enjoyed a boom period that coincides with these two developments in the profession. History stock was rising in American culture at large. The boom was most pronounced in the academic marketplace, but it was not confined to that world. It also penetrated the world of the publishers, and to some degree the worlds of the foundations, the intellectuals, even the politicians, not to mention a large and unsophisticated lay reading public that likes its history with colored illustrations. This picture admittedly runs counter to that painted in 1964 by a distinguished committee of the American Historical Association. Concerned particularly over what they felt to be

[14] John D. Hicks, *My Life with History* (Lincoln, Neb., 1968), 354; Roy F. Nichols, *A Historian's Progress* (New York, 1968), 299–300; Dexter Perkins, *Yield of the Years* (Boston, 1969), 204, 233, 235.
[15] Richard Hofstadter is certainly one exception.

neglect by the foundations, this committee complained that history was "too little honored," "too much taken for granted," and "consistently underestimated." But even they noted with sartisfaction that "history and English literature are the two most powerful major studies in many of our leading universities and colleges—and the prime elective studies too."[16]

Perhaps it would be well first to clear up some confusion about that not wholly captive nor altogether predictable market, the college student, graduate ad undergraduate. During the huge expansion in higher education that took place in the first half of this century, the numbers of students in both the humanities and the sciences increased enormously. But while the humanities as a whole and the natural sciences suffered a relative decline in the percentage of degrees granted, history consistently held its own in this respect.[17] English and foreign languages declined to about a quarter of their former relative strength; the natural sciences suffered smaller losses, while the social sciences scored rapid gains. In the meantime, from 1901 to 1953, history succeeded in maintaining a constant level. In the next sixteen years, down through 1968, all of these fields have enjoyed a relative increase in the percentage of degrees granted, but none so large as history and the language group, both of which nearly doubled the percentage they granted in 1953.[18] So much for numbers and percentages; quality is a more difficult matter. We are informed on good authority, however, that in the competitive recruitment of talent, history has been able to win to graduate study a larger percentage of seniors who distinguished themselves in that field than it once did.[19]

The more students, the more professors. The membership of the American Historical Association, stalled for some years before

[16] American Council of Learned Societies, *Report of the Commission on the Humanities* (New York, 1964), 114.

[17] W. David Maxwell, "A Methodological Hypothesis for the Plight of the Humanities," *American Association of University Professor Bulletin*, LIV (Spring 1968), 78–80.

[18] Paul L. Ward, "The Plight of the Humanities," *ibid.* (Autumn 1968), 397.

[19] Dexter Perkins and John L. Snell, *The Education of Historians in the United States* (New York, 1962), 38.

1953 at about five thousand, more than tripled in the next dozen years. Te prodigious increase in membership was matched by a proliferation of activities, staff members, committees, and publications. The growing size and the additional number of the Association's *Review* reflected in part the enormous increase in the number of history books written and the obligation to review them. The total number of history titles published in the United States in 1968 was three times the total for 1950.[20] The number of periodicals in the country devoted to history of all kinds, including popular, patriotic, and local, has almost doubled since 1946.[21] The responsiveness of the foundations to the appeal of historians, though still quite niggardly, multiplied sevenfold in five years.[22] In the 1960's two opposing candidates for President of the United States wrote, or at least published, history books of a sort with, in one case the presumed and in the other the explicitly avowed, intent of enhancing the appeal of the politician-authors as intellectuals.[23] And in two administrations of that decade, the White House "intellectual," a new adornment of the executive office, was a prominent American historian. Such were the emoluments, the bounties, and the bonuses of the great history boom.

Booms do not last forever, and it would now seem prudent to examine the prospects and portents of the recent one. In so doing I would try to avoid the role of alarmist. I am not charging

[20] *American Library Annual* (New York, 1950), 80; *Bowker Annual Library and Book Information* (New York, 1969), 36. Granted much imprecision about what constituted a "history" title, the number so designated increased from 516 in 1950 to 1,528 in 1968.

[21] *Ulrich's International Periodicals: A Classified Guide to a Selected List of Current Periodicals, Foreign and Domestic*, ed. Eileen Graves (New York, 1947–69). Sixty-six new journals were founded between 1947 and 1956.

[22] "Foundation Grants," *Foundation News* (Mar., Sept. 1963; Mar., Sept. 1968). This includes only grants over ten thousand dollars and does not include renewals or grants not reported to the *News*. It does include grants for restoration and preservation of historic sites. Grants increased from one million dollars in 1963 to seven million dollars in 1968, but they fell precipitantly to three million dolars in 1969. (*Ibid.* [Sept.–Oct. 1969].)

[23] John F. Kennedy, *Profiles in Courage* (New York, 1956); Richard M. Nixon, *Six Crises* (New York, 1962). In the preface of the latter work (p. xi), the author writes that his opponent has advised him that such a book "tends to elevate [the politician] in popular esteem to the respected status of an 'intellectual.'"

the profession at large with giddiness or complacency or delusions of grandeur—failings often characteristic of boom psychology. It is reassuring to remember that throughout this period of boom and bustle, inflated markets and popular attention, there have been some American historians who have gone about their self-assigned tasks of scholarship undeterred, drawing mainly on inner resources. The quality and importance of the work they have done will probably bear favorable comparison with the historical scholarship of any previous period. Granting all that, I do feel obliged, nevertheless, to report certain signs of trouble. They are confined mainly to three overlapping areas: the academic world, the intellectual community, and the profession itself.

Within the academy the conventional barometer of departmental fortunes (for what it is worth) is student patronage, and in significant quarters that barometer has been falling lately for history. Measured by percentage of degrees granted, as we have seen, history has for the last sixteen years enjoyed an unprecedented increase in students. This may well continue for some time in terms of national averages. But a sampling of indicators that lie back of the degree stage, a look at figures on course enrollments, departmental majors, and the attitudes of pre-college students would suggest a somewhat different prospect. A survey of the sixty-four American institutions that currently graduate the highest percentage of their students in arts and sciences as history majors (those with at least three times the national average) indicates that well over half of those responding, twenty-five out of forty-three, suffered a decline in student patronage in the last two years. In the minority group of eighteen that reported no significant change or actual increase of student interest fall most of the small denominational colleges in the oddly assorted sample thus defined. On the other hand heavy losses in undergraduate history course enrollment in the last two academic years, losses ranging from 27 to 34 percent, occurred at Harvard, Yale, Stanford, and Amherst. Among eastern institutions, Princeton, Brandeis, Smith, Swarthmore, Williams, Hamilton, Haverford, Georgetown, and Fordham reported substantial but smaller losses in their history courses. In other parts of the country, with a much smaller proportion of colleges graduating the specified percentage of history majors, several institutions of high quality included in the survey also reported declining student interest in history. Generalizations based on these findings are difficult to formulate and can be quite misleading. Several institutions cite local and temporary conditions to explain their losses. These changes, moreover, are too recent to provide any reliable projection for the future. They do occur, however, often in their most pronounced form, in some of the most sensitive zones of American academic life and can scarcely be dismissed as insignificant.[24]

More indicative about the future of the past and future student interest in history are the attitudes of the oncoming generation of college students. A recent poll shows that of the twenty-one subjects in their curriculum on which they were questioned, American high school students regarded history as the "most irrelevant."[25] The planners of their curriculums and the writers of their textbooks would seem to share the aversion of the students. Time and attention once devoted to history have rapidly given way to current affairs and social studies. Serving as a member of the California Statewide Social Sciences Study Committee, Charles Sellers reports that, "Virtually no one except the history professors on this large and representative committee saw much value in retaining history in the curriculum at all."[26]

The changing whims and cultural styles of college students and adolescents have recently become the subject of a massive literature of which I am not a master. The aversion to history may be a minor symptom of more arcane ailments. The monotonous recurrence of the word "relevance" in student parlance does,

[24] The decline in student patronage of history at Oxford and Cambridge Universities has also been sharp since the Second World War, but it was spread over a longer period. The comparisons in the American survey are between figures for 1966–1967 and 1968–1969.

[25] Poll by Louis Harris and Associates, Inc., of "100 schools in representative cities, suburbs, small towns and rural areas," for *Life*, LVI (May 16, 1969), 23, 31.

[26] Charles G. Sellers, "Is History on the Way out of the Schools and Do Historians Care?" *Social Education*, XXXIII (May 1969), 510.

however, require some notice from the historian. Highly subjective and capable of as many meanings as it has users, the term "relevance" seems to express an inarticulate existentialism, a headlong immediatism of the "here" and "now" that is impatient with any "there" and "then" that do not have an obvious bearing on present preoccupations or personal problems. In accounting for the defection from history courses, Harvard mentions "a very substantial increase" of undergraduate concentrators in the government department; Yale and several others refer to a rising popularity of psychology, Princeton to a boom in sociology. These shifts of undergraduate tastes may, of course, be quite temporary. The current vogue of combining Cavalier hairstyles with Roundhead earnestness may well revert once more to tonsorial roundheadedness and attitudinal cavalierness. As a cultural indicator, the undergraduate passion for "relevance" may have less to do with the long-range future of the past than with the short-range future of the job market for historians.

The declining status of history in the intellectual community at large is a more serious matter. Most disturbing of all is the anti-history animus that emanates from quarters generally assumed to be in friendly alliance with history: the arts and humanities. The tradition of literary animus may be traced back to Friedrich Nietzsche, Henrik Ibsen, and André Gide, but nothing before quite equals the rebellion against history among more recent and contemporary men of letters. Foremost among the rebels are the French existentialists André Malraux, Albert Camus, and the early Jean-Paul Sartre, though their attitudes have precedents in Paul Valery, James Joyce, and Thomas Mann. For Joyce's Stephen Dedalus history was a "nightmare" from which he must awaken. The tyranny of historical consciousness is a recurrent theme in modern literature. It is implicit in William Carlos Williams' plea for immediacy: "History, history! We fools, what do we know or care?" And it is explicit in his renunciation of history as "a tyranny over the souls of the dead—and so the imaginations of the living." Camus, a cultural hero of the young, spoke candidly of his indifference to history and contemptuously of "the evil of history." Sartre wove the same bias through his early fiction and philosophy.[27] What some of the foremost men of letters in our culture have been saying for some time without our special heeding is that history as currently written is bland, banal, or Philistine, that it is often morally obtuse, aesthetically archaic, and intellectually insipid. The historian's pretensions as artist are regarded as pathetic if not ludicrous. Among fashionable playwrights and fiction writers such as Kingsley Amis, Angus Wilson, and Edward Albee these attitudes have become a cliché. In their plays and novels the historian is a stock figure of ridicule, regularly kicked about the stage as part of the evening's entertainment.[28]

The scientists have been more circumspect and less vehement and articulate in verbalizing their aversions and suspicions toward history. But as the anthropologists move in from the far side and the psychologists, sociologists, and political scientists encroach from the hither side upon the territory of human experience that historians normally think of as their private preserve, cries of impatience and dismay arise from the invaders on both flanks. Complaints of methodological naïveté, conceptual vagueness, ambiguous premises, and outmoded generalizations pour in. If this is the science to which historians profess part-time allegiance, they are saying, it is bad science or outmoded and archaic science—late nineteenth-century science at best. The space devoted to history in the *International Encyclopedia of the Social Sciences,* published in 1968, is strikingly less than the amount in its precursor of 1930. Biographies of historians are markedly fewer than those in other disciplines represented, and of the fifty historians included among the six hundred subjects of biographies only six did their work in the United States.[29] What scientists

27 Sartre underwent a later "conversion to history" according to Leonard Krieger, "History and Existentialism in Sartre," in *The Critical Spirit: Essays in Honor of Herbert Marcuse,* ed. Kurt H. Wolff and Barrington Moore, Jr. (Boston, 1967), 239–66. Camus himself came eventually to base values in history.

28 Hayden V. White, "The Burden of History," *History and Theory,* V (No. 2, 1966), 115–23.

29 See review of the *International Encyclopedia of the Social Sciences,* ed. David L. Sills (17 vols., New York, 1968), by Thomas C. Cochran in *American Historical Review,* LXXIV (June 1969), 1573–76.

are implying in various ways is that history as now practiced is as far out of touch with modern science as men of letters are explicitly saying that history is isolated or alienated from modern art.[30]

Among philosophers there are still reputable champions such as Sir Isaiah Berlin, who put up a formidable defense for the autonomy of history as a discipline *sui generis*.[31] Others are increasingly skeptical of these claims. They are suggesting that the middle ground the historian occupied in the nineteenth century between the romantic artists' fear of science and the positivistic scientists' ignorance of art may no longer exist, nor may the extreme dissimilarity of art and science still be assumed by the historian, nor may his self-appointed function as mediator between the two. It has even been suggested that the historian's prestige among intellectuals of the nineteenth century was culturally determined, that the conception of history then current was itself the product of ephemeral historical circumstances, the passing of which may well have deprived history of its status, its autonomy, and its traditional defenses. "In short," according to one harsh judgment, "everywhere there is resentment over what appears to be the historian's bad faith in claiming the privileges of both the artist and the scientist while refusing to submit to critical standards currently obtaining in either art or science."[32]

Some of these attacks, including the last quoted, were exaggerated and open to effective rejoinder, and some of the critics and their disciplines were not above criticism themselves. But in so far as contemporary historians have been at all aware of criticisms by artists, scientists, and philosophers, they have often (though not always) fallen back on the old Fabian strategy of fending off the scientists with the assertion that history was a kind of art given to the uses of intuition beyond the ken of science, and fending off the artists by maintaining that history was

[30] The critique of history by behavioralists is ably presented by Robert F. Berkhofer, Jr., *A Behavioral Approach to Historical Analysis* (New York, 1969).

[31] Isaiah Berlin, "History and Theory: The Concept of Scientific Theory," *History and Theory*, I (No. 1, 1960), 1–31.

[32] White, "Burden of History," 112.

a kind of science limited by analytical methods inappropriate to artistic manipulation. A "guild," a "craft," we quaintly call it. Half scientist, half artist, the historian was a sort of centaur among the disciplines, a centaur with wings some would have it, the only academic discipline endowed with an authentic muse. Incapable of sustaining such fanciful poses, or unaware of the attacks that provoked them, the great majority of American historians became increasingly preoccupied with their fields of specialization and intradisciplinary matters. With some exceptions, by the mid-twentieth century American historians carried little weight and took little part in discussions preoccupying the intellectual community at large, even discussions pertaining to their own discipline. Whatever contemporary paintings they hung on their walls or modern literature they kept on their shelves, little of the spirit that informs these arts seemed to enter into the monographs the historians wrote.

More and more, historians in America sought refuge in their supposedly captive audience of students, or increasingly in the growing public they enjoyed among the laity. In the latter, many guildsmen took a special pride. Unlike other disciplines, they pointed out, history abjured a specialized jargon and spoke the language of the people. While other arts and sciences were growing more abstruse and occult, history was becoming more popular.[33] Excited by the prospect, historians took to the airwaves and the platform with campaigns of salesmanship. Within the guild a movement led by Allan Nevins and Conyers Read narrowly failed to secure sponsorship by the American Historical Association for their dream of a popular magazine of history. But the dream later materialized as a commercial success of fabulous proportions—slick, handsome, well edited, and bland.[34] Historians also reached the laity through the numerous book clubs, Civil War round tables, state and local history societies, and civic enthusiasm for restoring historic sites and commemorating centennials. The efforts to please popular taste and court popular es-

[33] See the presidential address of Allan Nevins, "Not Capulets, Not Montagus," *American Historical Review*, LXV (Jan. 1960), 253–70, esp. 255–57.
[34] Higham *et al.*, *History*, 80–84.

teem tended to encourage the qualities of blandness and banality complained of by the critics of history. They also tended to diminish the esteem in which the craft was held by sister disciplines and to put even more distance between historians and the intellectual community.

There is, moreover, a false security about the refuge sought in popular esteem. It is true that history as romantic entertainment or as "heritage" sustaining national pride has enjoyed great waves of popularity among Americans, especially those of the first half of the nineteenth century.[35] The assumption of a solid and continuing patronage for the profession anchored in a national devotion to history, however, fails to reckon with some old traits of national character. Accused by their critics of "not learning from history" and being indifferent to the past, spokesmen of the student movement reply: "But we say that there is no historical precedent for our generation."[36] So far as historical precedent for their attitudes toward the past is concerned, American students are poorly informed. There are many precedents for their attitude. They go back at least to the Jeffersonians, for some of whom the past seemed both misleading and irrelevant. For Thomas Jefferson himself the present was as independent of the past as the United States from England, and had no more authority over it. "We may consider each generation as a distinct nation," he wrote, and Jefferson once reckoned the length of a generation as nineteen years and the legitimacy of all laws and institutions, without consent of the living, as of the same duration.[37] Alexis de Tocqueville unerringly picked up the theme of generational disjuncture: "the tie that unites one generation to

[35] George H. Callcott, *History in the United States, 1800–1860* (Baltimore, 1969), esp. Chap. 11.

[36] Gregory H. Wierzynski summarizes interviews with students on twenty campuses in *Fortune*, LXXIX (Jan. 1969), 146.

[37] Daniel Boorstin, *The Lost World of Thomas Jefferson* (New York, 1948), 169, 204, 205, and Chap. IV, Sec. 4, entitled "The Sovereignty of the Present Generation"; but cf. H. Trevor Colbourn, *The Lamp of Experience: Whig History and the Intellectual Origins of the American Revolution* (Chapel Hill, N.C., 1963), 158, 167. The quoted statements of Jefferson do not do justice to his respect for history. On eighteenth-century attitudes toward history, see Peter Gay, *The Enlightenment: An Interpretation* (New York, 1966, 1969), II, 368–96.

another is relaxed or broken"; he wrote, "every man there loses all trace of the ideas of his forefathers or takes no heed of them." Or again, "In America, society seems to live from hand to mouth, like an army in the field."[38] According to R. W. B. Lewis, "the American myth saw life and history as just beginning . . . a divinely granted second chance for the human race." He quotes the *Democratic Review* of 1839 as saying, "Our national birth was the beginning of a new history . . . which separates us from the past and connects us with the future only."[39]

Our eighteenth-century ancestors, according to William Bartram, had a ceremony called the "busk," in which a whole town would periodically turn out to make a common bonfire of everything old, outworn, and discarded. Henry David Thoreau made a metaphoric extension of the busk into a social philosophy of "purifying destruction." "I have lived some thirty years on this planet," wrote Thoreau, "and I have yet to hear the first syllable of valuable or even earnest advice from my seniors," that is, anyone over thirty.[40] It may have been the tradition of the busk that inspired Nathaniel Hawthorne's fantasy of 1844, "Earth's Holocaust," a terrifying metaphor of the American urge toward purifying destruction. On a vast western prairie a huge throng gathered to light a cosmic bonfire of the world's "outworn trumpery," including the whole body of European literature and philosophy. "Now," declared their leader, "we shall get rid of the weight of dead men's thoughts."[41] Even Ralph Waldo Emerson, for all his apostrophe to history, declared that "All inquiry into antiquity . . . is the desire to do away with this . . . preposterous There or Then, and introduce in its place the Here and the Now."[42] The "Now Generation" is not without authentic ante-

[38] Alexis de Tocqueville, *Democracy in America,* ed. Phillips Bradley (2 vols., New York, 1956), II, 4; I, 212.

[39] R. W. B. Lewis, *The American Adam* (Chicago, 1955), 5, and Chap. I, entitled "The Case against the Past."

[40] Quoted in Thornton Wilder, "Toward an American Language," *Atlantic,* CXC (July 1952), 29.

[41] The difference between Hawthorne and Thoreau, as Lewis points out, was that the former knew that the holocaust did not touch the real source of oppression, the human heart. (Lewis, *American Adam,* 13–15.)

[42] *The Complete Essays and Other Writings of Ralph Waldo Emerson,* ed. Brooks Atkinson (New York, 1940), 127.

cedents. It would be possible to follow the theme of indifference or hostility toward the past through the corpus of American literature down to contemporary writers directly influenced by the existentialists. The fact is that if Americans may be said to have been born Lockeans, they can in this particular respect as readily be described as having been born existentialists—without the obligation to Sartre they owe to John Locke.[43]

In addition to this heritage of attitudes from the past about the past, American are the creators of wholly new disruptions between past and present. Even the committee of historians who a few years ago deplored and deprecated the effect of these forces admitted that "the world is now moving so fast that history of the knowable past seems to Americans more than ever irrelevant, out of date and useless."[44] Unlike agrarian, or craft, or commercial societies, industrial society, in the opinion of J. H. Plumb, really needs no past. For the industrial society, he writes, "The past becomes . . . a matter of curiosity, of nostalgia, a sentimentality. . . . The strength of the past in all aspects of life is far, far weaker than it was a generation ago: indeed few societies have ever had a past in such galloping dissolution as this."[45] But Plumb is evidently thinking of contemporary Britain or Europe, and we are constantly told that America and Europe are no longer living in the same historical era, that the United States has already broken through into something called the "post-industrial" or the "technetronic" age and is in daily confrontation with the unprecedented. In the American experience, other peoples of the world can read, for better or for worse, what is in store for them in the future—for most of them a very remote future—in which Americans are already living.

This future already exhibits more disjunction from the past than did the industrial era. One English interpretation of the

[43] For one of several southern exceptions to the national norm, see William Faulkner's Gavin Stevens in *Intruder in the Dust*: "The past is never dead. It is not even past."

[44] American Council of Learned Societies, *Report of the Commission on the Humanities*, 119.

[45] J. H. Plumb, *The Death of the Past* (Boston, 1970), 14–15; see also *ibid.*, 42–44.

first lunar landing, doubtless moved to rashness by the spectacle, pronounced it "the most brutal break that the world has known with its past 400 million years."[46] For a Carnegie, a Rhodes, a Krupp, a Rockefeller, or even a Henry Ford the past was still fairly rich with sanctions. For their counterparts (if any) of the "postindustrial" world it is hard to see what the past provides in the way of sanctions. The new spiritual environment, on the other hand, is not wholly strange or entirely uncongenial to the American. "Americans are abstract," writes Thornton Wilder. "They are disconnected," from place as well as from past. "There is only one way in which an American can feel himself to be in relation to other Americans—when he is united with them in a project, caught up in an idea and propelled with them toward the future. . . . 'I am,' he says, 'because my plans characterize me.' "[47] An essential element of American identity, one of "the principal sources of identity strength," according to Erik Erikson, is "a sense of anticipated future."[48] And in the words of the *Democratic Review* already quoted, our history "separates us from the past and connects us with the future only." Henry James was under the impression that America "had no past" and as "the next best thing" was hell-bent on substituting "a magnificent compensatory future."[49] Perhaps the outworn faith in progress was only one expression of a deeper national commitment. What William James saw as our "platitudinous optimism" and H. G. Wells called our "optimistic fatalism" could become in Henry Adams a rather lurid and apocalyptic catastrophism without essential inconsistency with the future-oriented bent of American character.[50]

A profession that sets itself up as custodian of the past

[46] *Economist,* July 19, 1969, 13.

[47] From his Charles Eliot Norton Lectures at Harvard University, in *Atlantic,* CXC (July 1952), 31.

[48] Erik Erikson, "Memorandum on Youth," in *Toward the Year 2000: Work in Progress,* ed. Daniel Bell (Boston, 1968), 231–32.

[49] Quoted in H. G. Wells, *The Future of America* (New York, 1906), 5.

[50] On the historian and the future, see Henry Adams, *The Education of Henry Adams* (Boston, 1918), 395. Offering Tocqueville and Adams as examples, Hofstadter has observed that, "At their best, the interpretative historians have gone to the past with some passionate concern for the future. . . ." (*Progressive Historians,* 465.)

among a people with such peculiar attitudes toward the past, a people that has characteristically sought identity in the future, would seem to have little ground for complacency—about either the future of the past or the future of the craft that deals with the past. Complacency in these matters would seem all the more inappropriate in a period of radical disjunctures between past and present, and so would withdrawal of the historian from the continuous discussions of these disjunctures carried on in the intellectual community. Deafness or indifference toward criticism of the guild, whether it comes from artists, scientists, or philosophers, or from our own students, would appear to be singularly perilous at this time. The last resort of Philistinism would be for professional historians to take refuge from intellectual problems and critical attacks in what remains of popular sentimentality and nostalgia about the past.

Plumb attempts to draw "a sharp distinction between the past and history." The past as he conceives of it is always used to sanction or sanctify authority, to control or motivate societies or classes, to endow elites and nations with a sense of destiny and mission, and therefore to bemuse and coerce and exploit. "Nothing has been so corruptly used as concepts of the past," he writes, and he is ready "to toll the bell for the past which is dying." The demise of the past, however, "does not deny a future for history." History is not an ideology, and it is not the past. It is an intellectual process, a discipline that is still growing. Its future and true function are "to cleanse the story of mankind from the deceiving visions of a purposeful past."[51]

There are admittedly some ambiguities in this contrast between history and the past. But American historians, particularly those whose subject is the history of their own country, have often been careless and sometimes even oblivious of the more elemental distinctions between the two. In their quest for a "usable past" they have fallen into what J. R. Pole calls "the American extension of the Whig interpretation of history."[52] An

[51] Plumb, *Death of the Past*, 11, 17, 50.
[52] J. R. Pole, "The American Past: Is It Still Usable?" *Journal of American Studies*, I (Apr. 1967), 63.

instrumentalist view of historiography, this interpretation regards history as an instrument of political or social action. It assumes that the United States stands for certain values and that it is the duty of the historian in his study of the past to discover, record, and celebrate these values. This position has had both radical and conservative advocates, but none more explicit than the conservative Conyers Read, who in his presidential address to the American Historical Association of 1949 enlisted the historian in the cold war. As he saw it, "the first prerequisite of a historian is a sound social philosophy," and "As historians we must carry back into our scrutiny of the past" our political faith. He advocated social controls over historians and demanded that we "accept and endorse such controls as are essential for the preservation of our way of life." They would be, he assured us, "no menace to essential freedoms." This meant that "we recognize certain fundamental values as beyond dispute," values that we "must defend against all assaults, historical or otherwise."[53]

Those Americans who pursue the usable past have unconsciously assumed a space-time continuum that confuses forebears with descendants and homogenizes time past with time present. Whether they are conservatives with friendly and affectionate feelings toward the past or radicals with cynical and iconoclastic attitudes, the resulting confusion is the same. A fatal betrayal of the craft would be to permit the profession of history to become inextricably entangled with the future of the past, the purposeful past of the rationalizers, the justifiers, and the propagandists. Anyway, it is no good any longer urging upon a chaotic era of discontinuities and disruptions a specious time past continuum—not with the classic American continuity myths of security and invincibility, of success and innocence crumbling about our heads. Without some continuities the social fabric would disintegrate. Many continuities, of course, persist. But ours is essentially an age of disjuncture, not of continuity. Indifference to these conditions and insensitivity to any light that the world of art or sci-

---

[53] Conyers Read, "The Social Responsibilities of the Historian," *American Historical Review*, LV (Jan. 1950), 284–85.

ence or philosophy may throw upon them would be a disservice to the craft.

"It is not inconceivable," wrote Marc Bloch shortly before his tragic death, that our civilization "may, one day, turn away from history, and historians would do well to reflect upon this possibility."[54] We have seen that the future of history, its status in the academic world, and its prestige in the intellectual community have been seriously questioned of late. Referring to the future of another branch of learning, Berlin writes, "There exist only two good reasons for the demise of a discipline: one is that its central presuppositions . . . are no longer accepted. . . . The other is that new disciplines have come to perform the work originally undertaken by the older study."[55] Such was the fate, he points out, that overtook astrology, alchemy, and phrenology, among others, on which their offspring performed a species of parricide. History would not seem destined for that fate.

Marc Bloch had the audacity "to claim for history the indulgence due to all new ventures." While history has remained "quietly loyal to its glorious Hellenic name," he wrote, it has "grown old in embryo" as myth and legend, chronicle and romantic storytelling, but it is "still very young as a rational attempt at analysis."[56] In its new phase it bears little more resemblance to the embryo than astronomy to astrology or chemistry to alchemy. Unlike the sciences, however, history did not change its name with its phases. One result is that it has been falsely judged by the antiquity of the old Greek name as well as by association with an antique subject matter. Unlike the sciences also, history has not been periodically endowed with "a common paradigm" that is said to have "freed the scientific community from the need constantly to re-examine its first principles."[57] Given the nature of the craft, history probably never will be so freed or so en-

[54] Marc Bloch, *The Historian's Craft* (New York, 1964), 5.
[55] Isaiah Berlin, "Does Political Theory Still Exist?" in *Philosophy, Politics and Society,* ed. Peter Laslett and W. G. Runciman, 2d Ser. (New York, 1962), 1–2.
[56] Bloch, *Historian's Craft,* 13.
[57] Thomas S. Kuhn, *The Structure of Scientific Revolutions* (Chicago, 1962), 162.

dowed. "The uncertainties of our science must not, I think," wrote Bloch, "be hidden from the curiosity of the world. They are our excuse for being." He urged professional historians, "above all the younger ones, to reflect upon these hesitancies, these incessant soul-searchings, of our craft."[58] In the new era of soul-searching for which our guild seems destined, it is well to keep his valiant example in mind.

Exercises in self-doubt and self-criticism are not new to the craft. They need never become self-destructive. After all allowance for its shortcomings, all admission of outrageous pretensions, and all deference to the achievements of other arts and sciences, history may still claim legitimate and vital roles unfilled by other disciplines. These roles multiply rather than diminish in times such as our own, times of striking disjuncture between past and present. For it is in just such times as these that anachronisms proliferate, and when they cease to be harmless myths and grow into rigid dogmas over which nations go to war and races of men tear at each other's throats. Anachronisms are the peculiar concern of historians, and as causes for concern and peril they were never more numerous, more menacing than they are in our time. The historian is peculiarly fitted also to serve as mediator between man's limitations and his aspirations, between his dreams of what ought to be and the limits of what, in the light of what has been, can be. There is no other branch of learning better qualified to mediate between man's daydream of the future and his nightmare of the past, or, for that matter, between his nightmare of the future and his daydream of the past. So long as man remains recognizably human, he will remain a creature with both a past and a future. A creature so long described as earthbound and so newly transcending those bounds, so giddy over his spectacular innovations, so guilt-ridden about his past, and so anxiety-ridden about the present and the future is not a creature who can safely turn away from history.

[58] Bloch, *Historian's Craft*, 51.

Afterthoughts

In so far as my address of 1969 dealt with the future rather than the past it engaged in the unhistorical enterprise of prophecy. Since then twenty years of the future have slipped into the past and have thus become subject to historical investigation. How do the prophecies stand up? Predictions expressed in numbers and percentages are not necessarily the most important, but they are usually the ones most readily tested. Of such projections, those suggesting a future decline in the number of college students attracted to history had received the most attention, caused the most concern, and were the first to be challenged. Paul L. Ward, Executive Secretary of the American Historical Association, took pleasure in assuring its members, as soon as the figures were available, that in 1970–71, the year following my pessimistic prediction, the number of bachelor's degrees in history awarded in the country, instead of declining, actually increased. In fact the number was "the highest ever," and this on top of eighteen years of unprecedented increase. The figures suggested that the study of history in the academy might be "launched on something of a plateau," a very high one at that.[1]

The year 1970–71 did indeed set a record for degrees granted. But I had prefaced my predictions by saying that the increase in history degrees "may well continue for some time," and that I was relying upon "indicators that lie back of the degree stage," such as the attitudes of pre-college students and class enrollments in outstanding colleges. The decline that was already manifest in those quarters was not registered in degrees granted until 1971–72, but then and thereafter those more tangible indicators continued to drop for fifteen years, with no assurance of recovery yet. The "plateau" had really dropped off, gradually at first, then plunged downward precipitately. Starting with the peak year and looking at the figures every fifth year thereafter, degrees in 1970–71 were 44,663; in 1975–76 they had dropped

[1] Paul L. Ward in *American Historical Association Newsletter* (November 1972), 50.

28,400, by 1980–81 another 10,000 to 18,301, and in 1985–86
to 16,413. But those are absolute figures in years that registered
sharp increases in total college enrollments and degrees. As a
percentage of degrees in all fields the plunge of those in history
was much more dramatic than the decline in numbers: from 5.3
percent of the total in 1970–71 to 1.7 percent in 1985–86. The
sad thing about doctoral degrees, earned by future teachers of
declining history classes, was that the decline began later: in
1972–73 at 1,215, it fell to 563 by 1985–86.[2]

An official of the history guild thought he saw "reason for
optimism" in a slight upturn in number and percentages of
lower and higher history degrees in 1985–86, the first in more
than fifteen years. Even so, he admits, "the discipline is far from
recovering from its losses." The number of new Ph.Ds in history
increased slightly, but remained 53.7 percent below the peak
level of 1973, and "full recovery remains a distant goal."[3] Still,
the job market for historians was improving, and there were
other, if less tangible reasons for encouragement. If the great
decline in student patronage of history struck first in Eastern
universities of high rank, the current boom in those same institutions may presage a general recovery. At Harvard, Yale, Princeton, and a few other universities, history majors and enrollments
have been soaring of late as never before, and history departments
in some institutions exceed all their sister disciplines in student
appeal.

Nowhere are there signs to signal the return of the guild's
boom mentality of the 1940s and 1950s. But there are a few signs
that inspire quiet confidence. One is an unexpected improvement
of relations with the non-academic public. This is manifest
notably in an impressive recent gain in the market for serious
history books. These are not popularizations by amateurs, but
scholarly works on large subjects—the rise and fall of ancient and
modern empires, comprehensive work on the American Civil
War, path-breaking biographies of world figures. They are not

[2] "A Revival for History?" *Perspectives, American Historical Newsletter*
(March 1988), 9–10.
[3] Ibid.

works of the sort that encourage blandness and banality. The courage mustered for such undertakings is itself a sign of health in the profession. The present status of history in the intellectual community at large is harder to assess, but it must have improved with the fading influence of the generation of French intellectuals that professed such a strong anti-history bias.

Undergraduate tastes, market fluctuations, and intellectual fashions come and go. The deeper traits of national character repeated over the generations will remain to be reckoned with in the long run. They include the attitudes toward history voiced by Jefferson, perceived by Tocqueville, and repeated by Emerson, Thoreau, and their successors down the years in pronouncements quoted above. The "New Generation" had authentic historical antecedents. That generation, which now enjoys tenure or is of tenurable age, may be expected to perpetuate some of its favorite convictions in the minds of oncoming generations.

2

Clio With Soul

The circumstances surrounding the delivery of the following paper, also given in 1969 as a presidential address, this one to the Organization of American Historians, were comparable with those described for the previous paper. The tensions this time, however, were more closely related to the subject of my address, which was the controversies then raging around black history, its writing and teaching. Universities were then belatedly hurrying to integrate black history and historians into the curriculum with new courses and programs in great numbers. Just as all this was taking place black intellectuals were loudly demanding black withdrawal, separation, nationalism, exclusion of all whites, and pre-emption of all teaching and monopoly of all writing of black history by blacks. I took precisely the opposite position, contending that "Negro history is too important to be left entirely to black historians," that "race and color are neither a qualification nor a disqualification for historians" and "the righteousness of a cause is not a license for arrogance." I knew that blacks had heckled and denounced other speakers at the meeting who agreed with me, and I was expecting trouble. Who can forget the academic scene of those times? Dashikis were the uniform of the day, Swahili the lingua franca, Afros the prevailing hair style, and jive talk the medium of intellectual discourse. They did not shout me down, but neither did

*they—at least at that time—pay the slightest heed to my ad-
monitions.*

ALL WHO WRITE or teach American history are aware by now
of the demand for more attention to the part that Negro people
have played. It may come quietly from a distressed college dean,
or it may come peremptorily and noisily from militant student
protest. In any case the demand is insistent that we move over
and make room. With whatever grace they can muster and whatever resources they command, historians as teachers are responding one way or another. New colleagues are recruited (black if
humanly possible), new courses listed ("Black" or "Afro" in the
title), new textbooks written, new lectures prepared. Or, in a
pinch, old colleagues may have to be pressured and reconditioned
and old lectures hastily revised. The adjustment is often awkward
and sometimes rather frantic, but American academic institutions
are responding, each in its own style and fashion—clumsily, belatedly, heartily, or half-heartedly, as the case may be.

We are concerned here, however, not with the institutional
response and its problems nor even primarily with the social
purpose and the overdue ends of justice sought, as important as
these things unquestionably are. Rather we are concerned for the
moment with the professional problems the movement poses,
particularly with the impact, good, bad, or indifferent, it will
have—is having, has had—upon the writing and reinterpretation
of American history. Will it warp as much as it will correct? Will
it substitute a new racism for an old? Will historians be able to
absorb and control the outraged moral passions released and bend
to the social purposes dictated without losing balance and betraying principle? Or will the historian's moral engagement compromise the integrity of his craft? Granting inevitable losses in
detachment, will the gains in moral insight outbalance the losses?

On the positive side, corrective influences may be scored up
as incremental gain immediately apparent. In the past a certain
moral obtuseness and intellectual irresponsibility regarding the

Negro people have cropped up again and again in our most respectable historical literature. The tendency appeared very early, but one does not have to go back so far as the romantic school, or even so far as the scientific school and its smugness about Teutonic institutions, for instances. Frederick Jackson Turner could write in his famous paper on "The Significance of the Frontier" that "when American history comes to be rightly viewed it will be seen that the slavery question is an incident."[1] And Charles A. Beard took the view that the results of Negro suffrage and political strivings during Reconstruction "would have been ludicrous if they had not been pitiable."[2] Even historians with abolitionist backgrounds combined their antislavery views with white supremacy and anti-Negro assumptions.[3] One consequence of having Negro critics or colleagues looking over one's shoulder or having more Negro historians is that such embarrassing white-supremacy and ethnocentric gaffes are likely to become much rarer in the pages of respected historians. This is not to say that the profession will thus be purged of moral obtuseness and intellectual irresponsibility. These shortcomings are likely to remain constants in the historical profession as in other parts of the human community. But they are likely to find different forms of expression.

In spite of the warning admonitions of Herbert Butterfield and others about the moral interpretation of history, Negro history seems destined to remain the moral storm center of American historiography. It is hard to see how it could very well be otherwise, at least for some time to come. Slavery was, after all, the basic moral paradox of American history. It was what Dr. Samuel Johnson had in mind when he asked: "How is it

[1] Frederick Jackson Turner, *The Frontier in American History* (New York, 1920), 24.

[2] Charles A. Beard, *American Government and Politics* (New York, 1911), 86.

[3] For examples see W. E. Burghardt Du Bois, "The Propaganda of History," *Black Reconstruction in America: An Essay Toward a History of the Part Which Black Folk Played in the Attempt to Reconstruct Democracy in America, 1860–1880* (New York, 1935), 711–29; and Benjamin Quarles, "What the Historian Owes the Negro," *Saturday Review*, XLIX (Sept. 3, 1966), 10–13.

that we hear the loudest *yelps* for liberty among the drivers of Negroes?" But the paradox is older and deeper than the temporary embarrassments of 1776, of slaveholders yelping for liberty, writing the Declaration of Independence, and fighting for the natural rights of man. Back of that were the European dreamers of America as an idyllic Arcadia, the New Jerusalem, the Promised Land, the world's new hope of rebirth, fulfillment, and redemption. Before the dreamers came the discoverer of America, who returned from one of his voyages with a cargo of Indian slaves. After him came the explorers and colonizers who competed in the lucrative African slave trade and brought millions of slaves to the New World. It is, in fact, difficult to see how Europeans could have colonized America and exploited its resources otherwise. David B. Davis has phrased the paradox perfectly: "How was one to reconcile the brute fact that slavery was an intrinsic part of the American experience with the image of the New World as uncorrupted nature, as a source of redemption from the burdens of history, as a paradise which promised fulfillment of man's highest aspirations?"[4]

One way of dealing with the problem was that of J. Hector St. John de Crèvecoeur, who wrote the classic statement of the American idyll of democratic fulfillment. "What then is the American, this new man?" was his famous question. And his answer was: "He is either an European, or the descendent of an European. . . ."[5] Crèvecoeur simply defined the Negro out of American identity. It is significant that the tacit exclusion went unnoticed for nearly two centuries.[6] Arthur M. Schlesinger, Sr., took the title and text of his presidential address to the American Historical Association in 1942 from this passage of Crèvecoeur without referring to its racial exclusion.[7] Crèvecoeur's precedent

[4] David B. Davis, *The Problem of Slavery in Western Culture* (Ithaca, 1966), 10; also Chapter I, "The Historical Problem: Slavery and the Meaning of America," 3–28.

[5] J. Hector St. John de Crèvecoeur, *Letters from an American Farmer* (New York, 1945), 43.

[6] Winthrop D. Jordan, *White Over Black: American Tttitudes Toward the Negro, 1550–1810* (Chapel Hill, 1968), 340–41.

[7] Arthur M. Schlesinger, " 'What Then Is the American, This New Man?' " *American Historical Review,* XLVIII (Jan. 1943), 225–44.

was widely followed in the writing of American history. It might be called the "invisible man" solution.

Another way of dealing with Davis's problem of brute fact and idyllic image was that of Beard and Turner. They recognized the Negro's existence all right, but they either ignored moral conflicts and paradoxes in moral values forced by his existence and status, or they attempted to reduce them to other and morally neutral categories of explanation. Referring to Beard, W. E. B. Du Bois remarked that one has the "comfortable feeling that nothing right or wrong is involved."[8] Beard and Turner are merely two conspicuous examples of the numerous practitioners of what might be called the moral-neutrality approach.

Neither the invisible-man solution nor the moral-neutrality approach is any longer acceptable. Moral engagement ranging upward to total commitment now predominates. This approach divides into overlapping though distinguishable categories. One is embraced in the general class of paternalistic historiography, but divides broadly into northern and southern schools. Northern-type paternalism is usually the more self-conscious. One representative of this school assures the Brother in Black that "Negroes are, after all, only white men with black skins, nothing more, nothing less," endowed natively with all the putative white attributes of courage, manhood, rebelliousness, and love of liberty. Another concedes the deplorable reality of the "Sambo personality," but attributes it to potency of the plantation master as white father image and to other misfortunes. Others console the Negro for not producing more Nat Turners and slave rebellions by offering ingenious theories to explain his accommodation to slavery. Still others assure him that he would have been better advised to have chosen men of Iberian and Catholic background rather than those of English and Protestant heritage as masters of the plantation school.

The modern Southern paternalist, falling back on his regional heritage, takes to the role more naturally and with less self-consciousness. He disavows the Phillipsian concept of the

[8] Du Bois, *Black Reconstruction*, 714–15.

benevolent plantation school for Africans, but proceeds as if the school actually worked admirably, with some exceptions, and turned out graduates fully prepared for freedom and equality. Any shortcomings or failings on the part of the blacks are attributed to delinquencies of the "responsible" whites, the paternalists. These assumptions result in a charitable picture of the freedmen during emancipation and Reconstruction and the era following. Instead of a "white man with a black skin," the Negro is elected an honorary southerner by paternalists below the Potomac.

Moral preoccupations and problems shape the character of much that is written about the Negro and race relations by modern white historians, but they are predominantly the preoccupations and moral problems of the white man. His conscience burdened with guilt over his own people's record of injustice and brutality toward the black man, the white historian often writes in a mood of contrition and remorse as if in expiation of racial guilt or flagellation of the guilty. In this connection it is well to recall Butterfield's observation that "since moral indignation corrupts the agent who possesses it and is not calculated to reform the man who is the object of it, the demand for it—in the politician and in the historian for example—is really a demand for an illegitimate form of power." It is "a tactical weapon," says Butterfield, valued for its power "to rouse irrational fervour and extraordinary malevolence against some enemy."[9] It is a weapon that is especially useful in polemics—polemics of region against region, party against party, and class against class.

This is not to deny to the historian the role of moral critic or to dismiss what has been written out of deep concern for moral values.[10] The history of the Negro people and race relations has profited more from the insights and challenges of this type of writing in the last two decades than from the scholarship of the preceding and much longer era of moral neutrality and obtuseness. Nor is it to deny the value of what white historians have

[9] Herbert Butterfield, *History and Human Relations* (London, 1951), 110.

[10] John Higham, "Beyond Consensus: The Historian as Moral Critic," *American Historical Review*, LXVII (April 1962), 609–25.

contributed to the understanding of Negro history. For better or for worse, the great majority of scholars working in this field have been and will continue to be white. Without their contribution, Negro history would be far more impoverished and neglected than it now is.

Granting the value of the part white historians have played in this field, the Negro still has understandable causes for dissatisfaction. For however sympathetic they may be, white historians with few exceptions are primarily concerned with the moral, social, political, and economic problems of white men and their past. They are prone to present to the Negro as *his* history the record of what the white man believed, thought, legislated, did and did not do *about* the Negro. The Negro is a passive element, the man to whom things happen. He is the object rather than the subject of this kind of history. It is filled with the infamies and the philanthropies, the brutalities and the charities, the laws, customs, prejudices, policies, politics, crusades, and laws of whites *about* blacks. "Racial attitudes" or "American attitudes" in a title mean white attitudes. "The Negro Image" means the image in white minds. In this type of history, abolitionists, Radical Republicans, and carpetbaggers are all of the same pale pigmentation. A famous history of the Underground Railroad virtually omitted reference to the blacks, who incurred most of the risks, did most of the work, and suffered nearly all the casualties.[11] The largest and most comprehensive book on the antislavery movement could spare only nine pages for the black abolitionists.[12] Not until the civil rights workers of the 1960s do the prime movers and shakers of Negro history take on a darker hue in the history books, and not in all of them at that.

Negro history in this tradition—and many Negro historians themselves followed the tradition, virtually the only one available in university seminars—was an enclave, a cause or a result, a

[11] Wilbur H. Siebert, *The Underground Railroad from Slavery to Freedom* (New York, 1898). See Larry Gara, *The Liberty Line: The Legend of the Underground Railroad* (Lexington, 1961), for a critique of this and similar works on the subject.

[12] Dwight Lowell Dumond, *Antislavery: The Crusade for Freedom in America* (Ann Arbor, 1961), 326–34.

commentary on or an elaboration of white history. Black history *was* white history. Denied a past of his own, the Negro was given to understand that whatever history and culture he possessed was supplied by his association with the dominant race in the New World and its European background. Thoroughly Europo-centric in outlook, American whites subscribed completely to the myth that European culture, *their* culture, was so overwhelmingly superior that no other could survive under exposure to it. They also shared the European stereotypes, built up by three centuries of slave traders and elaborated by nineteenth- and twentieth-century European imperialists, of an Africa of darkness, savagery, bestiality, and degradation. Not only was the African stripped of this degrading heritage on American shores and left cultureless, a Black Adam in a new garden, but also he was viewed as doubly fortunate in being rescued from naked barbarism and simultaneously clothed with a superior culture. The "myth of the Negro past" was that he had no past.[13]

So compelling was this myth, so lacking any persuasive evidence to the contrary, so universally prevalent the stereotypes of Africans in their American world that until very recently Negroes adopted it unquestioningly themselves. Carter Woodson remarked in 1937 that "Negroes themselves accept as a compliment the theory of a complete break with Africa, for above all things they do not care to be known as resembling in any way these 'terrible Africans.' "[14] And Du Bois wrote that NAACP members had a "fierce repugnance toward anything African. . . . Beyond this they felt themselves Americans, not Africans. They resented and feared any coupling with Africa."[15] White friends of the Negro defended him against any slurs associating him with Africa as if against insults. And Negroes commonly used the words "African" and "black" as epithets of an opprobrious sort. They were *Americans* with nothing to do with Africa or its black-

[13] Melville J. Herskovits, *The Myth of the Negro Past* (New York, 1941), 227, 298–99.
[14] Carter Woodson, review of Melville J. Herskovits, *Life in a Haitian Village, Journal of Negro History*, XXII (July 1937), 367.
[15] W. E. Burghardt Du Bois, *Dusk of Dawn: An Essay Toward an Autobiography of a Race Concept* (New York, 1940), 275.

ness, nakedness, and savagery. Africa, like slavery, was something to be forgotten, denied, suppressed. With an older American pedigree and a far better claim than first and second generation immigrants of other ethnic groups, Negroes could protest the remoteness of their foreign origins and the exclusiveness of their American identity. "Once for all," wrote Du Bois in 1919, "let us realize that we are Americans, that we were brought here with the earliest settlers, and that the very sort of civilization from which we came made the complete adoption of Western modes and customs imperative if we were to survive at all. In brief, there is nothing so indigeneous [*sic*] so completely 'made in America' as we."[16] Until very recently these were the received opinions, the prevailing attitudes of most Negro Americans.

A few years ago a French writer used the word *"décôlonisation"* in the title of a book on the contemporary movement for Negro rights in America.[17] While the analogy that this word suggests is misleading in important respects, it does call attention to the wider environment of the national experience. The dismantling of white supremacy since World War II has been a worldwide phenomenon. The adjustment of European powers to this revolution has appropriately been called decolonization, since this is the political effect it has had on their many possessions in Asia, Africa, and the Caribbean Sea. The outward trappings, the political symbols, the pomp and ceremony of decolonization doubtless contained a considerable amount of collective ego gratification for the ethnic groups concerned. These included the lowering of old flags and the raising of new ones, the drawing of national boundaries, the establishment of new armies, navies, and air forces with new uniforms, foreign embassies, and seats in the United Nations—the full protocol of national sovereignty in the European tradition. The result has been the appearance of thirty-two new black nations, seventeen of them in the year 1960 in Africa alone, and many tiny ones in the Caribbean. But even more gratifying perhaps was the physical as well as symbolic

[16] Quoted in Harold R. Isaacs, *The New World of Negro Americans* (New York, 1963), 222; see also 106–07, 171 on Negro rejection of Africa.
[17] Daniel Guérin, *Décôlonisation du Noir Américain* (Paris, 1963).

withdrawal of the dominant whites, together with the debasement of their authority and the destruction of the hated paraphernalia of exclusiveness and discrimination. We know from the writings of Frantz Fanon of Martinique and others how much of the colonial syndrome of dependency, inferiority, and self-hatred lingered behind the new facade of national sovereignty and how little the life of the masses was affected.[18] But the gratifications were there, too, and for the ruling-class elites these were no doubt considerable.

The dismantling of white supremacy was simultaneously taking place in the United States, but the process was accompanied by no such pomp and circumstance and no such debasement of white authority and power. What did take place in America was far less dramatic. It came in the form of judicial decisions, legislative acts, and executive orders by duly constituted authority that remained unshaken in the possession of power. It came with "all deliberate speed," a speed so deliberate as to appear glacial or illusory. The outward manifestations were the gradual disappearance of the little signs, "White" and "Colored," and the gradual appearance of token black faces in clubs, schools, universities, and boards of directors. Some of the tokens were more impressive: a cabinet portfolio, a Supreme Court appointment, a seat in the Senate, the office of mayor. By comparison with the immediately preceding era in America, these developments were striking indeed. But by contrast with the rituals and symbols of decolonization in Africa and the Caribbean, they took on a much paler cast. And while the outcome abroad was separation and independence for black people, the outcome for black people at home was desegregation and integration—or rather the renewal of unfulfilled promises of them.[19]

While Africa was being transformed from degraded European colonies to aggressively independent nations with famous

[18] Frantz Fanon, *Black Skin, White Masks* (New York, 1967), 83–108; O. Mannoni, *Prospero and Caliban: The Psychology of Colonizations* (London, 1956).

[19] Isaacs, *New World of Negro Americans*, 6–9.

heroes of liberation and a conspicuous visibility on the world scene, American Negro attitudes toward the ancestral homeland changed profoundly. The traditional indifference or repugnance for things African, the shame and abhorrence of association with Africa, gave way to fascinated interest, pride, and a sense of identification. The art, folklore, music, dance, even the speech and clothing of Africa have taken on a new glamor and emotional significance for people who have never seen that continent and will never set foot on it. Instead of concealing marks of African identification, many young people increasingly emphasize, invent, or exaggerate them in dress, speech, or hair style.

We are destined to hear a great deal more about Africa from Afro-Americans as time goes on. This will find its way into historical writing, and some manifestations may seem rather bizarre. Before we assume a posture of outrage or ridicule, it might be well to put this phenomenon into historical perspective. We might recall, for example, that the "scientific" school at the end of the last century placed great emphasis on "Teutonic" and "Anglo-Saxon" tribal customs and institutions and that in doing so it was dipping several centuries deeper into the past for primitive origins than the Afro-Americans are now. The Irish nationalists of the twentieth century in decreeing the use of Gaelic were attempting the revival of a language a good deal less alive than Swahili. While Hebrew has more scholarly uses, its study in America is also dictated by the needs of ethnic identity.

The assimilation of European ethnic groups in America throughout the history of immigration has not only been a story of deculturation and acculturation—the shedding of foreign ways and the adoption of new values. It has also been a story of fierce struggles to assert and maintain ethnic interests and identity.[20] One key element in that struggle has been the group's sense of its past. Each immigrant group of any size established its historical societies and journals in which filiopietism has free rein.

[20] Nathan Glazer and Daniel Patrick Moynihan, *Beyond the Melting Pot: The Negroes, Puerto Ricans, Jews, Italians, and Irish of New York City* (New York, 1963), 13–19.

According to Marcus Hansen, more than 400 Norwegian journals have been established from time to time in America.[21] Not
only the Norwegians but also the Irish and the Jews have contested with Italians the claim to the discovery of America. These
assertions of group pride in a common past, mythic or real, have
accompanied a strong urge for assimilation and integration in
American society. In the opinion of the anthropologist Melville J.
Herskovits, "the extent to which the past of a people is regarded
as praiseworthy, their own self-esteem will be high and the
opinion of others will be favorable."[22]

The priests who taught the children of the Irish slums that
St. Brendan, Bishop of Clonfert, discovered America in the sixth
century,[23] or the rabbis who taught their charges in the Jewish
slums that the Indians were the lost tribes of Israel,[24] or the
Bohemians and Poles and Swedes and Italians who assured the
children that it was *their* countrymen who saved the day at
Bunker Hill or Bull Run or the Bloody Angle were not advancing the cause of history. But they *were* providing defenses against
the WASP myths of the schoolbooks and some sense of group
identity and pride and self-esteem to slum dwellers who were, in
turn, regarded by the Best People as the scum of the earth.[25]

Denied a praiseworthy past or for that matter a past of any
sort that is peculiarly their own, Negro Americans have consequently been denied such defenses and self-esteem as these resources have provided other and less vulnerable American groups.
Now that they are seeking to build defenses of their own and a
past of their own, they are likely to repeat many of the ventures
in mythmaking and filiopietism in which other minorities, including the WASPs, have indulged.

[21] Marcus Lee Hansen, *The Immigrant in American History* (Cambridge, 1940), 28.
[22] Herskovits, *Myth of the Negro Past,* 299.
[23] Edward O'Meagher Condon, *The Irish Race in America* (New York,
1887), 3.
[24] Peter Wiernik, *History of Jews in America: From the Period of the
Discovery of America to the Present Time* (New York, 1912), 14.
[25] Edward N. Saveth, *American Historians and European Immigrants,
1815–1925* (New York, 1948); Arthur M. Schlesinger, Jr., "Nationalism
and History," *Journal of Negro History,* LIV (1969), 19–31.

One of their temptations will be to follow the exciting example of their brothers in Africa who are now in search of national identity for brand-new nation-states.[26] Nationalists have always invoked history in their cause and abused it for their purposes. No nations have been so prone to this use of history as new nations. Unable to rely on habituation of custom by which old states claim legitimacy and the loyalty of their citizens, new-born nations (our own for example) invoke history to justify their revolutions and the legitimacy of new rulers. Like their American kin, the Africans had also been denied a past of their own, for European historians of the imperialist countries held that the continent, at least the sub-Saharan part, had no history before the coming of the white man. Historians of the new African states have not been backward in laying counterclaims and asserting the antiquity of their history and its importance, even its centrality in the human adventure. Inevitably some black patriots have been carried away by their theme. One Ghanian historian, for example, goes so far as to assert that Moses and Buddha were Egyptian Negroes, that Christianity sprang from Sudanic tribes, and that Nietzsche, Bergson, Marx, and the existentialists were all reflections of Bantu philosophy.[27] How much of this overwrought nationalism of the emergent African states will take root in American soil remains to be seen. Already something like it has found expression in cults of black nationalism and is seeking lodgement in the academies.

It seems possible that the new pride in Africa's achievements, identification with its people and their history, and the discovery of ancestral roots in its culture could contribute richly to the self-discovery and positive group identity of a great American minority. What had been suppressed or regarded with shame in this American subculture could now be openly expressed with

[26] The stimulus to nationalism was not all one way. For earlier influences of Negro Americans on the rise of nationalism in Africa, see George Shepperson, "Notes on Negro American Influences on the Emergence of African Nationalism," *Journal of African History,* I (1960), 299–312.

[27] Immanuel Wallerstein, "The Search for National Identity in West Africa: The New History," Werner J. Cahnman and Alfin Boskoff (eds.), *Sociology and History: Theory and Research* (New York, 1964), 303–13.

confidence and pride. The extent of African survivals in Negro-American culture has been debated for a generation by anthropologists.[28] No doubt such survivals have been exaggerated and admittedly there are fewer in the United States than in Latin America and the West Indies. But the acknowledged or imagined African survivals in religious and marital practices, in motor habits, in speaking, walking, burden carrying, and dancing, however the anthropologists may assess them, have gained new sanction and a swinging momentum.

It seems to me that the reclaimed African heritage could give a third dimension to the tragically two-dimensional man of the Du Bois metaphor. "One ever feels his two-ness," he wrote, "—an American, a Negro; two souls, two thoughts, two unreconciled strivings; two warring ideals in one dark body. . . ." Du Bois thought that, "The history of the American Negro is the history of this strife . . ." and that "this double-consciousness, this sense of always looking at one's self through the eyes of others" was his tragedy.[29] The recovery of an African past and a third dimension of identity might have a healing effect on the schizoid "two-ness," the 'two-soul" cleavage of the Negro mind.

There are, unhappily, less desirable consequences conceivable for the preoccupation with Africa as a clue to racial identity. For in the hands of nationalist cults, it can readily become a mystique of skin color and exclusiveness, of alienation and withdrawal. It can foster a new separatism, an inverted segregation, a black apartheid. It can seek group solidarity and identity by the rejection of the White Devil and all his works simply because of white association. This is part of what Erik Erikson meant by "negative identity," the affirmation of identity by what one is not. With reference to that concept, he remarked on "the un-

[28] Herskovits, *Myth of the Negro Past*; E. Franklin Frazier, *The Negro in the United States* (New York, 1949), 1–21; Isaacs, *New World of Negro Americans*, 109–13; John A. Davis, "The Influence of Africans on American Culture," *Annals of the American Academy of Political and Social Science*, 354 (July 1964), 75–83.

[29] W. E. Burghardt Du Bois, *The Souls of Black Folk: Essays and Sketches* (Chicago, 1903), 3–4.

pleasant fact that our god-given identities often live off the degradation of others."[30] The most profound insight to be gained from Winthrop D. Jordan's study of American attitudes toward the Negro from English origins to the early nineteenth century is precisely the "negative identity" use that Europeans and white Americans made of Africans. To achieve their own group identity and unity, they systematically debased the Negro to a symbol of the barbarism and licentiousness to which they feared life in the wilderness might reduce Europeans themselves. The Negro thus became, as Jordan says, "a counter image for the European, a vivid reminder of the dangers facing transplanted Europeans, the living embodiment of what they must never allow themselves to become."[31] American society and identity were thus based on white supremacy. It would be one of the most appalling ironies of American history if the victims of this system of human debasement should in their own quest for identity become its imitators.

One manifestation of black nationalism in academic life is the cry that only blacks are truly qualified to write or to interpret or to teach the black experience. In the special sense that, other things being equal, those who have undergone an experience are best qualified to understand it, there is some truth in this claim. George A. Myers, the Negro friend and faithful correspondent of James Ford Rhodes, pleaded with the historian to do justice to the Negro, but doubted his capacity to do so. "You cannot fully appreciate this," he wrote, "because you have never been discriminated against."[32] Since white historians have written most of American history, including the part assigned the Negroes, it was inevitable that they should have determined the concepts, priorities, values, and interpretations of American historiography

[30] Erik Erikson, "The Concept of Identity in Race Relations: Notes and Queries," *Daedalus* (Winter 1966), 154–56.

[31] Jordan, *White Over Black*, 110.

[32] George A. Myers to James Ford Rhodes, Jan. 8, 1918, and Sept. 23, 1915, John A. Garraty, ed., *The Barber and the Historian: The Correspondence of George A. Myers and James Ford Rhodes, 1910–1923* (Columbus, 1956), 78, 32–33.

and that the values of the white man should have generally prevailed over those of the black man. This situation calls for correction and represents a present challenge to Negro historians.

American history, the white man's version, could profit from an infusion of "soul." It could be an essential corrective in line with the tradition of countervailing forces in American historiography. It was in that tradition that new immigrant historians revised first-family and old-stock history, that Jewish scholars challenged WASP interpretations, that western challengers confronted New England complacencies, Yankee heretics upset southern skeptics attacked Yankee myths, and the younger generation, since the beginning, assaulted the authority of the old. Negro historians have an opportunity and a duty in the same tradition.

An obligation to be a corrective influence is one thing, but a mandate for the exclusive preemption of a subject by reason of racial qualification is quite another. They cannot have it both ways. Either black history is an essential part of American history and must be included by all American historians, or it is unessential and can be segregated and left to black historians. But Negro history is too important to be left entirely to Negro historians. To disqualify historians from writing Negro history on the grounds of race is to subscribe to an extreme brand of racism. It is to ignore not only the substantial corrective and revisionary contributions to Negro history made by white Americans but also those of foreign white scholars such as Gilberto Freyre of Brazil, Fernando Ortiz of Cuba, Charles Verlinden of Belgium, and Gunnar Myrdal of Sweden. To export this idea of racial qualifications for writing history to Latin America is to expose its narrow parochialism. The United States is unique, so far as I know, in drawing an arbitrary line that classifies everyone as either black or white and calls all people with any apparent African intermixture "Negroes" or "blacks." In Latin America and the Caribbean, the gradations of color, hair, and features—often very fine gradations—are all important. Some Americans who present themselves as qualified by color to write "black" history would mystify many Latin Americans, since by their standards such people are not black at all, and deem themselves so only by unconsciously adopting white racist myths peculiar to the United States.[33]

The fact is that there are few countries left in the New World that are not multiracial in population. In many of them racial intermixture and intermarriage are prevalent. To impose the rule of racial qualification for historians of such multiracial societies as those of Trinidad, Cuba, Jamaica, Brazil, or Hawaii would be to leave them without a history. What passes for racial history is often the history of the relations between races—master and slave, imperialist and colonist, exploiter and exploited, and all the political, economic, sexual, and cultural relations, and their infinitely varied intermixtures. To leave all the history of these relations in the hands of the masters, the imperialists, or the exploiters would result in biased history. But to segregate historical subjects along racial lines and pair them with racially qualified historians would result in fantastically abstract history. This is all the more true since it is the relations, attitudes, and interactions between races that are the most controversial and perhaps the most significant aspects of racial history.

Some would maintain that the essential qualification is not racial but cultural and that membership in the Afro-American subculture is essential to the understanding and interpretation of the subtleties of speech, cuisine, song, dance, folklore, and music composing it. There may be truth in this. I am not about to suggest that the Caucasian is a black man with a white skin, for he is something less and something more than that. I am prepared to maintain, however, that, so far as their culture is concerned, all Americans are part Negro. Some are more so than others, of course, but the essential qualification is not color or race. When I said "all Americans," unlike Crèvecoeur, I included Afro-Americans. They are part Negro, too, but only part. So far as their culture is concerned they are more American than Afro and far more alien in Africa than they are at home, as virtually all pilgrims to Africa have discovered.[34]

---

[33] H. Hoetink, *The Two Variants in Caribbean Race Relations: A Contribution to the Sociology of Segmented Societies* (New York, 1961), 31–46.

[34] Harold R. Isaacs, *Emergent Americans: A Report on 'Crossroads Africa'*

Many old black families of Philadelphia and Boston are less African in culture than many whites of the South. The southern white "acculturation" began long ago and may be traced in the lamentations of planters that their children talked like Negroes, sang Negro songs, preferred Negro music at their dances, and danced like Negroes. It was observed by travelers like Frederick L. Olmsted, who was "struck with the close co-habitation and association of black and white . . . black and white faces constantly thrust out of doors, to see the train go by."[35] It is still a moot question whether white revivalist behavior—shouts, jerks, "unknown tongues," possession, and the rest—is a reflex of Africanism or vice versa. Even the sophisticated Mary Boykin Chesnut, on attending a Negro church at her plantation, admitted that she "wept bitterly" and added that "I would very much have liked to shout, too."[36] But as Herskovits says, "Whether Negroes borrowed from white or whites from Negroes, in this or any other aspect of culture, it must always be remembered that the borrowing was never achieved without resultant change in whatever was borrowed."[37] If there was a "black experience" and a "white experience," there was also a "gray experience."

Modern white parents have a complaint that differs from that of the antebellum planters, but resembles it. For where the old planter's children took on their African acculturation unconsciously by a process of osmosis, the contemporary collegiate swinger, protester, and rebel is a deliberate, assiduous, and often egregiously servile imitator. It was Langston Hughes' lament that "You've taken my blues and gone . . ." and he was probably justified in his complaint in the same poem that ". . . you fixed 'em / So they don't sound like me. . . ." But if so, it was certainly for no lack of effort on the part of the young white imitator, "The White Negro." His is but the latest contribution to the "gray experience."

(New York, 1961), 128–31; Isaacs, *New World of Negro Americans*, 261–70, 294.

[35] Frederick Law Olmsted, *A Journey in the Seaboard Slave States, With Remarks on Their Economy* (London, 1856), 17.

[36] Mary Boykin Chesnut, *A Diary from Dixie* (Boston, 1949), 149.

[37] Herskovits, *Myth of the Negro Past*, 225, 231.

Whether the revision of Negro history is undertaken by black historians or white historians, or preferably by both, they will be mindful of the need for correcting ancient indignities, ethnocentric slights, and paternalistic patronizing, not to mention calculated insults, callous indifference, and blind ignorance. They will want to see full justice done at long last to Negro achievements and contributions, to black leaders and heroes, black slaves and freedmen, black poets and preachers.

As for white historians, I doubt that their contribution to this revision would best be guided by impulses of compensatory exaggeration. The genuine achievements of Negro Americans throughout our history are substantial enough in view of the terrible handicaps under which they labored. They should receive the credit that they have been denied. But during the greater part of the struggle for power and place and fame that make up so much of history, black men were kept in chains and illiteracy and subject thereafter to crippling debasement and deprivation. The number of landmarks and monuments they were able to leave on the history of their country was necessarily limited. It is a misguided form of white philanthropy and paternalism that would attempt to compensate by exaggerating or by celebrating ever more obscure and deservedly neglected figures of the past. Equally misguided are impulses of self-flagellation and guilt that encourage the deprecation of all things European or white in our civilization and turn its history into a chorus of *mea culpas*. The demogoguery, the cant, and the charlatanry of historians in the service of a fashionable cause can at times rival that of politicians.[38] Also suspect is the standard assumption, supported by a long New England tradition, that this subject can be properly discussed only with an attitude of humorless solemnity. Anything so full of tears as the black experience, and anything so full of the absurd as the relations between the races in America, cannot be wholly devoid of existential laughter. I think this is what Ralph Ellison meant by the Negro's "tragicomic attitude toward

[38] Julian P. Boyd, *Between the Spur and Bridle* (New York, 1968), an address to the Association of American University Presses.

the universe."[39] The humor need not come at anyone's expense, but whatever the cost to piety, it should never be entirely excluded from discourse on this subject.

The Negro historian under present circumstances labors under a special set of pressures and temptations. One that will require moral fiber to resist is the temptation to gratify the white liberal's masochistic cravings, his servile yearnings to be punished. This is indeed a tempting market, but historians would do well to leave it to the theater of the absurd. Another temptation, given present license and indulgence, is to give uninhibited voice to such sentiments as Du Bois expressed in his declaration: "I believe in the Negro race, in the beauty of its genius, the sweetness of its soul. . . ."[40] A sincere sentiment, no doubt. But before releasing such pronouncements for publication it might be advisable to substitute the word "white" for the word "Negro" and play it back for sound: "I believe in the *white* race, in the beauty of its genius, the sweetness of its soul. . . ." At present, the celebratory impulse runs powerfully through the historiography of this field. Now is the time to praise famous men. Now is a time to do honor to heroes, justice to the obscure, and to demonstrate beyond doubt that the downtrodden seethed constantly with resistance to oppression and hostility to their oppressors. The demand for such history is understandable. But the historian will keep in mind that the stage of history was never peopled exclusively by heroes, villains, and oppressed innocents, that scamps and timeservers and anti-heroes have always played their parts. He might be reminded also that the charlatans and knaves and rakehells of Malcolm X's Harlem were probably as numerous as their white counterparts and represent a neglected field of Negro history.

It is to be hoped that white as well as black historians will reserve some place for irony as well as for humor. If so, they will risk the charge of heresy by pointing out in passing that Haiti, the first Negro republic of modern history, though born of a slave rebellion, promptly established and for a long time maintained an

39 Ralph Ellison, *Shadow and Act* (New York, 1964), 131.
40 W. E. B. Du Bois, *Darkwater* (New York, 1920), 3.

oppressive system of forced labor remarkably similar to state slavery; that Liberia, the second Negro republic, named for liberty, dedicated to freedom, and ruled by former slaves from the United States, established a flourishing African slave trade; and that Kwame Nkrumah, dictator of Ghana, with a misguided instinct for symbolism, selected as his official residence at Accra the Christiansborg Castle, one time barracoon from which his ancestors had sold their kinsmen into slavery.

These instances are not adduced to alleviate the guilt of the white man, who rightfully bears the greater burden. I would subscribe in general to the admonition of Barrington Moore, Jr., that, "For all students of human society, sympathy with the victims of historical processes and skepticism about the victors' claims provide essential safeguards against being taken in by the dominant mythology."[41] In all the annals of Africa there could scarcely be a more ironic myth of history than that of the New World republic which reconciled human slavery with natural rights and equality, and on the backs of black slaves set up the New Jerusalem, the world's best hope for freedom. The mythic African counterparts look pale beside the American example. They do serve, however, as reminders that the victims as well as the victors of the historical process are caught in the human predicament.

Joseph Conrad once remarked that women, children, and revolutionaries have no taste for irony. These are certainly not the most propitious times for the cultivation of that taste. Not only is it an abomination to revolutionaries, but also equally abhorrent are mixed motives, ambivalence, paradox, and complexity in any department. In times like these the historian will be hard put to it to maintain his creed that the righteousness of a cause is not a license for arrogance, that the passion for justice is not a substitute for reason, that race and color are neither a qualification nor a disqualification for historians, that myths, however therapeutic, are not to be confused with history, and that it is possible to be perfectly serious without being oppressively solemn.

[41] Barrington Moore, Jr., *Social Origins of Dictatorship and Democracy: Lord and Peasant in the Making of the Modern World* (Boston, 1966), 523.

To defend this position under the circumstances will require a certain amount of what some call "cool" and others, "grace"— grace under pressure.

Afterthoughts

Neither black nor white historians remained frozen for very long in the postures I attributed to them years ago. Much has changed since then, and with the changes have come alterations in the mood, the temper, the expectations, and the style of black history. Gone are the dashikis and the Afros. Rarely is heard a Swahili word, and jive talk is also a rarity—at least around the seminar table. Nor do Black Panthers any longer patrol the corridors. The newly decolonized African nations that once inspired black nationalism over here prove to be less inspiring now that they are so often plagued with famine, civil war, and dictatorship.

Dropouts have thinned the ranks of those who once professed eagerness to write the new black history. Some who were once conspicuous as spokesmen and leaders of the movement have proved less effective as scholars and writers. And if scholars and writers do not make the best agitators, militant agitators are rarely the best qualified scholars. As people sorted themselves out according to their talents and predilections, the style and manner of black historians and the character and prospects for black history changed quite markedly. A few figures from the piping times of revolution lingered on, and phrases from their messianic rhetoric still turn up occasionally in monographs. Some wavering between the antithetical goals of non-violent assimilation and militant separatism may be detected here and there. Those tendencies, however, are rather more prevalent among the non-publishing than among publishing black historians. Those of the latter kind usually steer clear of the old racial slogans and postures. If they profess any ideological interpretation at all it is more likely to be neo-Marxist than ethnic or racial.[1]

[1] August Meier and Elliott Rudwick, *Black History and the Historical Profession, 1915–1980* (Urbana and Chicago, 1986), 294–308.

Black historians in the last two decades have shared with their colleagues the precipitate decline of their discipline in the academy. Enrollments in black history courses have dropped even faster. Reckoned in terms of doctorates earned in history, black candidates were awarded 38 percent fewer in 1985–86 than they had earned twelve years earlier, and they received only 4 percent of the total number granted.[2] Less is heard of late about the need for black history's being written and taught exclusively by blacks. More work by blacks now reaches beyond racial confines for subject matter, relates the Afro-American to the Euro-American experience, and integrates it with American history. The contribution of blacks has already made it impossible to think of American history as the story of white men or to think of black history as what whites did, or did not do, or thought or believed, or hoped about blacks. Assenting to my suggestion that black history is too important to be left exclusively to black historians, John Hope Franklin remarked casually that "He could have added that any aspect of American history was too important to be left in the hands of any one group of historians."[3] *Touché!*

The most profound historical experience of Afro-Americans has yet to be fully appreciated and understood for its uniqueness. This was their long confrontation with the white man through the centuries of his greatest arrogance, when his will could not be seriously challenged anywhere in the world. And unlike the subject races of Asia, India, Africa, and the Indies, who were always a majority facing a white minority, often a small minority, the subject race in America faced its ordeal with white supremacy as an isolated minority confronting a majority, in bondage and out. Only a people who have endured and survived such an ordeal could have marshaled the collective patience, restraint, maturity, and determination they so often displayed under intense provocation during their great twentieth-century movement for liberation.

[2] *Perspectives: American Historical Association Newsletter* XXVI (March 1988), 9–10.
[3] John Hope Franklin, "Afro-American History: State of the Art," *Journal of American History* 75 (June 1988), 162–73.

Nathan Huggins wonders if Afro-American history is not "too discordant with progressive assumptions to be comfortably incorporated into the American story," a story in which all problems have solutions, with "each today better than all yesterdays." As he points out, "All national histories are not so optimistic and progressive as our own." In contrast with "the dominant American story," he believes the Afro-American experience has to be "told in terms of failed hopes, frustrated and ambiguous victories, dreams deferred." In what he believes to be its unlikely integration with the dominant national legend, the new narrative would "resonate to a more experienced, a wiser, nation."[4]

The great majority of Afro-Americans, however, share with a minority of non-black Americans a regional heritage relatively unencumbered with "optimistic and progressive" assumptions, with a collective experience that does not support the national myths and legends of success, abundance, innocence, and invincibility. The Southern background of most black Americans might prove an advantage in making black history part of American history. Thinking of these possibilities many years ago, I wrote: "There *are* Americans, after all, who were not 'born free.' They are also Southerners. They have yet to achieve articulate expression of their uniquely un-American experience. . . . The Negro has yet to do that. His first step will be an acknowledgement that he is also a Southerner as well as an American."[5]

[4] Nathan I. Huggins, in Darlene Clark Hine, ed., *The State of Afro-American History, Past, Present, and Future* (Baton Rouge, 1986), 167.

[5] *The Burden of Southern History* (Baton Rouge, 1960), 22.

3

The Future
of Southern History

For all the reference to future and present, the main preoccupation of the following paper, published in 1975, was really with the past, a past not all that recent either. The past I bore in mind was the previous half-century, during the early decades of which Southern history as then written was something of an embarrassment. As written and taught in those years it served generally to defend, legitimize, and rationalize the social order founded by the rulers who overthrew Reconstruction and to some extent the order that preceded it. Anyone professing Southern history as a calling was naturally assumed to be a conservative and a strict conformist. The subject was usually avoided by all historians except Southerners and by many of them as well. Moral opprobrium of an order rivaling abolitionists for eloquence continued to pour down from Yankeedom on Southern sinners. Anyone seeking to chronicle or explain the South's past was likely to be regarded as an apologist or worse. The changes that transformed the subject from an embarrassment to a source of pride, from a stagnant local enterprise to a mine of riches attracting enterprisers from all over, were indeed most welcome. Especially when it became evident that the intentions of those hailing from afar were not necessarily opprobrious. And these developments were welcomed

*with special warmth by a Southern historian who had devoted
a long career to revisions of the old story under all the handicaps that preceded the welcome change.*

THE CLOSEST THE HISTORIAN CAN LEGITIMATELY GET to making
pronouncements about the future is the recent past, and the
closer the recent past gets to the present, the more insecure the
historian feels in whatever he has to say about it. His instinct is
to withdraw from the present, which is the brink of the future,
and put distance between himself and the brink to gain the security he likes to call "perspective." The trouble with the future
from the historian's point of view is that it has not happened yet.
Whatever glimpses beyond the brink I shall venture here will be
afforded from a point well back from the edge.

My first impression of the recent past of Southern history is
that there has been more of it. Here I speak in crudely quantitative terms of sheer number and volume of publications during
the last twenty years or so. For that observation to have much
meaning, it would have to be endowed with that cherished quality of "perspective." It would have to be placed in context of
productivity in other fields of history, indeed in other fields of
learning. The 1960s were exceptionally prosperous years for
universities and for scholarship. Foundations and government
agencies were generous with funds, graduate schools were
crowded, jobs were plentiful. It is likely that productivity increased markedly in many disciplines, including other fields of
history besides Southern history. Whether Southern history was
exceptional in this respect, and if so to what degree, it would be
premature to say. All that seems possible at this time is a few tentative soundings and estimates.

With apologies for citing a personal experience, I might offer the recent historiography of the brief period between Reconstruction and the First World War. In 1951 there appeared a
volume treating that period entitled *Origins of the New South*.
Twenty years later a second edition was published that included

a supplementary bibliography prepared by Charles B. Dew, who compiled a critical list of works on this field which had appeared in the two decades since the original edition was published. A comparison of the bibliography of 1951 with that of 1971 is rather startling. A valid comparison requires elimination of the half of the list of 1951 that covered primary sources, government documents, newspapers, periodicals, and such materials. A comparison confined to secondary works of scholarship, however, discloses only 16 pages listing such works in the first edition and 112 pages in the second, and a count of individual titles comes to 311 in the one and 1,905 in the other.[1]

I hasten to say that this does not necessarily prove that more than six times the number of works were produced in the period between 1951 and 1971 than were published in the period of more than three times that length since 1913. For one thing the original bibliographer was probably more selective than the second, and for another the second bibliographer was probably more thorough and systematic than the first. I am at least sure that the second was more scrupulous in rounding up dissertation titles—granting there were more such titles to be rounded up in the latter period.

Allowing for these and other probable discrepancies in the comparison and for the delinquencies of the party of the first part, I am still persuaded that the contrast is significant. While I doubt that the ratio of productivity between the periods was quite six to one, I would feel confident in guessing that considerably more scholarly works on the New South era were produced in the two decades following 1951 than had been produced in all the years preceding, perhaps twice as many, perhaps more than that.

In all these estimates and those that follow it is well to keep in mind how brief has been the enterprise of scholarly investigation of Southern history. Putting aside the literature on the

---

[1] C. Vann Woodward, *Origins of the New South, 1877–1913* (Baton Rouge, L.S.U. Press, 1971); see the original bibliography excluding primary works, pp. 499–515; Charles B. Dew's "Critical Essay on Recent Works," pp. 517–628.

Southern Confederacy, especially its military aspects, and that on the local history of various Southern states, David Potter remarked in 1961 that "the history of the South as a region—of the whole vast area below the Potomac, viewed as a single entity for the whole time from the settlement of Jamestown to the present—is largely a product of the last five decades."[2] In that foreshortened perspective, it is less surprising that the products of two decades can account for such a large proportion of the whole. Especially so when it is recalled that those years came in the period after most of the learned journals of the field were launched, the great research collections were established, and courses and seminars in the subject had gained recognition in the leading universities of the country. Earlier historians of the South had labored without many of these advantages.

Whether activity on the post-Reconstruction period has been representative of productivity on other periods of Southern history it is difficult to say. No comparison of bibliographies such as those used for the New South period has been attempted for any other period. Were such comparisons available, they might well prove that other periods have outstripped the one observed. For what it is worth, my impression is that at least in the last fifteen years publications on the antebellum period, the Civil War, and Reconstruction have exceeded in number those on the period following. I have also been impressed with recent activity in colonial history, and the Revolution would seem to be undergoing a somewhat artificially stimulated boom that is, of course, national rather than regional.

So far we have spoken only in crudely quantitative terms— titles listed, books published, productivity in the market and manufacturing sense. These terms are not appropriate to the measurement of products of the mind. They do not even prove that the mind is involved. In too many instances it is not. The mindlessness of much academic productivity is all too apparent. If I have appeared to be rather casual in my quantification methods

---

[2] David M. Potter, "The Enigma of the South," *Yale Review* 51 (1961), reprinted in his *The South and the Sectional Conflict* (Baton Rouge: L.S.U. Press, 1968), p. 3.

so far, it is attributable not merely to laziness but also to contempt for numbers as evidence of things of the mind. They may constitute mere evidence of misdirected energy or lax and low standards on the part of professors, editors, publishers, and critics. My guess is that these latter influences play a large part in accounting for bulging bibliographies and publishers' lists in recent years.

Any serious reckoning of the progress and future of a field of learning will shun numbers and turn from criteria of quantity to criteria of quality. These are, of course, even more difficult to apply and to agree upon. I can report, however, a considerable amount of agreement among knowledgeable critics with high standards that there has indeed been a gratifying improvement in quality. One evidence of improvement is found in the learned journals, and I quote the present managing editor of the *Journal of Southern History* as follows:

> On the whole, I agree that there has been an improvement in the quality of the *Journal* articles over the years. There are fewer narrative and descriptive articles and more interpretative ones; there are more articles on blacks and slavery with a more balanced approach; there are more articles on urban history and more on the recent South; and there are more sophisticated quantitative articles. Much of the material is in a sense less southern than it is writing about topics relating to the South.[3]

I have undertaken no survey of professors offering graduate and undergraduate courses in Southern history, but I suspect that the experience of many in selecting essential secondary works for required reading would correspond with my own—viz., that a large percentage of such books in the required list have been published in the last twenty years. In my own list of required books for a year-long graduate course, for example, 14 of a total of 29 fall in that category. I hope this does not merely betray a

[3] S. W. Higginbotham to C. Vann Woodward, January 3, 1975. The same editor indulges in a bit of harmless quantifying in his annual report of October 1974. While in the year 1964–65 he received 99 articles, rejected 81, and accepted 18, in the year 1973–74 he received 142, rejected 132, and accepted 7. He speaks ominously of "a large backlog, which is only gradually being reduced."

vulgar bias for the contemporary as against the old—a bias especially repugnant in historians—and I do not think it is that. At
least a lot of old-timers, including U. B. Phillips and Charles
Sydnor still retain honored places. It would be interesting and
possibly revealing to see how many of what are now considered
the most essential or important scholarly books on Southern history are missing from Rembert Patrick and Arthur Link, *Writing
Southern History*[4]—not because that excellent study of historiography ignored or overlooked them, but simply because they were
published later—that is, since 1965. My guess is that it might
take more than the fingers of one hand to number them. And
again I disavow the vulgar bias of contemporaneity.

Whether one finds this impressionistic evidence persuasive
or not, it will be my assumption that something unusual has happened recently to a field of scholarship long considered parochial,
out of the mainstream, marginal in importance, and comparatively
dormant. What has happened, I believe, is that this field has suddenly emerged in a position of central importance in national history, disclosed more relevance to the history of foreign peoples
than any other American field, and attracted more than its share
of first-rate talent. In addition, or as a consequence, it explodes
with innovations in interpretations, findings, revisions, and meth-
odology, and discharges a flow of intellectual excitement that
spills over into other fields.

My second assumption is that this is a phenomenon of
American academic and intellectual life that calls for explanation of a kind to which the historian himself is peculiarly qualified to contribute. A start on this task is the main purpose of this
essay. An incidental hope is that the effort might also lift a corner of the curtain that veils the future of the field of Southern
history.

It will necessarily be an exercise in multiple causation, for
the explanation is complex. The causes might be divided tenta-
tively into two categories—the fortuitous and the inherent. By the

---

[4] Rembert Patrick and Arthur S. Link, eds., *Writing Southern History:
Essays in Historiography in Honor of Fletcher M. Green* (Baton Rouge:
L.S.U. Press, 1965).

fortuitous I mean the unforeseeable accidents of history, the shifting fortunes of chance and coincidence, the unearned increments. By the inherent I mean causes more directly attributable to the nature and riches of the subject—of Southern history itself. It will quickly become apparent that this dichotomy is of limited usefulness because the fortuitous and the inherent tend to overlap and intertwine. Since there is likely to be less controversy about the unearned than the earned, the rewards of chance than those of merit, it might be best to turn first to the fortuitous.

It was not chance that brought on the Civil Rights Movement, the drive for Negro rights, the demand for the study of black history and culture, or the great northward and cityward migration of millions of Southern black people. But it was chance or coincidence that all these events served to stimulate interest and work in Southern history. That certainly was not the intention of these upheavals. But anything touching Afro-American experience leads inevitably back to Southern history, and black history is inextricably interwoven with white.

Undoubtedly much of the historical writing inspired by those movements was superficial, propagandistic, or chauvinistic. On the other hand, without the direct or indirect stimulus of the social upheavals it is impossible to explain or even imagine the subsequent advances of serious scholarship in the history of slavery, abolitionism, emancipation, sectional conflict, reconstruction, segregation, and race relations—not to mention progress in the neglected field of black history more strictly defined. The main, if not exclusive, historical theater for all these subjects, of course, lay below the Mason and Dixon line.

For a century after the Civil War the South was an importer and consumer of cultural determinants and subjects for historical investigation—the North the exporter. The Southern historian was consequently concerned with the impact of such importations as big business, the corporation, Wall Street, urbanization, progressivism, and radicalism. A common response was that the South also had its urban problems, progressivism, and radicalism—even its frontier democracy: that the South was "American too." More recently the balance of trade in cultural determinants seems to be swinging the other way, with the South the growing exporter, the North the main importer. For one thing, the South has exported millions of its black people and along with them patterns of culture, housing, schooling, poverty, segregation, and politics—generally called "urban problems"—that had long been considered peculiarly Southern. By 1975 they were more commonly associated with Boston than with Little Rock. It has been seriously suggested that Northern politics is being "southernized." Increasingly, the North looks to the South for the historical roots of its problems, as the South had once looked to the North. To a degree Southern history has been nationalized as a subject of concern.

This is one, but by no means the only, reason for the rapid recent influx of non-Southern historians into the field of Southern history. In the old days there were always a few Northern historians who kept a hand in Southern history. Some of them, like Albert Hart, George Bancroft, or Dwight L. Dumond, whose chief concern was to set Southerners right "on the goose," continued the old tradition of sectional debate and confrontation. Others like William A. Dunning and later Paul L. Buck carried on the nationalist tradition of sectional reconciliation. In the main, however, Southern history was written and taught by Southerners. When the editors of the multivolume *History of the South* planned their series in the 1930s, every one of the ten authors originally selected was a Southerner. It has not been so many years since Northern visitors to a meeting of the Southern Historical Association were relatively rare. One met Southerners and heard papers by Southerners. All that has changed. The attendance at a Southern Association meeting is now little more regional in character than one of the national association meetings, and the same applies to the authors of the papers. In the scholarship of certain fields, notably slavery, Reconstruction, and social history, non-Southerners have taken the lead and set the pace. Fortuitous or not, this has surely been a powerful cause of the renaissance in Southern history.

More clearly fortuitous and unearned as well as more subtle was the heritage of the Southern Literary Renaissance. Although its heyday was over before the boom in Southern history was well started, it served as an example and inspiration in several ways. For one thing the men of letters demonstrated beyond doubt that there was nothing in the subject matter of Southern history that prevented it from being treated with utmost seriousness by men of higher talent or from commanding the attention and capturing the imagination of the reading world at home and abroad. If historians had been inhibited by the feeling that their subject was somehow too discredited or parochial or backward or degraded to deserve the highest concern, they could banish their doubts. The novelists and dramatists taught historians other lessons, if any needed them: that to understand they need not justify, that to recount or recapture the past was not to celebrate it, and that defense had best be left to propagandists. The hallmark of the highest Southern fiction was history-mindedness. Historians could derive such pride as they might from evidence that their own muse won homage from craftsmen who served another muse with such fidelity and distinction.

There was yet another means at hand for overcoming the sense of parochialism and isolation under which Southern historians once labored. This was the rather recent discovery of the possibilities of comparative history with which the Southern experience was peculiarly endowed. And here we shift from the category of the fortuitous to that of inherent causes. For a long time the South suffered under the sense of the irrelevance of its past, a past that was out of step, a throwback to forgotten eras, a perverse survival of bygone styles and ways into modern times. In that way the modern South thought of its experience of aristocracy and hierarchy, of slavery and patriarchy, of paternalism and deference, of race and caste, of personalism and the familial ambiance, of colonial dependence and economic backwardness. Of course, the South's point of reference as the supposed norm in all those matters was the Northern or non-Southern part of the United States. What the South forgot was the North's boasted exceptionalism, its pride in escaping the ills that plagued the South's experience and that of other unfortunate peoples, together with its well-grounded myths of affluence, innocence, and invincibility—The American Way. What the South has recently discovered is that in the very peculiarities of its past that it had long considered eccentric, irrelevant, and out of step, the South's historic experience was more relevant and in step with many other peoples of the world and their heritage than was the history of the North. If any history was eccentric and out of step, in this respect, it was that of the rest of the country.

The South could claim shared experiences and institutions with many Old World peoples, but its closer claims lay to commonality and historic kinships with New World societies. The South was the major member of the great community of nations and colonies that made up Plantation America. That vast cultural community stretched eastward from Texas along the Gulf and through the Caribbean to remote Barbados, and southward from Virginia to far-off São Paulo. With dozens of societies once under the flags of several empires the Southern states shared the experience of slavery and plantation, the presence and influence of large numbers of people of African origins, styles of racial subordination and intermingling, and styles of aristocracy, patriarchy, paternalism, authority, caste, and deference, patterns of abolition, emancipation, and reconstruction, and post-manumission experiments with apprenticeship, sharecropping, and peonage. The antebellum South was the largest, wealthiest, and most powerful of the Plantation America societies. It clung to slavery longer than most, but not so long as Brazil and Cuba, and it was the only one of them that chose to fight an all-or-nothing war for survival.

The South, like most societies, sought to understand its past in part by comparison. It was only belatedly that it discovered that in picking the North it had chosen an incongruous partner for comparative purposes. Only lately and more logically has it turned for comparative illumination of its past to those countrires of old Plantation America which had shared so many aspects of it. The result has been much more light upon the South's history than could be shed by comparisons with Massachusetts, Michigan, or Minnesota. Suggestive studies have been made comparing slavery in Virginia and Cuba, South Carolina with Barbados and

Jamaica, and various aspects of the history of race relations by comparing the South with Brazil and with Caribbean societies.[5] So far, New England and the Middle West seem to have inspired no such comparative history, and short of the sociological abstractions of mobility, demography, and technology, it is difficult to know where such opportunities lie or where suitable comparative partners for such an enterprise might be found. The point is that Southern history has benefited singularly from this line of inquiry because of its special character and that this development has contributed significantly to its enlivenment as a field of study.

The next explanatory variable, to borrow a sociologism, might be said to combine the fortuitous and the inherent. At least elements of each category play a part in the explanation. Here the categories overlap and intertwine. On the fortuitous side is a secular slump in the national morale cycle. This happens whenever the national myths of affluence, innocence, and invincibility are seriously threatened, especially when all three are jeopardized simultaneously as they have been by the combination of depression, Watergate, and South Vietnam—to mention only a few of several such menaces to myths. A familiar side effect of such slumps in the morale cycle is a falling off in Yankeedom of the normal enthusiasm for such perennial historical themes as progress in urbanization and industrialization, technological advance, the westward movement, immigration, ethnic voting, social mobility, and the rise of the middle class.

As usual when that happens, historians turn away from familiar themes of the bland, the homogeneous, and the hopeful that sustain nation myths and seek contrasting themes. This may take any of several directions. The oldest alternative, the one William R. Taylor chronicles in *Cavalier and Yankee*,[6] is es-

[5] Herbert S. Klein, *Slavery in the Americas: A Comparative Study of Virginia and Cuba* (Chicago: University of Chicago Press, 1967); Carl N. Degler, *Neither Black nor White: Slavery and Race Relations in Brazil and the United States* (New York: Macmillan, 1971); and Philip D. Curtin, *The Atlantic Slave Trade: A Census* (Madison: University of Wisconsin Press, 1969).

[6] William R. Taylor, *Cavalier and Yankee: The Old South and American National Character* (New York: G. Braziller, 1961).

capist and romantic, the quest for lost grandeur: silver on polished mahogany, white-columned porticoes, and, to quote a forgotten poet, "pistol-hearted horsemen who could ride like jolly centaurs under the hot stars." It still has lingering appeal for some, but other alternatives take priority. One is the search for what went wrong, the moral lesson, the serpent in the garden, the American genesis of wickedness and perversity. Broader still is the simple need for something different, some striking contrast to the bland, the hopeful, the homogeneous—even something wickedly un-American, darkly tragic, or catastrophic. All these "explanatory variables" fall in the category of the fortuitous.

The consequences, however, take us at once into the category of the inherent. Where else could the seekers more logically turn for that which they sought than to the history of the South and its notoriously inherent qualities? Where else, within national boundaries, could they have found so abundantly available all the varieties of contrast? Both the substance and the trappings of grandeur were there, and also the serpent, the perversity, the wickedness of aristocracy, the inequality, the towering pretensions and the precipitous fall, the catastrophe and the tragedy—all as un-American as one could well wish. As for the pall of blandness, homogeneity, and cheerful optimism, the rise and fall of the slave empire and the heritage of defeat that followed provide the perfect contrast. Between master and slave or white and black there were few ambiguities in the line of authority, little blurring of class lines, and no nonsense about homogeneity and equality on those fronts. The myths of affluence, innocence, and invincibility strike few roots in such soil.

The attractions of these riches have been irresistible to many seekers from above the Potomac and the Ohio—seekers of the exotic, seekers for new moral lessons to teach the South, seekers for startling new interpretations of its history. They have swelled the ranks of non-Southerners in the field and contributed substantially to the recent expansion of activity in Southern history. Their stay will probably be as temporary as the impulse and the needs that attracted them southward. Many of our scholar carpetbaggers will soon withdraw with what they came to get. They will leave behind many contributions, some of undoubted value, but in the process of evaluating the whole it might be well to count our spoons, so to speak, and take a close look at the fine print in the documents bequeathing the legacy they left.

Among the many types of newcomers attracted southward recently, none were so strongly attached to the field and none left a more ironic legacy than the newly spawned tribe variously named quantifiers, econometricians, or cliometricians. Whether the explanation is mainly of the fortuitous or the inherent type, the fact is there seems to be a fatal attraction and a durable relationship between the quantifiers and Southern history, particularly but not exclusively the history of slavery. From the very inception of the econometric movement with the famous essay by Conrad and Meyer on the profitability problem in 1957[7] down to the ambitious volumes of Fogel and Engerman in 1974[8] and the deluge of controversial criticism and comment, pro and con, precipitated by their work since then, the field of battle has lain below the Potomac. It has not been North versus South, but rather a battle waged on Southern soil between factions of an alien army. A few Southerners were recruited in their ranks, but mainly Southerners have remained noncombatant if fascinated spectators. No other theater of scholarly historical activity of all the varied Southern theaters has attracted so much attention or prompted so many bets on the outcome as this. Few of the spectators have mastered the weaponry or understood the tactics of the new warfare, but they had no trouble grasping the issues involved.

The stakes have not been so high since Grant and Lee squared off in the Wilderness. What was at issue was the outcome of a renewed debate over virtually all the ancient issues of the furious nineteenth-century sectional conflict that ended in the blanket moral indictment of Southern society. All the old issues were dragged forth: cruelty, slave breeding, brutal punishment, the whip and the branding bar, family separation, child

---

[7] Alfred H. Conrad and John R. Meyer, "The Economics of Slavery in the Ante Bellum South," *Journal of Political Economy* 66 (April 1958): 95–130.
[8] Robert W. Fogel and Stanley L. Engerman, *Time on the Cross: The Economics of American Negro Slavery* (Boston: Little, Brown, 1974).

sales, sexual exploitation, feeding, clothing, housing, medication, the horrors of the slave block and the slave trade, the whole abolitionist bill of indictment. Only this time the contestants were not fierce-eyed abolitionists and infuriated planters, but factions of fierce-eyed econometricians ranged in confrontation behind their batteries of computers.

The tide of battle swayed back and forth, and the outcome seemed doubtful. First Manassas raised false hopes and perhaps Vicksburg and Gettysburg were still to come. It would be a long war. But during the campaigns of '74 and '75 hopes soared along the Rappahannock and rebel yells echoed all the way to the Mississippi. It looked for a time as if Generals Fogel and Engerman and their disciplined regiments had turned the flank of opposing forces and were driving all before them. They had the advantage of numbers, and numbers counted—so to speak. Numbers were said to prove that slaves of the South were well fed, adequately clothed, comfortably housed, and reasonably well medicated. Materially they enjoyed many advantages over contemporary industrial free labor in the North and Europe, since they received larger real wages, had longer life expectancy, and a lower percentage of their output was withheld from them as profits. Brutality was rare, whippings were few, broken families were exceptional, child sales minimal, family integrity was carefully fostered, and slave breeding was virtually nonexistent. Under expert planter management and dedicated overseers, the majority of them black, slave labor far outstripped free agricultural workers of the North in efficiency and productivity and accounted for one of the wealthiest, most productive, and rapidly growing economies in the world. And furthermore, the 70 percent of whites who owned no slaves and the slaves themselves, to a degree, are said to have shared these blessings.

Many of these points were strongly contested, and pockets of resistance that were overrun in the general advance put up determined defense behind the lines. They were expecting reinforcements and their ammunition was not yet exhausted. On the other hand, the broad strategic advances seem rather more secure: that slavery was highly profitable, slave labor comparatively efficient and highly productive, and the Southern economy, at least in the closing decade of the old regime, extremely wealthy, sanguine about the future, and booming along at a great rate. Most of the shooting that continued among the hosts of quantification was not over these major points, but rather over the correct explanation: whether the stick or the carrot, the cowhide whip or the Protestant ethic. This is not the place to assess the merits or predict the outcome of this running war between cliometricians.

The only concern here is to estimate its impact upon the field of Southern history and particularly upon the Southerners who write and teach in this field. There can be little doubt that the work of the quantifiers has contributed substantially to the recent revival of interest and work in slavery and related subjects. Indeed it has altered the whole landscape of the old field. The question is how Southern historians will respond, particularly to the bold revisionism that professes to lift the whole subject out of the plane of moral recrimination in which it has so long languished.

Before making this timid foray into the future, however, the historian would characteristically halt for "perspective." First we should recall that when the cliometricians unexpectedly appeared with reinforcements, the South had scarcely emerged from the dugouts into which it was driven by the long barrage of moral charges ensuing from the civil rights movement, desegregation, and black liberation. During that long siege any head lifted was promptly shot down. To explain or account for any and all of the ills that beset the black people in the Northern ghettos—deterioration of the black family, desertion of black fathers, mounting welfare rolls, soaring crime rates, increasing drug addiction, multiplying dropouts, and declining school performance—the answer was always the same: "Look away! look away! look away! Dixie Land!" It was all due to evils of long ago and far away—slavery, racism, peonage, or whatnot, way down South in the land of cotton—which, of course, could not possibly be remedied by further strains on the city budget of Boston or New York, and which could not in any reasonable way be attributed to the shortcomings of the free enterprise system and the deterioration of industrial capitalism.

But even before the recent siege, Southern historians had long cowered under a lower-keyed sniping from members of their own guild up North that intensified in the 1950s. The pattern of fire is familiar to aging survivors of that era. It did not appear planned or deliberate or even consciously malicious. Nevertheless, among a prominent school of historians, whatever appeared retrograde in national history, whether among the Founding Fathers, the Jacksonians, the Populists, the Bryanites, or the Progressives, was somehow attributable to Southern votes or influence. The tendency is familiar to any reader of the more popular books on Populism and Progressivism. As for those movements that lay clearly beyond the pale—fundamentalism, prohibition, mobism, McCarthyism—the South was assumed to be more directly responsible. To this school of historians the debit side of Tocqueville's tally sheets on democracy lay almost entirely below the Potomac. To extremists of the school the South was "marvelously useful as a mirror in which the nation can see its blemishes magnified," or "a kind of Fort Knox of prejudice—where the nation has always stored the bulk of its bigotry."[9]

Subjected to a generation or more of such treatment, with a heritage of the sort stretching even further back, Southern historians gradually acquired a vocational handicap, a permanent stance of apology and a posture of defensiveness often complicated by writer's cramp and in severe cases total paralysis. Their lectures and writings often limped along with lamentations about how bad it all was, ritual citations of Thoreau, Emerson, and Sumner, and concessions about the good intentions of John Brown. A less common reaction to the same situations on the part of a few historians was a posture of defiant bellicosity. It is hard to say which produced the more unhealthy climate for the professional welfare of historians, which shackles curtailed their freedom the more.

Then suddenly the cliometricians arrived on the scene wav-

[9] Howard Zinn, *The Southern Mystique* (New York: Knopf, 1964), pp. 217–263.

ing an emancipation proclamation. Brushing aside questions of the legitimacy of the document, they promised to liberate the oppressed, strike off their shackles, turn the tables, throw abolitionists and neo-abolitionists on the defensive, and vindicate the South. The question is how would the liberated react? Crippled by generations of bondage, were they prepared for freedom? Were they ready for equality? Might they not abuse it? Might they not interpret freedom as freedom from work, freedom from observance of the established canons of their craft, even freedom from the canons of historical evidence? Might they not acclaim the "higher law" doctrine of their liberators? What were the anarchical consequences of putting the bottom rail on top?

Before the new freedmen celebrate their Day of Jubilee prematurely, they should remember that the war that promises their liberation still rages and that the fortunes of war may change. Already serious questions are raised about the authority of the emancipation proclamation. It has been dismissed as executive fiat, lacking legislative approval and popular support, and probably unconstitutional. It undoubtedly deprives privileged classes of long-cherished rights and immunities which they will stubbornly defend and subverts the moral order that separates good and evil along established geographical lines. All these matters still await adjudication, and some call for the slow processes of constitutional change.

Finally, to abandon strained metaphors, I would simply caution fellow Southern historians against being the first to embrace the latest fashions, especially those demanding total revision. They should have observed from past instances that quantification almost invariably proves that things were not so bad before the revolution—any revolution. That is why radicals shun quantification like the plague. It is, on the other hand, a favorite resort of *ci-devant* radicals. We have enough to be grateful for from the quantifiers without uncritically accepting gifts with both hands. They have enormously enlivened and helped to rejuvenate large parts of Southern history. They have also had an important hand in lifting the fog of provincialism that had obscured the significance of the field.

Other forces have, as we have seen, contributed mightily to all these desirable ends. We have already mentioned the contributions of the Southern Renaissance in letters, the enrichment brought by comparative history, the intensified interest in black history, and the recruitment of many Northern historians of talent. The list would not be complete without mentioning the contributions of the new American school of revisionary Marxists. Renouncing with scorn the propagandistic history and vulgar determinism of the older generation of American Marxists, the revisionists have brought the zest and independence of an Oedipal rebellion to their rediscovery of Southern history. With refreshing logic and boldness Eugene D. Genovese asks how Marxists can consistently contend that morals are determined by class interests and then withhold from planter statesmen and leaders the admiration due them for the loyalty, courage, and devotion with which they served their class. The historical works of the new American Marxists have been predominantly concerned so far with Southern history and related subjects. The whole field has profited from their intervention.

With all these windfalls and endowments from both fortuitous and inherent sources, it is little wonder that Southern history should have forged to the front in recent years and become the most active frontier of American historical scholarship. It might also be reasonably designated the most intellectually stimulating and innovative field, the one in which new techniques are most often tried and tested, where ideological skirmishing is liveliest, on which movements for racial and social justice impinge most readily, and to which Northern historians most naturaly turn to escape the blandness of consensus and the drabness of homogeneity.

In full awareness of such riches, the Southern historian who is also a Southerner, white or black, has special reason for pride in his field—though none for complacency in its present state of development. Endowed with ample riches, he can afford to extend generous hospitality, even to strangers and outsiders—even if their ways are a bit eccentric and their accents rather strange. There is plenty for all down on the old plantation. Its resources are such that the historian should have no fear of exhausting them by overwork. He should feel sufficient security in his heritage never to be tempted to raise his voice in argument over its worth. As a historian with proper respect for his muse, he would never stoop to pick up ancestral polemics of the proslavery or antislavery argument. He has more important things to do. For the small domain of history he calls his own has more than its share of the triumphs and the anguish, the honor and the shame, the comedy and the tragedy that are the classic subjects of great history.

Afterthoughts

Fifteen years beyond the brink of the future at which the essay above cautiously halted, further steps have more than confirmed hopes for continued advances in Southern history. In fact the pace seems to have quickened since then. In terms of sheer productivity the new pace is suggested by a recently published two-volume bibliography, more than 1800 pages in length, confined to the subject of black slavery in the New World.[1] Another indication of expansion in the broader field is a massive reassessment entitled *Interpreting Southern History*, published in 1987.[2] This valuable book replaces one of comparable size and scope that appeared in 1965 under the title *Writing Southern History*.[3] The more recent volume gives predominant attention to work published since its predecessor appeared and tends to justify the emphasis by stressing the relative importance of recent work.

From evidence of this sort and that personally encountered in continuing work in the field, I have the impression that interest in Southern history is by no means on the decline and, mea-

[1] John David Smith, *Black Slavery in the Americas: An Interdisciplinary Bibliography, 1865–1980* (2 vols., Westport, Conn., 1982).
[2] John B. Boles and Evelyn Thomas Nolan (eds.), *Interpreting Southern History: Historiographical Essays in Honor of Sanford Higginbotham* (Baton Rouge, 1987).
[3] Arthur S. Link and Rembert W. Patrick (eds.), *Writing Southern History: Essays in Historiography in Honor of Fletcher M. Green* (Baton Rouge, 1965).

sured crudely in volume of work produced, is in fact growing as never before. For what impressions are worth, I would also venture the opinion that improvements in quality have, in some degree at least, matched increases in quantity. Some of the finest works we have on the subject are products of the last two decades.

Other gratifying impressions are not lacking. The characteristics that once made the historiography of the South rather "an embarrassment" have largely disappeared. These include the old defensiveness, its use to legitimize the status quo, and the popular inference that anyone who made it a profession was a conformist and a native son. Parochial rivalries within the guild resulted in the identification of products according to regional or racial or ideological identity of authors are no longer as meaningful as they once were. Northern historians continue to be attracted southward by subject matter and sources, but they are rarely stigmatized as carpetbaggers or their native friends as scalawags. Blacks write white history as well as black, and native whites have lost nervousness about integrating the two. Econometricians write narrative history, and neo-Maxists are known to cite neo-Confederates.

The expanding scope of comparative studies is suggested in the title of the 1800-page bibliography on slavery cited above, which is not limited to the South but embraces all "the Americas" and includes interdisciplinary works as well. Other hemispheres and continents have been penetrated by comparisons of forced labor in the South with that in South Africa and Russia.[4] "Parochialism" is hardly the word to characterize a field that inspires so many world-wide comparisons and cosmopolitan interests.

---

[4] Peter Kolchin, *Unfree Labor: American Slavery and Russian Serfdom* (Cambridge, Mass., and London, 1987); John W. Cell, *The Highest Stage of White Supremacy: The Origins of Segregation in South Africa and the American South* (Cambridge, Eng., 1982).

II

REINTERPRETATIONS

In their task of interpreting the relationship of past to present, historians have usually felt called upon to stress similarities, continuities, and precedents and to discount sharp departures, disjunctures, and anomalies. Given the usual pace of historical change—even the quickened pace of modern history up to quite recent times—traditional emphasis on continuities and similarities seemed appropriate enough. Beginning before midcentury, however, with the unprecedented accelerations of the rate of change resulting from Second World War, and with terrifying innovations and discontinuities tumbling one over another, historians with any awareness of how much was being replaced are obliged to shift their emphasis from continuities to discontinuities. Continuities remained, of course, but instead of calling for deference to precedent and stressing similarities and lessons of the past for the present, historians now must warn against misleading precedent and false similarities between past and present, and caution against the "lessons of history." In fulfillment of these unwonted obligations, one must use whatever special advantages come to hand. Among these surely is that enjoyed by survivors who participated in both the superseded past and the unprecedented present. The three essays that follow are attempts to bring to bear that perspective on some anachronistic views of history and its uses.

4

The Age
of Reinterpretation

The three examples chosen here to illustrate the need for historical reinterpretation could be described as the recent, sudden, and simultaneous end of three eras: (1) the era of free security in America, (2) a much longer era of human warfare and weaponry, and (3) the age of European dominance in world affairs. All three momentous developments were interrelated and appeared toward the end of the Second World War. All had profound implications for the decisions of statesmen on policy, grand strategy, and world affairs. And yet these decisions continued to be shaped fatefully by assumptions and expectations derived from bygone ages and anachronistic conceptions of their history. A prime concern of historians should be reinterpretation to overcome anachronisms.

INNUMERABLE INFLUENCES have inspired the reinterpretation of history. The most common of late would appear to have been those originating within the intellectual community, or within the historical guild itself, rather than with the impact of historical events. Influences of the predominant sort include new theories, new methods, and new sources. Of special importance in recent years has been the example of other disciplines and sciences, old ones such as philosophy and biology with new theories, or new ones such as psychology and sociology with new approaches to old problems.

With no intended disparagement for prevailing and recent types of revision, the present essay concerns itself almost exclusively with reinterpretations that are inspired by historical events and have little to do with new theories, new methods, or new disciplines. The suggested opportunities for reinterpretation are, in fact, related to historical events so recent that nearly all of them have occurred since the summer of 1945. As responsible human beings we are rightly concerned first of all with the impact of these events upon the present and immediate future. But as historians we are, or we should be, concerned with their effect upon our view of the past as well. These events have come with a concentration and violence for which the term "revolution" is usually reserved. It is a revolution, or perhaps a set of revolutions, for which we have not yet found a name. My thesis is that these developments will and should raise new questions about the past and affect our reading of large areas of history, and my belief is that future revisions may be extensive enough to justify calling the coming era of historiography an age of reinterpretation. The first illustration happens to come mainly from American history, but this should not obscure the broader scope of the revolution, which has no national limitations.

Throughout most of its history the United States has enjoyed a remarkable degree of military security, physical security from hostile attack and invasion. This security was not only remarkably effective, but relatively free. Free security was based in part on nature's gift of three vast bodies of water interposed between this country and any other power that might constitute a serious menace to its safety. There was not only the Atlantic to the east and the Pacific to the west, but a third body of water, considered so impenetrable as to make us virtually unaware of its importance, the Arctic Ocean and its great ice cap to the north. The security thus provided was free in the sense that it was enjoyed as a bounty of nature in place of the elaborate and costly chains of fortifications and even more expensive armies and navies that took a heavy toll of the treasuries of less fortunate countries and placed severe tax burdens upon the backs of their people. The costly navy that policed and defended the Atlantic was manned and paid for by British subjects for more than a century, while Americans enjoyed the added security afforded without added cost to themselves. In 1861 the United States was maintaining the second largest merchant marine in the world without benefit of a battle fleet. At that time there were only 7,600 men in the United States Navy as compared with more than ten times that number in the British Navy.[1]

Geographic isolation by oceans was not, of course, the only basis of free security. The absence of powerful rival nations on our borders or indeed within the same hemisphere made obvious contributions to free security. Spain was a decaying power, and her empire splintered into many small nations instead of combining into one strong nation. Other sources of free security came from what W. Stull Holt calls "the accidents of history."[2] There were many of these, but most of them derived from the European balance of power system. That system operated consistently to American advantage either by keeping European powers preoccupied or exhausted by their own wars, or discouraging them from intervening in the temptingly weak new nation from fear of each other. Across the Pacific no power strong enough to threaten the security of the United States emerged until the twentieth century.

[1] During Andrew Jackson's administration Alexis de Tocqueville described the situation in the following terms: "The President of the United States is the commander-in-chief of the army, but of an army composed of only six thousand men; he commands the fleet, but the fleet reckons but few sails; he conducts the foreign relations of the Union, but the United States are a nation without neighbors. Separated from the rest of the world by the ocean, and too weak as yet to aim at the dominion of the seas, they have no enemies, and their interests rarely come into contact with those of any other nation of the globe." *Democracy in America*, tr. Henry Reeve (2 vols.; New York, 1904), I, 120.

[2] This acknowledges the validity of criticisms of the first edition of this essay made by W. Stull Holt, "American Security and Historical and Geographical Accidents," in his *Historical Scholarship in the United States and Other Essays* (Seattle and London, 1967), 140–153.

Between the second war with England and World War II, the United States was blessed with a security so complete and so free that it was able virtually to do without an army and for the greater part of the period without a navy as well. Between the world war that ended in 1763 and the world wars of the twentieth century the only major military burdens placed upon the people were occasioned not by foreign threats but by domestic quarrels, the first to establish independence for the American colonies and the second to thwart independence for the southern states. After each of these civil wars, as after all the intervening war, Americans immediately dismantled their military establishment. They followed the same procedure after every succeeding war, down to World War II, and even after that they carried demobilization to dangerous extremes before reversing the policy.

The end of the era of free security has overtaken Americans so suddenly and swiftly that they have not brought themselves to face its practical implications, much less its bearing upon their history. Conventional aircraft and jet propulsion had shrunk the time dimension of the Atlantic and Pacific from weeks to hours by the mid-'fifties. But before military adjustment could be properly made to that revolution, the development of ballistic missiles shrank the two oceans further from hours to minutes. In the same period the hitherto impenetrable Arctic Ocean has not only been navigated by atomic-powered submarines under the ice cap, but has been shrunk in time width to dimensions of minutes and seconds by which we now measure the other oceans. The age of security and the age of free security ended almost simultaneously.

The proposition was advanced before a meeting of the American Historical Association in 1893 that "the first period of American history," a period of four centuries, was brought to an end by the disappearance of free land. Perhaps it is not premature to suggest that another epoch of American history was closed even more suddenly sixty years later by the disappearance of free security. It may be objected that security was never completely free and that the period when it came nearest to being so did not last very long. But one can reasonably ask as much latitude to speak in comparative and relative terms about free security as the theorists of free land enjoyed in their generalizations. Land was of course never completely free either, and the period when it came nearest to being so only dated from the Homestead Act of 1862, less than three decades before the end of the frontier era. In a comparative sense land may nevertheless be said to have been relatively free for a much longer period. In similar terms security may also be said to have been free until quite recently.

Military expenditures of the federal government have, of course, increased greatly and almost continuously since the last decade of the eighteenth century. Until very recently, however, they have not increased so rapidly as the government's nonmilitary expenditures. During the first century of the Republic's history, save in war years, annual military expenditures rarely came to as much as 1 percent of the gross national product, returned to that level a few years after World War I, and remained there until the Great Depression cut production back drastically. In the decade preceding Pearl Harbor, the percentage of federal expenditures devoted to military purposes fell lower than ever before in our history.[3]

Another measure of free security is the small demand that military service has made upon national manpower. Before World War I, apart from actual war periods and their immediate aftermath, it was an extremely rare year in which as many as 1 per cent of the total male population between the ages of twenty and thirty-nine saw military service. Between Reconstruction and the Spanish-American War there was no year in which as many as one-half of 1 per cent served in the

[3] M. Slade Kendrick, *A Century and a Half of Federal Expenditures*, Occasional Paper 48, National Bureau of Economic Research (New York, 1955), pp. 10–12, 28, 38, 40–42. For comparisons between military appropriations of the United States and other powers, 1820–1937, see Quincy Wright, *A Study of War* (2 vols.: Chicago, 1942), I, 666–72, Appendix XXII, esp. Tables 58, 59, and 60. The significant index of comparison is the proportion between military appropriations and national income. That proportion rose in the United States from 0.8 in 1914 to 1.5 in 1937, while in the same years it stood in Great Britain at 3.4 and 5.7; in France at 4.8 and 9.1; in Japan at 4.8 and 28.2; in Germany at 4.6 and 23.5; and in Russia at 6.3 and 26.4. This was the only period for which figures are given for all these powers.

armed forces.[4] The handful of men who made up the regular army during the nineteenth century were not employed in patrolling frontiers against foreign invasion, but chiefly in coping with a domestic police problem posed by the Indians. Upon the outbreak of the Civil War the United States Army numbered a few more than 16,000 men, and 183 of its 198 companies were spread among seventy-nine posts on the Indian frontier. The remaining fifteen companies were available for "defense" of the Canadian and Atlantic frontiers, and the incipient Confederate frontier.[5] The southern constabulary that patrolled the slaves was organized on military lines, but like the regular army it was concerned with a domestic police problem.

The contrast between free security and security costs of the present era scarcely requires emphasis. Military expenditures in 1957 and the years since have amounted to 10 per cent of the gross national product. By way of comparison, military expenditures in the 1880s were never over four-tenths of 1 percent. In spite of the vast increase of the gross national product during the last century, military costs have increased far faster and now represent ten to twenty times the percentage of the gross national product they represented in the peak years of the previous century.[6] Not counting payments to veterans, they now account for nearly 70 percent of the federal budget. The more advanced and improved military machinery paradoxically requires more instead of less manpower, both military and civilian. The Department of Defense and its branches employ more civilian workers now than did the entire federal government before the Great Depression. Indications are that we are only at the beginning instead of the culmination of expansion in costs and manpower for military purposes and that future expenditures will be larger still.

If historians waited until the disappearance of free land to recognize fully the influence of the frontier-and-free-land ex-

[4] Kendrick, *A Century and a Half of Federal Expenditures*, pp. 89–90. Before 1865 only white males of military age are included in these figures.

[5] Theodore Ropp, *War in the Modern World* (Durham, 1959), p. 157.

[6] Simon Kuznets, in Committee for Economic Development, *Problems of United States Economic Development* (2 vols.; New York, 1958), I, 29.

perience on American history, perhaps the even more sudden and dramatic disappearance of free security will encourage them to recognize the effect of another distinguishing influence upon our national history. I am not prepared to make any claims about the comparative importance of the two themes, nor do I wish to make or inspire any exaggerations of the influence of free security. But if the influence of free land may be considered significant in the shaping of American character and national history, it is possible that the effect of free security might profitably be studied for contributions to the same ends.

Certain traits that Americans generally regard as desirable, such as democracy, individualism, self-reliance, inventiveness, have been attributed in some measure to the frontier-and-free-land experience. It might be that the sunnier side of the national disposition—the sanguine temperament, the faith in the future,[7] what H. G. Wells once called our "optimistic fatalism"— is also related to a long era of habituation to military security that was effective, reliable, and virtually free. Optimism presupposes a future that is unusually benign and reliably congenial to man's enterprises. Anxieties about security have kept the growth of optimism within bounds among other peoples, but the relative absence of such anxieties in the past has helped, along with other factors, to make optimism a national philosophy in America. The freedom of American youth from the long period of training in military discipline that left its mark upon the youth of nations where it was a routine requirement could hardly have failed to make some contribution to the distinctiveness of national character.

Free security is related at various points to the development of the American economy. So long as an economy of scarcity prevailed in the land the gross national product was not far above the level of subsistence. While the margin was narrow, the demands of an expensive military establishment could have consumed so large a proportion of the surplus above subsistence as to slow capital formation seriously. Relative immunity from

[7] Boyd C. Shafer, "The American Heritage of Hope," *Mississippi Valley Historical Review*, XXXVII (Dec. 1950), 422–50.

this drain, at least under nineteenth-century conditions, enlarged opportunities for capital formation and increased productivity. Free security was surely related to light taxes and a permissive government, and they in turn had much to do with the development of the famous American living standard.

Not all the historic influences of free security have been so benign. Tocqueville's classic study of the national character attributes to democracy some familiar patterns of military conduct that might be profitably re-examined in the light of the free security thesis. Tocqueville finds, for example, that "the private soldiers remain most like civilians" in a democracy, that they chafe under discipline with "a restless and turbulent spirit," and that they are "ever ready to go back to their homes" when the fighting is over. With regard to the officer corps he observes that "among a democratic people the choicer minds of the nation are gradually drawn away from the military profession, to seek by other paths distinction, power, and especially wealth." He adds that "among democratic nations in time of peace the military profession is held in little honor and indifferently followed. This want of public favor is a heavy discouragement to the army."[8] Tocqueville may be correct in suggesting democracy as one explanation for these attitudes and patterns of behavior, but no explanation of American attitudes is complete that neglects a national disposition to look upon security as a natural right. What a people half consciously come to regard as a free gift of nature they are with difficulty persuaded to purchase at high cost in treasure, inconvenience, and harsh discipline. To reward with high honors, prestige, and secure status the professional military men who insist upon these sacrifices in time of peace comes hard to such people.

The heritage of free and easy security can also be detected behind the disposition to put living standard, private indulgence, and wasteful luxury ahead of vital security requirements. The same heritage can almost certainly be discerned at work in the tendency to plunge into wars first and prepare for them later. The historic background of security might help to explain, even

[8] Tocqueville, *Democracy in America*, II, 761–68.

if it cannot excuse, the irresponsibility of political leaders who make foreign commitments, coin bellicose slogans, and indulge in wild threats and promises without first providing the military means to back them up.

There are other aspects of American history besides demagogic diplomacy and military shortcomings that are not to be fully understood without reference to the history of free security. Among these surely is the American Civil War. The United States is the only major country since Cromwellian England that could afford the doubtful luxury of a full-scale civil war of four years without incurring the evils of foreign intervention and occupation. Had such evils been as much a foregone conclusion as they have been among other nations, it is doubtful that Americans would have proved as willing as they were to fall upon each other's throats. Needless to say, other inducements were operative.

It is doubtful, also, that Americans could have developed and indulged with the freedom they have their peculiar national attitudes toward power, had it not been for their special immunity from the more urgent and dire demands for the employment of power to assure national security and survival. Having this relative immunity, they were able to devise and experiment with elaborate devices to diffuse and atomize power. They divided it among the states and later among business corporations. They used such devices as checks and balances, separation of powers, and division of powers to deadlock power and to thwart positive action for long periods. The experience probably encouraged the tendency to regard power as bad in itself and any means of restraining or denying it as a positive good.

The national myth that America is an innocent nation in a wicked world is associated to some degree in its origins and perpetuation with the experience of free security. That which other nations had of necessity to seek by the sword and defend by incurring the guilt of using it was obtained by the Americans both freely and innocently, at least in their own eyes. They disavowed the engines and instruments of the power they did not need and proclaimed their innocence for not using them, while at the same time they passed judgment upon other nations for incurring the guilt inevitably associated with power. "We lived for a century," writes Reinhold Niebuhr, "not only in the illusion but in the reality of innocency in our foreign relations. We lacked the power in the first instance to become involved in the guilt of its use." But we sought to maintain the innocence of our national youth after acquiring power that was incompatible with it. We first concealed from ourselves the reality of power in our economic and technological might, but after it became undeniable, and after military strength was added to it, as Niebuhr says, "we sought for a time to preserve innocency by disavowing the responsibilities of power."[9] The urge to return to a free security age of innocence and the flight from responsibility and from the guilt of wielding power may be traced in elaborate efforts to maintain neutrality, in desperate struggles for isolationism and "America First," as well as in the idealistic plans of religious and secular pacifists.

So long as free land was fertile and arable, and so long as security was not only free but strong and effective, it is no wonder that the world seemed to be America's particular oyster. Now that both free land and free security have disappeared, it is not surprising that the American outlook has altered and the prospect has darkened. The contrast with the past was even sharper in the case of free security than in the instance of free land, for the transition was almost immediate from a security that was both free and effective to an attempt at security that was frightfully costly and seemed terrifyingly ineffective. The spell of the long past of free security might help to account for the faltering and bewildered way in which America faced its new perils and its new responsibilities.

This discussion leads naturally to a second and more extensive field of opportunity for reinterpretation, that of military history. In this field there are no national limitations and few limits of time and period. Military subjects have traditionally occupied a large share of the historian's attention, a dispropor-

[9] Reinhold Niebuhr, *The Irony of American History* (New York, 1952), p. 35.

tionate share in the opinion of some critics. Yet the military historian is now faced with the challenge of relating the whole history of his subject to the vast revolution in military weapons and strategic theory that has occurred in the past fifteen years. Primarily this revolution involves two phases: first, explosives, anl second, the means of delivering them upon a target. Both phases were inaugurated toward the end of World War II.

The revolution in explosives began when the primitive A-bomb was exploded by American forces over Hiroshima on August 6, 1945.[10] This was the first and, so far, the last such weapon but one ever fired in anger. That event alone marked the lurid dawn of a new age. But the entirely unprecedented pace of change in the weapons revolution has swept us far beyond that primitive dawn and broken the continuity of military tradition and history. Since 1945 we have passed from bombs reckoned in kilotons of TNT to those computed in megatons, the first of which was the hydrogen bomb exploded at Bikini on March 1, 1954, less than a decade after the A-bomb innovation. The twenty kiloton atomic bomb dropped over Nagasaki in 1945 had a thousand times the explosive power of the largest blockbuster used in World War II, but the twenty megaton thermonuclear bomb represents a thousand-fold increase over the Nagasaki bomb. One bomb half the twenty megaton size is estimated by Henry A. Kissinger to represent *"five times the explosive power of all the bombs dropped on Germany during the five years of war and one hundred times those dropped on Japan."*[11] And according to Oskar Morgenstern, "One single bomb can harbor a force greater than all the explosives used by all belligerents in World War II or even greater than all the energy ever used in any form in all previous wars of mankind put together."[12] But this would still not appear to be the ulti-

[10] Two rival dates for the opening of the nuclear age are December 2, 1942, when Enrico Fermi established a chain reaction in the Chicago laboratory, and July 16, 1945, when the test bomb was exploded in New Mexico.

[11] Henry A. Kissinger, *Nuclear Weapons and Foreign Policy* (New York, 1957), pp. 70–71. Italics in the original.

[12] Oskar Morgenstern, *The Question of National Defense* (New York, 1959), p. 10.

mate weapon, for it is now said that a country capable of manufacturing the megaton bomb is conceivably capable, should such madness possess it, of producing a "begaton" bomb. Reckoned in billions instead of millions of tons of TNT, it would presumably represent a thousand-fold increase, if such a thing is conceivable, over the megaton weapon.

The revolution in the means of delivering explosives upon targets, like the revolution in explosives, also began during World War II. Before the end of that war, the jet-propelled aircraft, the snorkel submarine, the supersonic rocket, and new devices for guiding ships, aircraft, or missiles were all in use. But also as in the case of the revolution in explosives, the revolution in agents of delivery accelerated at an unprecedented pace during the fifteen years following the war. The new jet aircraft became obsolescent in succeeding models before they were in production, sometimes before they came off the drafting boards. The snorkel submarine acquired atomic power and a range of more than fifty thousand miles without refueling. The expansion of rockets in size, range, and speed was even more revolutionary. The German V-2 in use against London during the last year of the war had a range of only about two hundred miles and a speed of only about five times that of sound. The intermediate range ballistic missile, capable of carrying a thermonuclear warhead, has a range of around fifteen hundred miles, and the intercontinental missile with similar capabilities has a range in excess of five thousand miles and flies at a rate on the order of twenty times the speed of sound. To appreciate the pace and extent of the revolution in agents of delivery, one should recall that in the long history of firearms, military technology was only able to increase the range of cannon from the few hundred yards of the primitive smoothbore to a maximum of less than eighty miles with the mightiest rifled guns. Then in less than fifteen years ranges became literally astronomical.

In all these measurements and samples of change in military technology it should be kept in mind that the revolution is still in progress and in some areas may well be only in its beginning stages. The line between the intercontinental rockets and some of the space rockets would seem to be a rather arbitrary one. The race for the development of the nuclear-powered plane may produce a craft capable of ranges limited in a practical way only by the endurance of the crew. The technological breakthrough has become a familiar phenomenon of the military revolution, and there is no justification for the assumption that we have seen the last of these developments.

To seek the meaning of this revolution in a comparison with that worked by the advent of firearms is misleading. The progress of the revolution brought on by gunpowder, first used in military operations in the early fourteenth century, was glacial by comparison. Only very gradually did the gun replace the sword, the arrow, the spear, and the battering ram. Flintlocks did not arrive until the seventeenth century, field artillery of significance until the eighteenth century, and it was not until the middle of the last century, more than five hundred years after the first military use of gunfire, that the era of modern firearms really opened. Military doctrine changed even more slowly.

The nuclear revolution is of a different order entirely. If strategic bombing with thermonuclear weapons occurs on an unrestricted scale now entirely possible with existing forces, it is quite likely to render subsequent operation of armies, navies, and air forces not only superfluous but unfeasible. It is not simply that huge concentrations of forces such as were used in major amphibious and land operations in the last world war present a vulnerable target themselves. Of more elemental importance is the fact that such armies, navies, and air forces require thriving industrial economies and huge bases and cannot operate when the cities of their home territories are smoking craters and their ports and bases are piles of radioactive rubble. As for the military effectiveness of survivors in the home territory, according to Bernard Brodie, "the *minimum* destruction and disorganization that one should expect from an unrestricted thermonuclear attack in the future is likely to be too high to

permit further meaningful mobilization of war-making capabilities over the short term."[13] Faith in the wartime potential of
the American industrial plant would appear to be another ca-
sualty of the revolution.

Historic changes in weapons, tactics, and strategy between
one war and the next, or even one century or one era and the
next in the past, become trivial in importance by comparison
with the gulf between the pre-atomic and the nuclear age of
strategic bombing. We are now able to view the past in a new
perspective. We can already see that the vast fleets that concentrated off the Normandy beaches and at Leyte Gulf, or the
massed armies that grappled in the Battle of the Bulge or across
the Russian steppes, or for that matter the old-fashioned bomber
squadrons that droned back and forth across the English Chan-
nel year after year dropping what the air force now contemptuously calls "iron bombs" were more closely related to a remote
past than to a foreseeable future. They did not, as they seemed
at the time, represent the beginning of a new age of warfare.
They represented instead the end of an old age, a very old age.

This is not to assume that unrestricted nuclear war is the
only type of military operations that are any longer conceivable,
nor that wars of limited objectives, limited geographic area, and
limited destructiveness are no longer possible. To make such assumptions, indeed, would be either to despair of the future of
civilized man or to subscribe to the theory that national differences will thenceforth be settled without resort to force. Even
assuming that limited wars may still be fought with "conventional" weapons, tactics, and strategy of the old era, there will
still be an important difference setting them apart from pre-
nuclear wars. Where major powers are directly or indirectly
involved, limited wars, or even support of or opposition to gue-
rilla forces, are now carried on under an umbrella of nuclear
power. The effects of that conditioning environment have only
been inconclusively tested, but it can scarcely be assumed that
they will prove inconsiderable.

The sudden transition from the old to the new age of war-

[13] Bernard Brodie, *Strategy in the Missile Age* (Princeton, 1959), p. 167.
See also pp. 147–49 on the comparison with the firearms revolution.

fare should not depreciate but actually enhance the role of the historian. We desperately need historical reinterpretation. The men who now determine policy, strategy, and tactics in the new age of warfare are inevitably influenced by their experience and training grounded on an earlier age of warfare and an outmoded interpretation of its history. The fact is that many of the precepts, principles, and values derived from past experience in wars can be tragically misleading in the new age. These include some of the so-called "unchanging principles of war" that are imbibed during training and discipline until they become almost "second nature" to the professional military man. Traditions that associate the new type of war with honor, valor, and glory are no longer quite relevant. The sacred doctrine of concentration and mass, applied at the critical point, has lost its traditional meaning.

The age-old assumption of a commander's freedom of choice once war was started can no longer be made. In previous ages, one could start a war and assume that his objectives, methods, or degree of commitment could be altered according to changing prospects of success or failure, or according to whether probable gains outweighed probable losses. Even as late as World War II one could still approach the abyss of barbarism or annihilation, take a look and turn back, settle for an armistice or a compromise, and bide one's time. Once resort is made to unrestricted nuclear war, there is no turning back.

The underpinnings of logic that have served historically to justify resort to war as the lesser of several evils have shifted or, in their traditional form, quite disappeared. Victory has been deprived of its historical meaning in total war with the new weapons, for the "victor" is likely to sustain such devastation as to lack the means of imposing his will upon the "vanquished." And yet to accomplish this end, according to Karl von Clausewitz, is the only rational motive of war. Democratic participation or consent in a war decision is rendered most unmeaningful at the very time popular involvement in the devastation of war has reached an unprecedented maximum.

The history of war and man's attitudes about it should be re-examined in the light of these developments. Attention has already been profitably directed in particular to the question of how and why total war came to appear the "normal" type of conflict between major powers.[14] Such investigation might reveal how military planning became divorced from political planning and war became an end in itself rather than a means of achieving more or less rational political ends. Given the destructive military capabilities presently at the disposal of major powers, it would seem to be more interesting than it has ever been before to learn how and why powers have been willing at some times in history to wage wars with more limited objectives than unconditional surrender, total victory, or complete annihilation of the enemy.

That mankind should have carried the values and precepts of the age of firearms into the thermonuclear age represents a far greater anachronism than the one represented by his carrying the values and precepts of the age of chivalry into the age of firearms. Anachronisms are pre-eminently the business of historians. The historic service that Cervantes performed with mockery in 1605, when he published the first volume of *Don Quixote,* three centuries after the advent of firearms, cannot with safety be deferred that long after the advent of nuclear weapons. Lacking a Cervantes, historians might with their own methods help to expose what may well be the most perilous anachronism in history.

On a grander scale, a third field of opportunity for historical reinterpretation has opened up since 1945. Too complex to be attributed to an event, it might better be ascribed to an avalanche of events, or a combination of avalanches. These avalanches go under such names as the collapse of Western imperialism, the revolt of the colored peoples of Asia and Africa, the rise of Eastern nationalism, the westward advance of the frontier of Russian hegemony, and the polarization of power between the Russian and American giants. All these developments and more have contributed to the shrinkage of Europe

---

[14] See, for example, Robert E. Osgood, *Limited War: The Challenge to American Strategy* (Chicago, 1957), and John U. Nef, *War and Human Progress: An Essay on the Rise of Industrial Civilization* (Cambridge, 1950).

in power and relative importance, and thus to what is probably the greatest of all opportunities for historical reinterpretation.

In recent years historians and other scholars have coined some striking phrases to describe Europe's plight: "the political collapse of Europe," "the un-making of Europe," "farewell to European history," "the passing of the European age," "the end of European history."[15] The tone of despair echoed from one of these phrases to another may well be called in question by the remarkable economic recovery and cultural resilience of Europe since 1945.* Crane Brinton is to an extent justified in taking to task the prophets of doom and calling attention to the rising birth rate, the material prosperity, and the intellectual activity in postwar Europe.[16] The end of European supremacy is not necessarily the end of Europe. The present argument, however, is not addressed to the question of the extent of cultural malaise in Europe nor to the validity of any of several cyclical theories of history. The point is simply one of relative power and influence, and no evidence so far presented disturbs the conclusion that an age of European pre-eminence in the world has come to a close. That age did not end overnight, nor does the explanation lie wholly in events of the last decade and a half, but awareness of the implications for history are only beginning to sink in.

Now that European power has dwindled or quite disappeared in Asia, Africa, and former insular dependencies, and now that Europe itself has become the theater for operations of non-European powers, their military bases, and power rivalries, the spell of an agelong European dominance begins to lift. It is difficult to realize how recently it was commonly assumed in

[15] Hajo Holborn, *The Political Collapse of Europe* (New York, 1951); Oscar Halecki, *The Limits and Divisions of European History* (New York, 1950); Alfred Weber, *Farewell to European History or the Conquest of Nihilism* (New Haven, 1948); Eric Fischer, *The Passing of the European Age* (Cambridge, 1948); Geoffrey Barraclough, *History in a Changing World* (Norman, 1956).

* Five years after the first version of this paper was published, Hugh Trevor-Roper in *The Rise of Christian Europe* wrote: "The history of the world, for the last five centuries, in so far as it has significance, has been European history."

[16] Crane Brinton, *The Temper of Western Europe* (Cambridge, 1953).

informed circles that the world was the proper theater for European enterprises and adventures, that world leadership was a European prerogative, that trends and fashions in arts, ideas, and sciences were as a matter of course set in Europe, that European political hegemony and economic ascendancy were taken for granted, and that history of any consequence was a commodity stamped, "Made in Europe." The corollaries of these assumptions were that non-Europeans, apart from a few societies composed primarily of peoples of European stock, stood in perpetual tutelage to Europe, that non-European cultures were decadent, arrested, primitive, or permanently inferior, and that progress was defined as successful imitation of the preferred European way of doing things.

The significance of all this for historiography lies in the fact that much of the history still read and believed and taught was written while these assumptions prevailed, and written by historians, non-European as well as European, who shared them. Three of the most productive and influential generations of historians in the whole history of Western culture, those between the Napoleonic Wars and World War I, coincided in time with the crest of European ascendancy and presumption. The generation between the world wars of the twentieth century generally shared the same assumptions. The contribution they made to the enrichment of historical scholarship is invaluable and should be cherished. But in so far as it rests on a set of assumptions no longer tenable, their work would seem to stand in need of extensive revision and reinterpretation.

On the needs for reinterpretation of the history of Europe itself it might be the prudent thing for an American historian to rely on the judgment of European historians, several of whom have already expressed themselves on the subject. Geoffrey Barraclough, for example, believes that "a total revision of European history [is] imperative." In this connection he has written, "Ever since the end of the war [of 1939–1945] a change has come over our conceptions of modern history. We no longer feel that we stand four square in a continuous tradition, and the view of history we have inherited . . . seems to have little relevance to our current problems and our current needs." In his opinion the trouble is that "we are dealing with a conception of European history which is out of focus and therefore misleading, because of the false emphasis and isolated prominence it gives to Western Europe, and which therefore needs revising not merely in its recent phases, but at every turn from the early middle ages onward."[17]

American historians will also have some reinterpreting to do, for in this as in so much of American cultural life, ideas were shaped by European examples and models. It should go without saying that American civilization is European derived. But the models of Europe-centered world history would seem to have restrained American historians from exploring the influence of their country upon European history and that of the world in general. There have been a few exceptions to the rule. One exception is R. R. Palmer, *The Age of the Democratic Revolution,* which demonstrates that an age traditionally called European shows the profound impact of the American Revolution on Europe. Another suggestive interpretation of the American influence on European history is Walter P. Webb, *The Great Frontier,* and yet another is Halvdan Koht, *The American Spirit in Europe.* Other neglected American themes of European history remain to be explored. The influence of European immigration on American history has received much attention. But the impact upon Europe itself of the emigration of 35,000,000 Europeans in the century between the Napoleonic Wars and World War I remains to be acknowledged except in a few countries and has still to receive its just share of attention in the pages of European history. The importance of the West as a safety valve for American society has undoubtedly been exaggerated. But the significance of America as a safety valve for Europe and the effect of the closing of that valve after World War I remain to be fully assessed. Apart from the United States, other offshoots and overseas establishments of European powers, including those in South America, Australia, and the British Commonwealth countries, will inevitably discover that they have

[17] Barraclough, *History in a Changing World,* pp. 9, 135, 178.

not been merely on the receiving end of the line of influence, but have had their own impact upon European and world history.

The same assumptions of Europocentric history have very largely shaped the interpretation of Asiatic, African, and other non-European history as well, for Europe successfully marketed its historiography abroad, along with its other cultural products, in remote and exotic climates. We may depend on it that the new opportunities for reinterpretation will not be lost upon New Delhi, Cairo, Tokyo, and Djakarta, to say nothing of Peking and Moscow. Already an Indian historian, K. M. Panikkar, has defined the period of European pre-eminence in the Orient as "the Vasco da Gama Epoch of Asian History." It began with the arrival of Da Gama at Calicut in 1498 and ended abruptly four and a half centuries later "with the withdrawal of British forces from India in 1947 and of the European navies from China in 1949." In the time dimensions of the Orient this could be regarded as only one of several episodes that have temporarily interrupted the flow of ancient civilizations. Relations between East and West continue and even increase in many ways, but, as Panikkar says, "the essential difference is that the basis of relationship has undergone a complete change . . . a revolutionary and qualitative change. . . ." The Indian historian concludes that "vitally important historical results may flow from this new confrontation" between East and West.[18]

One of the historical results to flow from the confrontation between East and West should be a new and revised view of world history. The ethnocentric, or Europocentric, view that has been held for so long a time in the West can hardly be expected to survive the sweeping change in East-West relationships. The "new confrontation" of which the Hindu historian writes is another event of the present that necessitates many reinterpretations of the past.

Three fields for historical reinterpretation have been sug-

[18] K. M. Panikkar, *Asia and Western Dominance: A Survey of the Vasco Da Gama Epoch of Asian History, 1498–1945* (London, 1953), pp. 11, 15.

gested: the first occasioned by the end of the age of free and effective security in America, the second by the end of an age of mass warfare, and the third by the end of the age of European hegemony. These subjects have been suggested to illustrate, not to exhaust, the list of possibilities for historical reinterpretation opened up since 1945. A complete list would not only be beyond the limits of this paper, but beyond the range of present vision. The need for reinterpretation is not always made immediately apparent by revolutionary events, while on the other hand such a need may easily be exaggerated by lack of sufficient perspective.

It may be noted that the ideological war between the Communist and the non-Communist worlds, which has occupied so large a share of public attention in recent years, has not been mentioned. It could well be that the Cold War will upset more traditional interpretations of history than the events listed above. It is even more probable, if we prove as myopic about our own times as historians have proved in the past, that we have overlooked or underestimated events that in future times will be accounted of far more historical significance than the noisier events we have noted. In such a situation the experienced historian will always take account of two powerful historical forces: the unforeseen and the unforeseeable. It may well turn out that new satellites for the earth will prove of more historical consequence than new satellites for earthly powers.

At least two objections to the proposal of reinterpreting history in the light of present events, however revolutionary, may be readily foreseen. The first is that the past is inviolable, that it is or should be unaffected by the present, and that it is the duty of the historian to guard its inviolability rather than to invade it with present preoccupations. But this would be to take an unhistorical view of historiography. Every major historical event has necessitated new views of the past and resulted in reinterpretations of history. This was surely true of the Reformation, of the discovery and exploration of the New World, of the Industrial Revolution, and of political upheavals such as the democratic and the communist revolutions. These events did not leave the past inviolate, nor the traditional interpretations of it sacrosanct. There is no reason to believe that present and future revolutions will do so.

A second objection may be that if the revolutionary changes used as illustrations represent such a drastic and sharp break with the past, they render history irrelevant and useless to the needs and concerns of the present and future: that history is bypassed by events and reduced to antiquarianism. The answer to this objection is that if history is bypassed and rendered irrelevant and antiquarian, it will be due in large measure to the view that historians take of their own craft. Writing more than half a century ago with regard to the disappearance of free land and its consequences in America, J. Franklin Jameson asked, "Can it be supposed that so great and so dramatic a transition . . . shall have no effect upon the questions which men ask concerning the past? Nothing can be more certain than that history must be prepared to respond to new demands. I do not think so ill of my profession as to suppose that American historians will not make gallant and intelligent attempts to meet the new requirements."[19]

The new demands and requirements to which Jameson urged historians to respond now come faster, more insistently, and in more momentous form than ever before. The historian, along with others, may be called upon soon to adjust his views to another age of discovery and exploration, one that transcends earthly limits. He is already confronted with a "population explosion" for which there is no precedent, not even a helpful analogy, and little but misleading counsel from classical theorists. In science and technology it is the age of the "breakthrough," when the curve of expansion suddenly becomes vertical on many fronts. Informed men of science speak of the possibility of tapping the ocean for unlimited food supplies, of curing the incurable diseases, of controlling the weather, and of developing limitless and virtually costless sources of power.

[19] J. Franklin Jameson, "The Future Uses of History" (1913), reprinted in *American Historical Review,* LXV (Oct. 1959), 69.

Historical thought is involved as soon as men confront change with anachronistic notions of the past. Anachronism, to repeat, is the special concern of the historian. If historians assume an intransigent attitude toward reinterpretation, they will deserve to be regarded as antiquarians and their history as irrelevant. The historian who can contemplate a single nuclear bomb that harbors more destructive energy and fury than mankind has managed to exert in all previous wars from the siege of Troy to the fall of Berlin and conclude that it has "no effect upon the questions which men ask concerning the past" would seem to be singularly deficient in historical imagination.

The present generation of historians has a special obligation and a unique opportunity. Every generation, of course, has a unique experience of history. "I had the advantage," wrote Goethe, "of being born in a time when the world was agitated by great movements, which have continued during my long life." But it is doubtful that any previous generation has witnessed quite the sweep and scope of change experienced by those who have a living memory of the two world wars of the twentieth century and the events that have followed. They carry with them into the new order a personal experience of the old. Americans among them will remember a time when security was assumed to be a natural right, free and unchallengeable. Among them also will be men of many nations who manned the ships and fought the battles of another age of warfare. And nearly all of this generation of historians will have been educated to believe that European culture was Civilization and that non-European races, if not natively inferior, were properly under perpetual tutelage. They will be the only generation of historians in history who will be able to interpret the old order to the new order with the advantage and authority derived from firsthand knowledge of the two ages and participation in both.

The historian sometimes forgets that he has professional problems in common with all storytellers. Of late he has tended to forget the most essential one of these—the problem of keeping his audience interested. So long as the story he had to tell contained no surprises, no unexpected turn of events, and lacked the elemental quality of suspense, the historian found his audience limited mainly to other historians, or captive students. While the newly dawned era adds new problems of its own to the historian's burden, it is lavish with its gifts of surprise and suspense for the use of the storyteller. If there are any readily recognizable characteristics of the new era, they are the fortuitous, the unpredictable, the adventitious, and the dynamic—all of them charged with surprise.

The new age bears another and more ominous gift for the historian, one that has not been conspicuous in historical writings since the works of the Christian fathers. This gift is the element of the catastrophic. The Church fathers, with their apocalyptic historiography, understood the dramatic advantage possessed by the storyteller who can keep his audience sitting on the edge of eternity. The modern secular historian, after submitting to a long cycle of historicism, has at last had this dramatic advantage restored. The restoration, to be sure, arrived under scientific rather than apocalyptic auspices. But the dramatic potentials were scarcely diminished by placing in human hands at one and the same time the Promethean fire as well as the divine prerogative of putting an end to the whole drama of human history.

Of one thing we may be sure. We come of an age that demands a great deal of historians. Of such a time Jacob Burckhardt once wrote, "The historical process is suddenly accelerated in terrifying fashion. Developments which otherwise take centuries seem to flit by like phantoms in months or weeks, and are fulfilled."[20] He could hardly have phrased a more apt description of our own time. It is doubtful that any age has manifested a greater thirst for historical meaning and historical interpretation and therefore made greater demands upon the historian. What is required is an answer to the questions about the past and its relation to the present and future that the accelerated process of history raises. If historians evade such

[20] Jacob Burckhardt, *Force and Freedom* (New York, 1955), p. 238.

questions, people will turn elsewhere for the answers, and modern historians will qualify for the definition that Tolstoy once formulated for academic historians of his own day. He called them deaf men replying to questions that nobody puts to them. If on the other hand they do address themselves seriously to the historical questions for which the new age demands answers, the period might justly come to be known in historiography as the age of reinterpretation.

5

The Aging
of America

The occasion for these reflections, the 1976 bicentennial of the American Revolution, which followed upon the debacle of Vietnam and Watergate, tended to obscure or overshadow the paradox I wanted to illustrate: the celebration of innocence and youth in the midst of realities of guilt and age. The same would have been true had the occasion been the 1987 bicentennial of the American Constitution, likewise paralleled by national embarrassments. The paradox might be legitimately illustrated by either the debacles of the 1970s or those of the 1980s. Two astute historians, Leo Marx and Ernest R. May, read prepared criticisms immediately following presentation of the paper. Both found flaws they thought worth my attention. Professor Marx suggested that I might have been led astray by methods with which I had "not hitherto been associated," the use of literary evidence characteristic of "the image-symbol-myth school of American studies." But this, alas, was not my original sin of the sort, only the last of several. I hope that in none of them have I confused metaphor with reality. He is quite right, however, that American responses to the Vietnam War were acti-

The original version of this paper was delivered as the J. Franklin Jameson Lecture, jointly sponsored by the American Historical Association and the Library of Congress.

*vated by things other than myth—including common sense—
and I may have been remiss in taking that for granted and not
saying so. Professor May is surely right that for most people
"national history has or can have some correspondence with
family history," and that for a great many citizens the American part of their family history began long after the Revolution.
But the latecomers have often proved the most devoted adherents of national myths. A native of Texas himself, Professor
May admits that "One of the most elaborate state programs for
the Bicentennial was that of Texas," a fact he finds "slightly
comical" since neither that state nor many of his ancestors had
any part in the Revolution. That, however, would seem to suggest more rather than less attention to myth.*

T HE GREAT AMERICAN BIRTHDAY PARTY OF 1976 is over. Visiting captains and kings have long since departed. A few belated revelers persist with scheduled ceremonials, but the main
celebration is behind us and the anniversary year has ended.
The time has come—as it inevitably does for all those of advanced years who join in the celebration of their own birth-
days—to admit of a certain ambiguity of feelings about what
exactly was being celebrated. On such occasions survival surely
justifies some self-congratulation—especially when one considers
the alternative. The fact remains, however, that all existence is
finite. And the question naturally arises, how much celebration
and how many congratulations are acceptable over the approach
of the inveitable. As Paul Valery observed in the seventh decade
of his life, "The future is like everything else, no longer what
it used to be."[1] So likewise the future of the past.

Regardless of what Americans thought they were celebrating with such enthusiasm and expense and international
cooperation, it is obvious that the chief significance of the occasion lay in the passing of a dramatically advanced milestone in
the aging of their nation—an advanced age even for nations. I

[1] Jackson Mathews, ed., *The Collected Works of Paul Valery* (New
York, 1962), 10: 171.

shall return later to the relativity of age among nations and promise to make due apologies for the analogies between human and national life and lifespan. In the meantime, however, I shall perversely continue to employ the analogies for limited and, I hope, valid purposes. The point about aging and the consciousness of it is introduced at this juncture to emphasize the contrast between the reality and the typical way in which Americans did in fact celebrate their bicentennial anniversary and the symbols they selected for what they found significant for them in the occasion.

What they spontaneously and almost universally preferred and doted upon were not the symbols of age and maturity, but rather the symbols of youth and innocence. Thousands of Americans marched in eighteenth-century uniforms and re-enacted youthful rebellions against parental authority. They paraded in quaint costumes and displayed antique weapons, implements, and vehicles. They made pilgrimages to the birthplace and the cradles of the republic—to Concord, Philadelphia, and Williamsburg. They admired eighteenth-century heroes and Founding Fathers. National news magazines printed colonial portraits on the covers, and one weekly published whole issues dated July 4, 1776 and September 26, 1789, reporting events of those weeks in slightly antiqued typography as if they had just happened. Sympathetic nations, and some not so sympathetic, took their cue from American whim and fantasy: from around the world governments dispatched old sailing vessels (with supplementary modern power) to American harbors. Suddenly and mysteriously the so-called tall ships became the prime symbols of whatever it was Americans yearned for, and they swarmed to the harbors, shores, and river banks by the millions in adoration.

It was all so different from the centennial celebration of 1876, where the most modern machines and technology were displayed at the Philadelphia Exposition as favored symbols. But the national mood of 1976 could hardly be described as nostalgic. Nostalgia was the happily inspired theme of the American exhibit of the International Expo at Montreal in 1976, filled with old movies, old hats, old clothes that people actually remembered. (It was the Russians who filled their exhibit at Montreal with the latest machines and technology like the Americans had a century before.) Memory and nostalgia, however, were not the appeal in 1976. It was something else, something quite different, some obscure and unconscious national impulse and need.

One recalls in this connection a remark of D. H. Lawrence about James Fenimore Cooper's Leatherstocking novels, that "they go backwards, from old age to golden youth. This is the true myth of America. She starts old, old, wrinkled and writhing in an old skin. And there is a gradual sloughing of the old skin, toward a new youth." And he repeats, "It is the myth of America."[2] Lawrence is not speaking of the reality, of course, but of the myth. There is a great deal in the record, both domestic and foreign, to support his theory of an America perceived as the land of youth, perennially seeking renewal, a new greening, the eternal Peter Pan among nations. So conceived, America is the land of beginnings, the country of the future, the place where things happen first, a nation of great expectations, and most of all the country of the young.

Among Americans Ralph Waldo Emerson, in his lecture "The Young American" in 1844, voiced the myth as well as any: "I call upon you, young men, be admonished, to obey your heart and be the nobility of this land. . . . Who should lead the leaders, but the young American . . . free, healthful, strong. . . . It is the country of the Future . . . a country of beginnings, of projects, of designs, of expectations."[3] He could return to the same theme twenty years later toward the end of the most terrible war in American history: "Everything on this side of the water inspires large and prospective action," he wrote in 1864. "America means opportunity, freedom, power . . . when we are reproached with vapouring by people of small home territory, like the English, I often think that ours is only the gait and bearing of a tall boy, a little too large for his trou-

[2] *Studies in Classic American Literature* (New York, 1951), 64.
[3] "The Young American," in F. I. Carpenter, ed., *Ralph Waldo Emerson: Representative Selections* . . . (New York, 1934), 165.

sers, by the side of small boys."[4] How "Uncle Sam" ever came to be represented as white-haired and white-bearded is a mystery wrapped in a paradox.

The archetypal hero of American literature is disclosed by R. W. B. Lewis's study, *The American Adam*, in the youthful innocence of Herman Melville's Redburn, his Pierre, and his Billy Budd, in Mark Twain's Huck Finn, in Henry James's Daisy Miller and his Isabel Archer, and later in tormented distortions of the Adamic prototypes such as F. Scott Fitzgerald's Jay Gatsby.[5] Kenneth S. Lynn has stressed "the psychic immaturity that inspired so many childish themes, childish characters, childish points of view" among classic American writers of the nineteenth and twentieth centuries. He ascribes this "immaturity of American literature," this "natural enthusiasm for avoiding problems rather than confronting them," to what he calls "the historical circumstances that fostered childishness in an entire civilization."[6] In *The Machine in the Garden*, Leo Marx subtly traces American yearnings for the pastoral ideal, the simple rural paradise, in conflict with persistent claims of industrialization and urban life.[7] Henry Nash Smith in his classic *Virgin Land* demonstrated how the myth of regeneration and renewal embodied in the symbol of the garden inspired not only writers and artists but farmers and immigrants, politicians and public policy, a whole society.[8] The insight shared by these scholars is the vision of a society eternally dedicated to innocence and youth and in some measure resisting maturity and denying age.

Foreign observers of America have often noted manifestations of the myth and sometimes shared its illusions. They include some who knew us best. Their testimony began quite early in our history when there was obviously more reason for identifying Americans with youth, but one does not have to go back

[4] E. W. Emerson and W. E. Forbes, eds., *Journals of Ralph Waldo Emerson with Annotations* (Boston, 1914), 10: 84.
[5] R. W. B. Lewis, *The American Adam* (Chicago, 1959), 128–129.
[6] "Adulthood in American Literature," *Daedalus*, 105, #4 (1976): 49–59.
[7] New York, 1964.
[8] New York, 1950.

to the seventeenth or eighteenth or even the nineteenth century for suitable examples. Here is George Santayana writing in 1920: "What sense is there in this feeling, which we all have, that the American is young?" he asked, doubtless thinking of his years of American residence. "His country is blessed with as many elderly people as any other, and his descent from Adam, or from the Darwinian rival of Adam, cannot be shorter than that of his European cousins. Nor are his ideas always very fresh. . . . In spite of what is old-fashioned in his more general ideas, the American is unmistakably young. . . . I am not sorry to have known him in his youth. The charm of youth . . . lies in nearness to the impulses of nature. . . . Even under the inevitable crust of age the soul remains young, and wherever it is able to break through, sprouts into something green and tender. We are all as young at heart as the most youthful American, but the seed in his case has fallen upon virgin soil. . . ."[9] It was the eternal greening of America again, and again the Virgin Land.

But now it is more than half a century later. Having just celebrated our nation's two-hundredth birthday, we might reasonably be expected to be somewhat more aware of "the inevitable crust of age" than we are of those "green and tender" sprouts. And yet through the crust of centuries the greening impulses still show. "Nations, like individuals," as I have said in another connection, "are slow in adjusting their mental habits to the process of aging. Patterns of thought, expectation, and self-image are normally fixed in youth and to persist past the age to which they are appropriate."[10] America would seem to have had more than its share of such problems, and some of them are still with her.

Perhaps this is the place to pause and admit that there are limits to the usefulness of any analogy between human and

---

[9] *Character and Opinion in the United States* (New York, 1956), 111–12.

[10] C. Vann Woodward, ed., *The Comparative Approach to American History* (New York, 1968), 346.

national life, between the biological and the institutional. There is no normal lifespan for nations, no foreordained cycle from birth through growth, decline, and death. Whatever use we make of this comparative frame of reference must therefore be figurative. With that acknowledgment, however, it is still possible to speak of the "aging" of nations and to think of their conduct in terms of their comparative age.

If we overlook the murky national origins of some oriental states, the one hundred and forty-odd more or less "sovereign" nations that at present hold seats in the United Nations General Assembly, along with the handful that are excluded, can be said to represent six fairly distinct generations of nation states. Of these the United States is the first born and considerably the oldest member of the second generation, which consists of offspring of the small family of European parent nations that made up the first generation of nations in the Western world. Their offspring in the New World spent their infancy in various stages of colonial dependency to "mother" countries. As "the first new nation," the United States achieved national independence so far in advance of her siblings to the south and north, nations which came along in the following century, as to constitute almost a separate generation by itself. Since then four more generations of new nations, three small ones and one very large, have successively made their appearance. A small third generation was born in central and southern Europe with the wave of romantic nationalism in the mid-nineteenth century, a fourth later in the Balkans out of a revolt against the Turks, and a fifth in Eastern Europe as an aftermath of the First World War. The sixth, and by far the largest, emerged in Africa, Asia, the Middle East, and the Caribbean in recent years largely as a consequence of the decolonization of European holdings in those parts of the world.

Order of birth and generational precedence are not the only ways of thinking of relative age among nations. Spain is one of the oldest among the first generations of Western nations. Yet this did not prevent King Juan Carlos I from telling a joint session of Congress in Washington that "Spain today is a young and renewed nation. Two-thirds of us are under 40 years of age," said the (then) thirty-eight-year-old monarch. "We are an old race, but at the same time a new people." A less superficial criterion than geriatric population is the continuity and age of the constitutional order of nations. Most nations, some of the oldest as well as many of the youngest, have undergone revolutions, sometimes successive revolutions, that have fundamentally changed their form of government and basic institutions. In this respect, American history has been singular. In terms of continuous constitutional existence without revolutionary disruption, the United States has the oldest, but one, of all existing governments—including those of the original parent nations.

By more than one criterion of relative antiquity, America can therefore be represented as standing in United Nations Plaza surrounded for the most part by puling infant nations, many of them with Oedipal problems about the "mother" country and most of them still in their constitutional diapers. Yet both at home and abroad the images of American youth and immaturity have persisted over the centuries. America is always said to be coming of age, or about to. As long ago as the seventeenth century, James Harrington prophesied that the American colonies would demand their independence "when they come of age." Two other Englishmen, Richard Price and Thomas Paine, both friends of the American cause in 1776, invoked the metaphor in eighteenth-century prophesies.[11] Prophets continued to labor the same "coming-of-age" figure of speech right down to our own times. In 1915, Van Wyck Brooks announced it in his *America's Coming of Age;* in 1920, Santayana speculated that the American "is perhaps now reaching his majority, and all I say may hardly apply at all tomorrow"; in 1927, Andre Siegfried seemed to confirm the prophecy in his *America Comes of Age;* in 1959, Henry F. May pictured a stage of the process in *The End of American Innocence;* most recently, Daniel Bell

[11] Quoted in Winthrop D. Jordan, "Searching for Adulthood in America," *Daedalus,* 105, #4 (1976): 5.

announced "The End of American Exceptionalism" in 1976. Repeatedly proclaimed, the rites of puberty seem perennially deferred.

"The youth of America is their oldest tradition," wrote Oscar Wilde. "It has been going on now for three hundred years." David Hackett Fischer quotes Wilde to that effect in his *Growing Old in America*, and calls him to terms for exaggerating by as much as a century. In doing so he has in mind the thesis of his own study, which I think he successfully proves, that there occurred in the late eighteenth century and afterward a "revolution in age relations" in America, a momentous transition from *gerontophilia* to *gerontophobia*. It might be symbolized by the change from powdered wig to toupee. Although they are not the same at all, there are undoubtedly connections between American attitudes toward youth and age, Fischer's subject, and the myth of the perennially youthful nation, the subject of this paper. Fischer does not explore these connections, but he does remark in passing that "America itself, as late as the mid-twentieth century, still thought of itself as a young nation even though it was more than three centuries old—in fact the oldest independent republic in the modern world."[12] I believe it continues to think of itself the same way in the last quarter of the twentieth century.

Explanations might be sought in numerous theories. The search would surely not overlook what on the surface might seem paradoxical—that unique antiquity and continuity of the American constitutional order, the unbrokenness of the eighteenth-century institutions. We are surrounded by them in Washington, some of them, as Daniel Boorstin has pointed out, housed in the original buildings or reconstructions and expansions of them—notably the White House and the two houses of Congress. Of the same age are the Supreme Court, the two-party system, the ancient names and doctrines, and above all the old Constitution, much amended and reinterpreted though

___

[12] New York, 1977 (he surely meant *two* centuries): 131. See especially ch. 2, "The Revolution in Age Relations, 1780–1820," and ch. 3, "The Cult of Youth in Modern America, 1780–1970."

it is.[13] They all contribute to the illusion of frozen time, of arrested change. "America was the exemplary once-born nation," Daniel Bell observed in the essay referred to above, "the land of sky-blue optimism in which the traditional ills of civilization were, as Emerson once said, merely the measles and whooping cough of growing up."[14] Under the same diagnosis, subsequent ills that are more regularly associated with maturity and aging could be similarly dismissed as infantile disorders of the Emersonian sort.

Another explanation might be sought in the experience and heritage of what I have called "free security" in American history. By that I mean the remarkable amount of military security that this country, unique among nations, enjoyed between the second war with England and the Second World War, largely as a bounty of nature and the accidents of geography and politics. It was a security so free, so exempt from the heavy price other nations had to pay for it, that Americans came to regard free security as a natural right.[15] Just as the infant is normally more secure in his world than the mature man is in his, so, as Reinhold Niebuhr has observed, "a strong America is less completely master of its own destiny [i.e., less secure] than was a comparatively weak America, rocking in the cradle of its continental security and serene in its infant innocence."[16] Nothing could have been more natural than a strong national impulse to recapture or return to that infant security and the innocence that supposedly accompanied it. Innocence was much more illusory than security as an endowment of national youth. Americans found it difficult to maintain the national myth that the United States is an innocent nation in a wicked world save by preserving the fantasy of youthful innocence.

Maturity may be legitimately reckoned by experience, but

[13] *The Genius of American Politics* (New York, 1958).
[14] "The End of American Exceptionalism," *The Public Interest*, #44 (1976): 223.
[15] C. Vann Woodward, "The Age of Reinterpretation," *AHR*, 66 (1960): 1–8.
[16] *The Irony of American History* (New York, 1952), 35, 74. In speaking of "the reality of innocency in our foreign relations," Niebuhr rather uncharacteristically brushed over some exceptions.

not simply by the amount of it or by the years that pass in acquiring it, by sheer age. The quality and character of experience must also figure in the reckoning, as well as the response evoked by the experience. Our historians fill many volumes with their accounts of the centuries of national experience, the complexities and problems of those years. Much of what they have written sustains the legend of American history as a success story. When it is written largely as an account of the white man's experience, when it neglects the losers for the winners, the story does indeed appear to become a string of triumphs and successes. Americans won their wars and solved their problems and prospered fabulously in the process. And when their victories, their triumphs, and their prosperity—the American Way of Life—are interpreted as the rewards of their virtue, history becomes a morality tale; and the myth of American invincibility, success, opulence, and innocence is seemingly vindicated.

"The American," remarked George Santayana back in 1920, "seems to bear lightly the sorrowful burden of human knowledge. In a word, he is young." Then he added as an afterthought that, of course, "The American has never yet had to face the trials of Job. Great crises, like the Civil War, he has known how to surmount victoriously; and now that he has surmounted a second great crisis victoriously [the First World War], it is possible that he may relapse, as he did in the other case, into an apparently complete absorption in material enterprise and prosperity. But if serious and irremediable tribulations ever overtook him, what would his attitude be?"[17] He continued to watch the American scene from abroad through the remaining years of his long life for an answer to his question about how Americans would respond to "serious and irremediable tribulations." Those of the Job-like seriousness he had in mind never came in his lifetime, of course, but he was not reassured by American hysteria over "a first touch of adversity," as he described the Great Depression of the 1930s. After the Second World War his American friends had scarcely got back home before they began sending him "coloured pictures of happiness, abundance,

[17] *Character and Opinion*, 111, 116.

youth, travel, and laughter [that] have transported me to a sort of dream-world where everything is a merry-go-round . . . a sort of youthful gaity, as if everybody were dressed in brand new clothes and rushing from one 'delightful' thing to another."[18]

It was not that Americans were still miraculously exempt from the great crises that afflicted the rest of the world. Americans experienced them too, but in a different way—remotely. Even the dismal Depression years and the Second World War were transformed in retrospect into triumphs of American power and will. Before their meaning had ever sunk home, God or History or Luck had, as always, come along and bailed them out with some ego-transporting triumph like the world-wide victories of 1945, the temporary monopoly of the ultimate weapon, and the Pax Americana—together with fabulous increments of national wealth and power and prestige and enhanced illusions of national virtue to boot. So that following hard on a withering winter for an aging faith came yet another spring, and the old creed seemed to be re-greening again and to flower more luxuriantly than ever for all its centuries of aging.

In remarking that Americans had displayed the ability "to surmount victoriously" great crises like the Civil War, Santayana failed to mention a large number of Americans who did not surmount that particular crisis victoriously. Their experience was quite different. The South as loser sustained historic encounters with defeat, failure, poverty, and guilt that embarrassed its later efforts to embrace the national myth of invincibility, success, opulence, and innocence. It was an experience more characteristic of the world's "sorrowful burden" from which Santayana thought Americans immune. This heritage found lodgment in the folk mind of the South and eventually gained expression in the work of a few of its brilliant writers. But that was not readily exportable, and the Northern market for it was limited. Even the French market was greater. What came through to Yankeedom instead was the spurious "New South"

[18] Santayana to Mrs. C. H. Toy, July 27, 1932 and to Mrs. David Little, September 23, 1949 in Daniel Cory, ed., *The Letters of George Santayana* (New York, 1955), 275, 384.

nationalism of the new ruling class, the plantocracy's bourgeois successors. So the South has failed its fellow countryman in a service of potential importance and even failed its own legitimate heritage in embracing the leadership and the spurious myths it has.

There were other losers, other Americans with a collective experience at fundamental variance with national myths. They included some of the oldest elements of the population, the enslaved and persecuted black people pre-eminently and other humiliated minorities of color, along with the rest of the impoverished. They also had something of importance of a cautionary nature to tell their fellow Americans about national pretensions of immunity from the forces of history, the faith that Americans were the darlings of divine destiny, and the delusion that they could control history for their own ends. But our own humiliated minorities have never been able to teach us what they learned at our own hands. The less wonder that, since the greatest teacher of humility in the history of religion never really learned how to teach humility very successfully to those who had never known humiliation themselves.

To put the mythic American experience in broader than domestic perspective it would be necessary to extend comparisons much wider than is possible here. We can only suggest the possibilities by thinking of the course of world history during the two centuries the conclusion of which we have just celebrated. When one thinks of the horror and anguish, the humiliation and tragedy that those two hundred years have inflicted upon the great peoples of the world—the Chinese, the Russians, the Japanese, the people of Indochina, the Hebrews, the Hindus, and the Muslims, the indigenous peoples of Africa and the Americas—even the nations of Western Europe, all of which have fallen under the heel of foreign military occupation at some time during that period—only then does one begin to appreciate the historical context of what has been called "American innocence." In all that long period, though America learned to contribute to those foreign horrors, never once, save in what was really an extension of our domestic quarrel with England, have foreign invaders set foot on American soil. No military occupation (save that of the South by Americans), no devastated cities (with the same exception), no mass deportation, mass rapes, mass executions, no class liquidations, no crematory ovens.

And surely no American would have it different, even for the loftiest educational reasons or the most sophisticated Machiavellian purposes. Besides, there is no assurance that the school of adversity teaches the right lessons. Nor does an adverse childhood assure any quicker or riper maturity than a happy one. Quite the contrary too often. The brief history of many of our junior republics testifies amply to the same unfortunate results among nations. It is doubtful that the defeated South was ever able to make its heritage of adversity contribute substantially to its maturity and wisdom save among a few individuals. That is not the point. The point is the skewed or eccentric perspective on history that our unique good fortune during most of our two centuries of national existence has fostered in America. That plus a deeply ingrained set of expectations that are scarcely the ideal preparation for the adversities normally encountered in, though not necessarily caused by, the course of aging. They would include some of what our Spanish philosopher called the trials of Job. As I have pointed out already, Americans have largely been spared those so far. But history may be presumed to have them still in store for us, and come they will in time.

As if in one of its moods of playful irony, history recently provided Americans with some relatively mild but instructive foretaste of the possibilities. The ironic turn of events came in the timing of the samples—just on the eve of our national celebration of two hundred years of unique good fortune that was the reward of virtue and righteousness. For one thing, the United States of America actually suffered defeat in a war. The implications are worth spelling out a bit, for it was the first war popularly perceived and partially admitted to have been lost. True, it was not a major war and it was fought on the opposite side of the globe without the slightest physical danger to Americans at home. Still it was a defeat, and as such a shattering blow to the national

myth of invincibility. Few face-saving opportunities were available
to temper the blow. It came at the peak of American military
power and pride and was sustained at the hands of a weak, undeveloped, and relatively unheard-of country in Southeast Asia
crippled by civil war and under Communist rule. Eventually
faced with a mutinous and demoralized army at the front and
rebellion at home, the defeated were compelled to do many of
the things traditionally required of the vanquished—eat their
words, swallow their pride, and do that which they had solemnly
sworn they would never do. It was, on the whole a most un-
American experience. "Peace with honor," it was called. Perhaps
the bitterest pill to swallow was the exposure of the emptiness of
moral pretensions used to justify the war and the shame with
which American foreign policy was covered in the eyes of the
world.

The ironic turn of events was not exhausted by introducing
the bicentennial anniversary with disgrace abroad, for accompanying that misfortune and coinciding with its climactic phases
occurred the exposure of by far the worst domestic disgraces in
the history of American government [up to that time, that is].
Starting in the White House at the very top, a spirit of lawless-
ness—condoning conspiratorial deception, obstruction of justice,
bribery, burglary, thuggery, perjury, a great variety of high crimes
and misdemeanors—infested a whole administration. Though the
crimes were often sordid and self-serving, their perpetrators defended themselves in a self-righteous spirit. Implicated and often
convicted of crimes were some of the chief governmental officials,
including two who had served as the highest law enforcement officers of the government, both of them as United States attorney
general. Acting personally and through his subordinates and
agents, the president misused for his political ends the Internal
Revenue Service, the Federal Bureau of Investigation, the Secret
Service, and the Central Intelligence Agency. Few agencies of the
executive branch of the government escaped the corrupting influence. The House Committee on the Judiciary, after hearings of
unprecedented length, found the president had "acted in a manner
contrary to his trust as President and subversive of constitutional

government, to the great prejudice of the cause of law and justice and to the manifest injury of the people of the United States," and declared that "such conduct warrants impeachment and trial, and removal from office."[19] Further disclosures were frustrated by the resignation and pardon of the president.

Ironic preliminaries of the bicentennial celebration were further compounded, however, by disclosures in other fields. Hard upon the vote for impeachement and the resignation and pardon of the president came charges of gross and frequent abuses of limited authority by intelligence agencies that made our own citizens targets of espionage. It was eventually confirmed that for twenty years beginning in 1953, the CIA had been illegally opening first-class mail, had in fact handled more than four million items in 1973, presumably its last year of operation in this field. In addition, the CIA maintained personal files on 10,000 citizens, a computer system containing 300,000 names of American organizations and citizens with no apparent connection with espionage, and a watch list of some 1,000 organzitions. It also engaged in unconstitutional wiretapping, bugging, and illegal examination of tax returns, and administered LSD to unsuspecting Americans.[20] As twin Big Brother of the CIA, the FBI was revealed to have been busy with comparable activities and to have been particularly zealous in hounding and persecuting leaders of protest and peace movements. Contemporaneous investigation at home and by foreign governments revealed that some of the largest American business corporations, including some with heavy government subsidies, have made a practice of bribing foreign officials with enormous sums. Disclosure of these bribes could topple friendly governments and threatened to topple one monarchy.

None of these American misfortunes such as Vietnam and Watergate should be thought of as inevitable or necessary symptoms, afflictions, or consequences of aging. Malaise, to be sure,

[19] *The Impeachment of Richard M. Nixon, President of the United States, Report of the Committee on the Judiciary,* House Document No. 93–339, 93rd Congress, 2d Sess. (Washington, 1974), 3.

[20] United States Commission on CIA Activities within the United States, *Report to the President* (Washington, 1975), 19–36.

illnesses of several sorts. But to my mind they do not evoke, as they have for some, images of Diocletian and late Roman calamities. Worse things have happened in recent times to regimes much younger than America's—for example those of India, China, or Russia—without setting off Spenglerian reflections. The only special correlation with age is that of being around long enough, which naturally incurs greater risk of getting in the way of such things happening.[21] It is not that they are historical anomalies, but that they are anomalous in the history of America. And there is quite enough odor of brimstone about them—about what is known, let alone what is still undisclosed—to prompt renewed speculations regarding George Santayana's question of how Americans, in their frozen posture of innocence and youth, would respond if over overtaken by "serious and irremediable tribulation." Odds are that old Job would have shrugged them off as trivial, and they have not yet been proven to be irremediable. But as I say, more than a whiff of sulphur still lingers about them, enough at least to suggest the test of Job's trials.

In their tortured response to the Vietnam War, the longest and most divisive in their history, Americans were divided ideologically between adherents of two main tenets of the American myth—that of invincibility and that of innocence. Many were caught somewhere in the middle, torn between the two, but virtually all—and especially those of the right and the left—adhered to the myth in some form. Behind the tenet of invincibility were aligned those of the right to whom the only conceivable end to an American war was victory. A defeat or a "no-win war" was to them so abhorrent that they rejected all thought of compromise, even negotiation, and were prepared to incur any amount of guilt, even resort to atomic weapons, to gain their ends. On the opposite side were those who, in addition to their genuine abomination of an unjust war, were so dedicated to the myth of national innocence that their abhorrence of guilt exceeded any concern for defeat. To restore lost innocence or stop the increment of intolerable guilt, some would renounce all future resort to force and military means in any circumstances. The myth of

[21] The decade of the 1980s would provide further examples of this sort.

innocence had special appeal for the new cult of youth, including the counterculture then engaged in yet another greening of America. The clash between the new cult of youth and innocence and the older culture of invincibility and success further intensified ideological warfare at home, but the struggle was for priority of myths, not for their renunciation.

The revelations of Watergate were an especially rude challenge to the myth of American innocence. So repugnant and gross were they that there was a strong disposition to disbelieve the plain and undeniable evidence or to connive tacitly in a conspiratorial cover-up. On April 25, 1973 there occurred an unforgettable telephone conversation between President Nixon and H. R. Haldeman. "Despite all the polls and all the rest," said the president, "I think there's still a hell of a lot of people out there, and from what I've seen they're—you know, they, they want to believe, that's the point, isn't it?"[22] He was right. They desperately wanted to believe, and they were prepared to go to almost any lengths to shore up the faith—innocence by "stonewalling," if it came to that. Had it not been for the unprecedented quantity and explicit character of the evidence—millions of words recorded electronically in the very tone, accent, and characteristic vocabulary of the accused—there can be little doubt who would have presided as head of state over the bicentennial year. Once the stonewalling ceased and the evidence was confronted, the old institutions of Senate, House, and federal judiciary, moved with gratifying firmness to perform their constitutional duties. Even so, even before all the trials were completed, the verdicts handed down, and the culprits sentenced or pardoned in advance, a strong national disposition was manifest to put the unfortunate matter out of mind and get on with business. In some circles it was considered poor taste to bring Watergate up at all, and in the ensuing presidential campaign the subject was virtually banned.

Although none of these ironic pranks that history played as prelude and accompaniment to the American Bicentennial can

---

[22] Unpublished court transcript quoted in Theodore H. White, *Breach of Faith: The Fall of Richard Nixon* (New York, 1974), 327.

really be classified with old Job's "irremediable tribulations," neither can they be dismissed as Emerson's "measles and whooping cough of growing up." Yet that would seem to be the predominant diagnosis—a problem for pediatrics, not one for geriatrics. The refusal to grow up can have serious consequences, and Americans still show symptoms of refusal. They would seem to stand poised on the brink of the third century of the national era and the third millennium of the Christian era, determinedly youthful, stonewall innocent. Or is it that in their private reading of the Book of Job Americans skipped the meat of the thing, missed the meaning of submission, and jumped to the epilogue? For there, you will recall, we are told that the Lord not only restored Job's fortunes but doubled his possessions. For good measure, the Almighty endowed him with fourteen thousand head of cattle, six thousand camels, a thousand yoke of oxen, a thousand she-asses, seven sons, three daughters of unsurpassed beauty, and another hundred and forty years of life to enjoy it all.

6

The Fall
of the American Adam

*Here again I deal with myth and use literary evidence, still
believing that these methods may not properly be denied historians and trying to be careful to acknowledge direful realities cloaked by mythic abstractions. Again the central myth is
innocence, "Adamic innocence," though this time counterposed
to constructs of collective guilt. The shift in predominance
from the one to the other and back again suggests a recurring
pattern of alternative moods. In 1981, when this paper was
read before a meeting of the American Academy of Arts and
Sciences, a new administration in Washington was hailing the
rebirth of national self-esteem, self-assurance, and collective innocence. Toward the end of that same administration, however,
signs of another shift in the cycle began to appear.*

I AM SPEAKING PRIMARILY OF THE PRESENT, but of attitudes toward the American past in the present and of how these attitudes
have undergone some significant changes. I am particularly concerned with the relatively recent inversion of traditional myths
and especially the shift from collective innocence toward collective guilt. For perspective on the extent of change and its relative

recency we do not have to go back very far. In fact we can rely on the testimony and views of a few worthy historians still much alive in the memories and in the affections of many people, including the present writer.

It was only a few decades ago that Samuel Eliot Morison could remark that the prevailing view of Americans toward their national past was "a friendly, almost affectionate attitude," and proclaim the existence of a "seller's market in early Americana," benignly and traditionally conceived. More recently the late Arthur M. Schlesinger wrote of how America had "held up a lamp to Europe and, more recently, to Asia and Africa." Writing of the American record of leadership in Western civilization during the two world wars and the Cold War, Allan Nevins could say, "It stands invested with all the radiance of the Periclean era, the Elizabethan era, and the era of Pitt and the long struggle against Napoleon." Toward the close of his book of memoirs, Dexter Perkins wrote in 1969, "I end this chapter with a paeon of praise to American democracy" and its citizens. "In their capacity for self-government, for the successful operation of one of the most difficult enterprises in the history of man, they can be proud of their past and hopeful of their future."

Samuel Flagg Bemis was somewhat more restrained about the present century, but for what he called "the great and happy successes" of the nineteenth century words all but failed him: "Oh, wondrous century, so fortuitously fortunate for our nation! Oh, happy, golden, bygone years of safety, in lucky innocence, apart from the world around us!" The Union had to be preserved at a cost, to be sure, but to my old colleague Professor Bemis, "the greatest achievement of American nationality was expansion of the nation across the empty continent to the shores of the 'other ocean.' It established the territorial basis of the United States as a world power and a bastion of freedom today . . . expansively perfected by peaceful diplomacy between 1783 and 1867"—one great succession of peaceful real estate transactions—save for the Mexican lapse.

I do not cite these professions of faith and pride in the national past to illustrate or characterize the views of the historians.

I quote them, of course, out of context. Each of them was capable of more sophisticated views of the past and the present, and we are indebted to all of them for critical assessments and interpretations of the aspects of American history in which they specialized. The more remarkable then, that all of them should have given voice to the myth of innocence of the American past. It would be possible to adduce other voices in support of the myth, but few more faithful to the tradition that extends back to George Bancroft and far beyond to the first chroniclers.

It was the virtues of the past the historians were praising, but the character of the modern period during which they voiced their pride in the past is worth recalling. That was a period of unprecedented American power, wealth, and prestige, a period of Pax Americana in which monopoly or predominant command of the ultimate weapon seemed for a while secure. The United States in the 1950s was at once the policeman of the world and the self-acclaimed model for revolutions of liberation. Influential books of the time bore such titles as *People of Plenty* and *The Affluent Society*. We were the *Redeemer Nation*, a country with a divinely assigned Errand, a World Mission. Americans commonly assumed their country to be the envy of all nations, and called it "the Galahad among nations."

Friendly critics there were, even then, to remind us of the moral risks of combining pretensions of innocency with unprecedented power and wealth. Reinhold Niebuhr warned of "ironic perils which compound the experiences of Babylon and Israel." Others spoke of "The Illusion of American Omnipotence" and of "The Arrogance of Power." They cautioned that the legend of American invincibility did not guarantee that all wars ended in victory, and that great power could not be wielded without incurring guilt. These admonitions may have had some impact on policy. But with a few exceptions the legend of an essentially innocent past held intact. Exceptions will be noted later. The remarkable thing is the degree to which the myth of Adamic innocency held together until it was in danger of being overwhelmed by a spreading conviction of national guilt.

Collective guilt has not enjoyed the long growing season or

the fertile seed bed of tradition from which the myth of national innocence has perennially sprung. It has nevertheless struck roots and flourished of late in a climate that seems specially suited to it. And it has been nourished by a public that evidently feels a need for its fruits. A seller's market for guilt now exists, only whetted, not satiated in the sixties. Though the demand may be inspired by recent events, the bargains in guilt are to be found mainly in the past. Ancestral atrocities and injustices, historic evils and inhumanities, and the brutalities and cruelties of past centuries can be acknowledged without assuming corresponding burdens of expiation. Ancient evils can thus be deplored and lamented, and pretensions of innocence scorned. But the grievances are antique and their perpetrators long gone. The guilt thus acknowledged can hardly be called red-handed.

The appreciating supply of historic guilt for the new market results not so much from revision of history or from new historic evidence as from the transposition of symbols and the inversion of myths. The new image of the past sometimes replaces the ethnocentrism of the mythmakers with that of its victims. Thus "discovery" of the New World becomes "invasion" thereof; "settlement" becomes "conquest," and Europeans the "savages." The "Virgin Land" becomes the "Widowed Land," the "howling wilderness" a desecrated Indian "hunting park." The "Garden of the World" becomes a "Waste Land," ravaged home of exterminated or endangered species. Professor Bemis's "empty continent" teems with outraged and betrayed First Americans. The advancement of the western frontier is sometimes pictured as a species of genocide, wave on wave of holocausts. One symbol that has been proposed to stand for the West so won is "A Pyramid of Skulls," Tartar model.

One of the ironies of the story is that the major burden of historic guilt was incurred in the age of innocence. Instead of ignoring the crimes, however, Americans of the earlier era often attacked and exposed them—not usually as collective guilt, but as the transgressions of individuals, groups, classes, sections—evils and injustices that threatened innocence and were to be corrected, punished, reformed, abolished. Slavery was the crime of southern slaveholders, injustice to Indians the fault of frontiersmen or their agents and influence. And so, with whatever justice or accuracy, specific evils were assigned to culprits such as Indian-haters, lords of the lash, lords of the loom, political bosses, big business, jingoes, "merchants of death," and "economic royalists." Guilt was something to be redressed, and its exposers looked to the future for expiation. The American jeremiad, as Sacvan Berkovitch tells us, both laments an apostasy and heralds a restoration.

The new guilt is different. It is something congenital, inherent, intrinsic, collective, something possibly inexpiable, and probably ineradicable. The first English settlers, south as well as north, arrived with it in their hearts, and they never should have come in the first place. Invasion was their initial offense. The pattern of collective rapacity and inhuman cruelty to darker peoples that characterized their westward conquests of the Pacific shores and on across the ocean ever westward through Asia is seen as existing from the very outset. From this point of view the line of precedents stretched from the slaughter of braves in the Pequot War of 1637 on for three centuries and more to Lieutenant Calley at My Lai, with little more than changes in the technology of annihilation. Thus interpreted, American history becomes primarily a history of oppression, and the focus is upon the oppressed. The latter vary in color or identity as the center of interest shifts from one of these groups to another. The most conspicuous among them of late have been the Afro-Americans, though popular concern with their grievances has not been unwavering and they have had to share attention from time to time with other groups.

The primary objective in all this would not seem to be so much the exposure of evil or the identification of transgressors as it is an oblique exercise in the analysis of national character. And yet "national" seems too comprehensive a word to be employed in its customary sense in this connection, for the characterizations are racially assigned or circumscribed, even though directed at the dominant or majority group. A favored characterization, often quoted and sometimes misused, is a famous definition of "the myth of the essential white America" by D. H. Lawrence, published in 1923. "The essential American soul," he writes, "is hard, isolate, stoic, and a killer. It has never yet melted. . . . This is the very intrinsic-most American. He is at the core of all the other flux and fluff"—such as love and democracy and equality.

The exercise of defining national (or racial) character in terms of guilt attributes takes on some peculiar traits in the American instance. It might be called, in a sense, unilateral. In most instances, that is, the guilt is to all appearances unshared, the offenses incurring it unprovoked, unique, and confined to the dominant group. If other nations have perpetrated comparable or worse offenses against *their* native population, black slaves and freedmen, racial minorities, neighboring countries, or remote Asian or African cultures, the opportunities for perspective by comparing the magnitude of the offenses and the number of casualties are passed over. Those American offenses that were confined to intraracial conflict, also go largely unremarked. That more American casualities were sustained in one battle of the Civil War than in all previous American wars, or that more Americans lost their lives in that war than in all subsequent wars of the nation goes unnoticed. Similar indifference in the national guilt market greets historic atrocities of one minority race against another, or intraracial mahem among minorities.

Rejection of collective innocence and embracing of collective guilt have not invariably dispelled national myths that accompanied or sustained the myth of innocence. Inverting myths may be a way of preserving them. The quest for guilt continues to seek new and far flung frontiers. When things go wrong in the Third World—and sometimes even in the Second—we are now taught to look inward for the cause. This teaching recalls by contrast the recent time when we were taught that America "held up a lamp" of hope to Asia and Africa. What has remained, if somewhat altered in the process, is the illusion of American omnipotence and moral responsibility and the cosmic self-centeredness of the national world view. "America," says a generally friendly Italian critic of ours, "is alone in the world."

Americans evidently have some special problems of a self-destructive nature in dealing with national guilt. If so, it is for no lack of guilt in the national and pre-national experience. The conquest of a continent, the dispossession and subjection of its natives, the exploitation of imported African slaves, the imposition of our will on other races and nations abroad, and the establishment of a brief Pax Americana by the world's most powerful nation are not exploits brought off without the incurring of guilt—impressive amounts of it. No intelligent citizen can have escaped awareness of this at some time. Still draped in legends of national infancy, myths of innocence, success, invincibility, and righteousness, however, we were caught short at the climax of our mythic national pretensions and exposed in deeds and failures that mocked all the old myths. It was then that the obsession with guilt took hold. Other nations with bloodier disgraces on their heads—Germany and her death camps; France and her Vichy, her Vietnam and her Algeria; Japan and her imperial conquests; not to mention Russia and China with their multimillions of domestic victims—all seemed to manage recovery without excesses of self-detestation or self-revilement.

It is a Freudian truism I will not presume to attest that the problem of guilt is as much within the heart as within the act, or even more so. Guilt looks inward. Psychoanalysts suggest that when a person inflicts punishment on himself, he should engage in historical recollection or exploration of the past to bring to consciousness and acceptance the cause of the guilt feelings. Presumably the same could be said of societies. We are also told on good authority that no one develops a sense of guilt without a punitive parent image—real or projectively imagined. We are guilty because we have not lived up to high standards represented by our parents. Or so we are told.

The curious thing about American experiments in self-therapy through the discovery and proclaiming of historic guilt is that it is the punitive progenitors themselves, the founding fathers and founding mothers, who have come to be regarded as the guilty parties—or at least the original sinners. As such they make rather poor punitive parent images, and provide their progeny with more escape from guilt than acceptance of it. When it is recent rather than historic transgression, the accusors conceive of it as the guilt of all. It is collective guilt. "When all are guilty," wrote Hannah Arendt, "no one is; confessions of collective guilt," she continues, "are the best possible safeguards against the discovery of culprits, and the very magnitude of the crime the best excuse for doing nothing."

Neither the old myth of innocence nor the self-therapy of historic or collective guilt has proved to be of much help to Americans with their problems. The sudden shift from the one extreme to the other may well portend a reaction in the opposite direction—and there are already some ominous signs of such a reaction. President Reagan and the opinion polls assured us that Americans have made a sudden recovery from their malaise, restored their self-esteem and self-confidence, and face the future and a skeptical world with old-time assurance. An aggressive foreign policy and bold commitments around the world indicate that changes have indeed taken place—whether the result of restored confidence or not. They suggest that the national conscience is preparing to take on new and unpredictable burdens.

If this means a swing back to the old myths, a return to fatuous complacency and self-righteousness, it is not likely to produce an equilibrium of spiritual well-being or a salutary balance in the American conscience. It might even contrive a spurious absolution of the very real guilt that so recently precipitated the obsession and cover with a mantle of counterfeit innocence the perpetrators themselves. That would be an ironic outcome, indeed.

Both the old myth of innocence and the obsession with its opposite would nevertheless seem destined to abide with us. They are deeply embedded in our tradition and in our literature. Perhaps the most profound and, to me, the most moving treatment of them in American letters is that of Robert Penn Warren in *Brother to Dragons*. You may recall that the subject of the dramatic dialogue of this book is the inhuman murder of a slave committed by two of Thomas Jefferson's nephews at their home in Jefferson's golden land of hope, the West. The crime is a matter of historical record. In *Brother to Dragons,* the author has Lucy, the sister of Thomas Jefferson and mother of his criminal nephews, say to Jefferson: "Dear Brother, the burden of innocence is heavier than the burden of guilt." But the poet goes on to make it evident that the latter burden is by no means a light one, for all that.

III

COMPARISONS
IN HISTORY

While comparative history has gained some reputability of late, and experiments in comparison have increased in number and boldness, most historians still manifest reticence and reservations about such ventures. Their attitude has reminded Raymond Grew, who edits a journal of comparative studies, of "the ambivalence of a good bourgeois toward the best wines: to appreciate them is a sign of good taste, but indulgence seems a little loose and wasteful." Indulgence is inhibited by other attitudes, some of them the result of misconceptions. One is the assumption that the sole purpose of comparison is the search for similarities. With their jealous regard for the unique and particular and their prevailing conviction of national distinctiveness and peculiarity, American historians have long been suspicious of quests for similarities. Marc Bloch, the great French champion of historical comparison, held "that primary interest of the comparative method is, on the contrary, the observation of differences."

Another misunderstanding is that the appropriate if not the only intelligible unit for historical comparison is the nation. So conceived, the comparative method could easily lend itself to the uses of nationalism and cultural chauvinism, especially when used invidiously. Of the four essays that follow, only the first uses the nation as the unit for comparison. While I believe that such comparison properly employed can serve to disabuse patriots of nationalist hubris and delusions of exceptionalism, I have no intention of suggesting that nations are the only, or the most appropriate, units. In fact the remaining three essays address other social institutions and entities for comparison, most of them to be found in this country only in the South. This follows from an assumption, long maintained, that the South has its historical misfortunes and calamities to thank for rich opportunities of comparison with foreign experience that are largely denied other parts of America. It is these other parts that can more justly boast of their "exceptionalism"—mainly their *in*comparable good fortune. And it is the "un-American" parts of the South's experience that makes a ready comparative partner for so much of the world that shares comparable misfortunes.

7

The Comparability
of American History

The following paper was written to introduce a book entitled
The Comparative Approach to American History *that appeared*
in 1968. Twenty-two other historians contributed as many es-
says on subjects chosen to provide opportunity for comparison
of the American experience with that of other peoples in such
historic episodes as colonial rule, revolutions, nation founding,
frontier advances, immigrations, slavery systems, civil wars, re-
constructions, racial dominations, empire building, world wars,
depressions, and cold wars. The authors were chosen for their
eminence in a particular field rather than their command of
the comparative method. Their contributions were of varied
merit, but they served in some measure, I believe, to foster the
growing interest in comparative history.

To LIMIT THE SUBJECT OF HISTORICAL STUDY within national
boundaries is always to invite the charge of narrow perspective
and historical nationalism. Historians of all nations have in some
measure incurred that risk, but Americans have been accused of
more than the normal share of this type of parochialism. They
are said to lay excessive claims to distinctiveness and uniqueness

in their national experience, to plead immunity from the influence of historical forces that have swept most other nations, to shun or deprecate comparisons between their history and that of other people, and to seek within their own borders all the significant forces that have shaped their history. These charges assume more sharpness and urgency as America approaches total involvement in world history. The striking paradox of a nation that professes historical parochialism and practices cosmopolitan involvement calls for attention from professional historians.

There is no denying a certain justification for such charges. It will appear on further analysis, however, that they have had more validity in some periods than in others, that there have always been exceptions among historians, and that of late a significant countercurrent has asserted itself in American historical thought.

From the start of settlement certain aspects of the American experience undoubtedly encouraged among the transplanted Europeans, and to some degree justified, an emphasis on distinctiveness and an aversion to comparison. This was for the settlers in many ways a *new* world. Both the uniqueness and the influence of free land and the fabled frontier that advanced steadily across the continent for three centuries have probably been exaggerated but they were impressive evidence of distinctiveness for those involved in the drama. Americans were slower to grasp the distinctive significance of their having skipped the feudal phase of history that was common to all the older nations and not wholly avoided by some of the newer ones. They thought they understood what Alexis de Tocqueville meant, however, when he wrote that they were "born equal." Whatever equality meant, the American brand was assumed at the time to be something distinctive.

Still another historic circumstance that Americans enjoyed for a long and crucial period without fully comprehending it was the blessing of military security that was not only effective but relatively free. It came as a bounty of nature and benign circumstance—the presence of vast oceans and the absence of powerful neighbors. The very absence of powerful and rival nations on the borders of the United States or, indeed, within its entire hemisphere was not only another circumstance that set the American experience apart as unique. It also removed a powerful incentive and stimulus for international comparison. Britain, America's nineteenth-century foreign standard of comparison, cultural irritant, and model, was across the wide Atlantic. Nearly all other nations lived constantly with the physical proximity of strong national rivals for territory, influence, prestige, markets, or priority in science, the arts and technology. While rivalries foster stereotypes, the comparative frame of reference is an ingrained habit of mind and sometimes a condition of survival among rival nations. For America alone among the major nations, this incentive for comparative analysis and reflection was long absent or physically remote.

As "the first new nation," the first to break from colonial status as well as the one to inaugurate the age of democratic revolution, America found no suitable models among her eighteenth-century contemporaries and few precedents for her experiments. Founding fathers often cited models of antiquity and theories of John Locke, but the patriot was impressed with the originality of their statecraft, and insistence on the uniqueness of national institutions became part of conventional patriotism.

Emphasis on uniqueness and distinctiveness, not only of national institutions but of national character, became an important means of asserting and defining national identity. The new nation suffered from an understandable insecurity of identity. Older nations were secure on this score in their common ethnic, or religious, or linguistic, or political heritage. Some nations could lay claim to unity in several of these important sources of identity and a few in all of them. The American nation could claim unity in none of them. With the exception of the aborigines, the Americans were immigrants or the descendants of immigrants from all parts of Europe, many parts of Africa, and some parts of Asia. Lacking a common racial, religious, linguistic, or political heritage, they had to look elsewhere for the bases of nationality. Their anxiety over this quest for national identity helps explain what David M. Potter has described as "a somewhat compulsive preoccupation with the question of their Americanism." This preoccupation has found expression in innumerable, often confusing and contradictory efforts to define the national character. Such attempts have naturally emphasized what was assumed to be unique or peculiar to America. The effect of such inquiries was to minimize comparability or to use comparison only to stress distinctiveness.

There were obvious reasons why a young and relatively undeveloped country might well shun comparisons between its history and that of old and mature nations, rich and glamorous with famous names, celebrated achievements, and venerable monuments. The risks of such comparisons were illustrated by Henry James, who undertook in the 1870's to "enumerate the items of high civilization as it exists in other countries, which are absent from the texture of American life." His inventory of missing items was not calculated to flatter the pride of patriots, though good Jacksonian democrats might shrug them off:

> No State, in the European sense of the word, and indeed barely a specific naitonal name. No sovereign,, no court, no personal loyalty, no aristocracy, no church, no clergy, no army, no diplomatic service, no country gentlemen, no palaces, no castles, nor manors nor old country houses, nor parsonages, nor thatched cottages, nor ivied ruins; no cathedrals, nor abbeys, nor little Norman churches; no great universities nor public schools—no Oxford, nor Eton, nor Harrow . . . no Epsom nor Ascot!

To invite comparison was to risk an exposure of pretensions, a withering of national pride or native complacency. The wide currency of the old chestnut that "comparisons are odious" was understandable under the circumstances. Americans have been notoriously eager throughout their history for praise of their institutions from foreign visitors, but they have also been sensitive to condescension and fearful of being patronized.

If there were forces at work in American history to discourage the comparative view, there were also certain circumstances that had a contrary effect. The very fact that America was a nation composed of the people of many nations meant that nearly all Americans were the heirs of more than one historical heritage—the American as well as that of the country or countries from which they or their forebears emigrated. The whole experience of emigration and immigration was charged with tensions of comparison. The decision to leave the Old World for the New often involved agonizing comparisons based on limited information and conjecture. Life for the first-generation immigrants was a daily round of comparisons, rueful or gratifying; and the second generation never ceased to hear "how it was in the Old Country." Well into the twentieth century, first-generation immigrants in vast numbers continued to repeat this exercise and to pass on to succeeding generations their comparative frame of reference. Some of the boldest recent experiments in American comparative history have been the works of historians who come of recent immigrant backgrounds.

Consciousness of the Old Country heritage and habituation to the comparative frame of reference tended to diminish in proportion to the remoteness of arrival in the New World and to decline more markedly after the first-generation immigrants. Identification with the country of origin tended also to be diffused and blurred as various nationalities interbred. J. Hector St. John de Crèvecoeur knew an American family in 1782 "whose grandfather was an Englishman, whose wife was Dutch, whose son married a French woman, and whose present four sons have now four wives of different nations." Most of the later generations rather arbitrarily settled upon one country (however many might actually have been involved) as the traditional place of family origin and spoke of themselves as being of "English stock," or "Italian background," or "Scandinavian extraction." Negro Americans, most of them descended from eighteenth-century arrivals whose African culture was largely obliterated by the slavery experience were the only ethnic exceptions to the American norm of multiple historical heritage, and interbreeding with whites mitigated the effect of this exception. Diffused, diminished, or conventionalized, the "Old Country" referent remained a part of the mental furniture of many Americans to some degree down through the generations. However cautious and reluctant the professional historian may be about comparisons, the layman has blandly indulged in them as a matter of course.

Among the historians themselves, broadly speaking, there has been over the centuries, until recent years, a declining consciousness of the European origins, context, and connections of American history. In general, and in particular the professionals among them, historians have tended to regard the fragment as the whole, to neglect the larger world for the offshoot, and to restrict their search for the compelling forces and dynamics of American history to their native soil. This has not always been true. Historians in the colonial period, when America was part of a thriving empire and they were closer to their European roots, were as acutely aware of the oppressions and conditions they had fled as they were of new problems they faced, of what they had brought with them as of what they had found on this side of the Atlantic. They knew they were a frontier, but they had not forgotten what they were a frontier of. In some ways the colonials were more cosmopolitan in outlook than their more sophisticated and worldly descendants.

Historians during the early years of the Republic, nationalistic and patriotic though they were, supported their exalted claims for American achievements in freedom, justice, and equality with comparative reference to the Old World, where they found these blessings less prevalent. The romantic school of historians in the middle and later nineteenth century may have been simple in outlook and untutored in method, but their books speak eloquently of broader and more cosmopolitan horizons than those their academic successors normally explored. Francis Parkman's great work, *France and England in North America,* is full of dramatic contrasts and comparisons and is profoundly conscious of European origins and influences. William Prescott's romantic narrative of Spanish conquests in the New World offers a comparison of frontier influences that contrast strikingly with frontier influences just north of the Rio Grande.

The first generation of professional academic historians in

America, who flourished in the last quarter of the nineteenth century, learned from their German masters a peculiarly Teutonic brand of comparative history. They were taught to look back to the German forests for the origins of "Anglo-Saxon" institutions and national character. The findings of this school fostered national pride and carried overtones of racial superiority. The methods of the Teutonic or "scientific" historians were not truly comparative, however, for what they were seeking were congenial similarities or flattering analogies and continuities. They closed their eyes to the contrasts and differences that are an essential part of comparative analysis. As a consequence they were betrayed into advancing sterile hypotheses and indefensible generalizations.

A devastating attack on the sterility and absurdities of the teachers of the germ theory was mounted by their own students. Their attack demolished the Teutonic hypothesis so thoroughly that it had few defenders after the turn of the century. This was a valuable service rendered by the new Progressive historians. But in throwing out the discredited and teleological uses of the comparative method made by the scientific school they discredited the valid uses as well and ended by virtually abandoning them. In effect they turned their backs on the larger world to concentrate on the fragment, to look inward subjectively for the answers to historical problems. They were given to dwelling on the newness of the New World and on what they were prone to suggest was the *in*comparable in American experience.

Frederick Jackson Turner, the famous exponent of the Frontier Thesis, took part in the attack on the Teutonic hypothesis and gave to the new school many of its distinguishing traits. Announcing that "the germ theory of politics has been sufficiently emphasized," he turned to his native West for the key to American development. It was not only the influence of Europe he deprecated, but that of the American East as well. "The true point of view in the history of this nation is not the Atlantic Coast," he wrote; "it is the Great West." Turner was predominantly an environmentalist and had little time for ideologies and theories. "American democracy was born of no theorist's dreams," he declared. It was not something imported from Europe. "It came out of the American forest . . ." Comparisons with what came out of the forests to the north and to the south of the American borders were left to others. "Neither the French nor the Spanish frontier is within the scope of the volume," he announced, Turner was more interested in what America did to Europeans than in what Europeans did to America. "The wilderness masters the colonist" he said. The enchanted wood was the great Americanizer, the generator of national identity. "Thus the advance of the frontier has meant a steady movement away from the influence of Europe, a steady growth of independence on American lines." It was clear that the historian rejoiced in this "steady movement" and believed that it indicated the proper direction of historical interpretation as well.

In this respect it would appear anomalous to bracket Charles A. Beard, another dominant figure of the Progressive school, with Turner. Beard had a rather more cosmopolitan style of thought and life. He enjoyed several years of study and work abroad, in England as a youth and in Japan in later life. Moreover, he studied and wrote European as well as American history. While both men employed economic interpretations, Turner's emphasis was on geographic environment and Beard's on class and interest conflicts, phenomena that lent themselves more readily to generalization and comparison. In writing of such conflicts in American history, Beard was aware in an abstract way of parallels in other lands. But in locating the dynamics that shaped American institutions and the development of democracy, Beard like Turner looked steadily within. The Beardean determinants were domestic conflicts between economic interests—agrarians and industrialists, holders of personal and real property, debtor and creditor, labor and capital, radicals and conservatives. He did not turn back to consider the inherited postulates, the given consensus of doctrine within which these domestic conflicts took place, and lacked therefore a comparative measure of the relatively narrow margins of difference between the opposing sides.

The work of Turner and Beard and that of Vernon Louis

Parrington, the intellectual historian who belonged to the same school, has been subjected to searching criticism in the last thirty years. None of the critics has so far attained an influence comparable with that exercised by the masters of the old school, however, and none has so far put forward a comprehensive reconstruction of American history to replace those attacked. While many of the findings and methods of the Progressive school have been rejected, the underlying assumptions of the inward determinants and the subjective nature of American historical analysis have been more rarely challenged and still have numerous adherents.

The recent vogue of American studies encouraging national boundaries to the study of culture, has probably had the effect of enhancing the subjective and inward tendency. The establishment of this discipline in a number of foreign universities in Europe and Asia has so far done little to alter the tendency, since foreign scholars have largely followed the lead of American interpretations. Europeans are increasingly willing to study American history but little inclined so far to subject it to comparative analysis.[1] "To teach American history in isolation," complains Geoffrey Barraclough, "as a separate branch of study parallel to European history, is to commit the very errors of which our teaching of European history has been guilty."

The end of American isolation and the explosive involvement of the United States in world politics and power struggles that came as a consequence of World War II have not left historians untouched. Government programs recruited teachers from American universities for foreign lectureships in universities around the globe, and hundreds of refugee scholars from abroad joined the American intellectual community. The intellectual capital of the country became host to the United Nations, and the political capital became a forum for debate of world problems.

One response of historians to the end of isolation has been a significant increase in the comparative approach to national his-

[1] One notable exception is J. R. Pole, *Political Representation in England and the Origins of the American Republic* (London and New York, 1966).

tory. This movement has not resulted in anything that could be called a "school." Nor have the comparative historians agreed upon any common method, fixed upon any typical subject of study, or arrived at any overriding hypothesis such as the Teutonic germ theory. The comparative studies that have been made have been highly individual, the methods experimental and diverse, the subjects of study scattered over many periods and fields, the findings broadly pluralistic and sometimes contradictory. If these historians have any common disposition, it might be an interest in the methods and studies of the social sciences, but some of them disavow and resist such interests and stick to traditional methods. And in spite of the expected and indeed predominant effect of turning historical thought outward, some of the comparative studies have had the tendency of enhancing the emphasis on uniqueness formerly associated with the subjective and inward analysis.

Daniel J. Boorstin is one practitioner of comparative history. To be sure, his study of American history is informed by wide acquaintance with European history and life and characterized by constant comparison and contrast. But the result is to stress the uniqueness of the American experience, to deny the importance or persistence of European influence and ideas and to turn inward again for the keys to American history. He pictures an American historical landscape littered with the wreckage of European plans, blueprints, theories, and grand designs, a graveyard of European categories, social distinctions, and sociological "laws." Americans owe nothing to "garret-spawned European illuminati" and have little gift for theorizing or interest in theory. Their political "genius" lay in inspired improvisation, free-wheeling pragmatism, versatile adaptation to brute fact, compelling circumstances, and practical problems. He echoes the Turnerian refrain "that American values spring from the circumstances of the New World, that these are the secret of the 'American Way of Life.'"

Louis Hartz, who makes comparative history the basis of his critique, believes that "the American historian at practically every stage has functioned quite inside the nation: he has tended to be an erudite reflection of the limited social perspective of the average American himself." Like Boorstin, he finds confirmation of "our national uniqueness" in comparison. "How can we know the uniqueness of anything," he asks, "except by contrasting it with what is not unique?" The failure of the Progressive historians lay in the fact that "they did not attempt the European correlations." Had they done so he thinks, they would have seen that all the domestic social conflict between "radicals" and "conservatives" which they described took place within a Lockean consensus. Since "America was grounded in escape from the European past" and succeeded in skipping the feudal stage, it had no *ancien régime* and therefore no real radicals to overthrow it and no reactionaries to restore it. Conservatives could, paradoxically, only conserve John Locke. Only by viewing America from the "outside," as did Tocqueville, does its true distinctiveness appear. From this perspective Hartz and his collaborators have produced a comparative study of the "fragmentation" of European culture and the development of new societies in Latin America, South Africa, Canada, and Australia, as well as the United States.

Another outlet for the comparative impulse has been to give a translatlantic dimension to historical experiences common to both America and Europe. One of the finest achievements of recent years in this field is Robert R. Palmer's *Age of Democratic Revolution,* which has the subtitle *A Political History of Europe and America, 1760–1800.* Reversing the conventional pattern of Europe transmitting and America receiving influences and ideas, Palmer stresses the American origins of an age of revolution and traces the profound impact the first of the democratic revolutions had upon the numerous European revolutions that followed. Also reflecting the transatlantic tendency of historiography are Alan Simpson's *Puritanism in Old and New England* (1955), Boyd Shafer's *Nationalism* (1955), and Felix Gilbert's *To the Farewell Address* (1964). Barrington Moore, Jr., has added transpacific to transatlantic comparisons in his *Social Origins of*

Dictatorship and Democracy (1966) to give modern world history a whole new conceptual framework.[2]

The comparative history so far mentioned has been done with traditional methods and, with the exception of Mr. Moore, by guild historians. Social scientists have increasingly invaded this field of late, and one of them, Seymour Martin Lipset, in *The First New Nation* (1963), pursues a bold line of wide-ranging comparison and analogy. Using concepts and methods developed by such social scientists as Karl Deutsch and Talcott Parsons, Lipset undertakes "to elucidate through comparative analysis some of the problems and some of the developmental processes that are common to all new nations." As was the case in the Age of Democratic Revolution, America as the "first new nation" is seen as teacher and initiator rather than pupil and follower, giving to latter-day new nations "clues as to how revolutionary equalitarian and populist values may eventually become incorporated into a stable nonauthoritarian polity."

The subject of slavery long caught in the grip of sectional recrimination, has recently been lifted to an international and intercontinental plane by comparative studies. The discussion of slavery has quickened in response to the sudden relevance of the contrasting cultural determinants, legal traditions, and religious practices of three continents and a hundred islands. Much credit for the stimulation of this discussion is due to Stanley M. Elkins, who in his *Slavery* (1959) not only made provocative comparisons between the institution under Latin-Catholic auspices and under Anglo-Saxon-Protestant control, but initiated a reconsideration of the impact of slavery upon Negro personality with daring psychological analogies, and spotlighted peculiarities of American abolitionists by a comparison with the British abolitionists. The comparative analysis has been broadened by anthropological contributions and refined by detailed studies of slavery in Brazil, Africa, and islands of the West Indies with various

---

[2] It should be noted in passing that a far larger proportion of historians in America work on the history of other nations than do historians in European countries, though this does not necessarily result in more comparative history.

national heritages. More recently David B. Davis' *The Problem of Slavery in Western Culture* (1966), a work of elegant scholarship and wide learning, has extended the range of comparative analysis of both slavery and thought about slavery back to the Greeks.

Secession, Civil War, and Reconstruction, usually considered culture-bound subjects of exclusively national negotiability, have profited from hints, suggestions, and limited experiments of a comparative nature. The stimulus of comparative analysis, they prove, need not be limited to the kind derived from formal and detailed comparisons. Overextended comparisons can in fact be self-defeating. If not pushed too far or elaborated too much, comparative reference can illuminate a discussion after the manner of an imaginative and disciplined use of simile, metaphor, or analogy. As in literary usage, the spirit of play is not without relevance in such exercises. In various essays David M. Potter has enriched our comprehension of the American sectional crisis by invoking suggestive comparisons with other separatist and unification movements and other conflicts between men's loyalties. Roy F. Nichols has rendered comparable service in an essay setting the American Civil War in the full context of numerous internal struggles over the location of power within the Anglo-American community going back to the Wars of the Roses. And Eric L. McKitrick has invaded the jealous parochial sovereignty of the Reconstruction field with reference to peace-making processes in Germany and Japan after World War II. These are but samples of the numerous experiments with comparative analysis in American historiography, and there are many others. Not all of them have been fully successful or entirely convincing, but the same may be said of more conventional types of history.

Once the stream of American history descends to the plains of industrial, mass society in the late nineteenth century the opportunities, temptations, and the available data for comparative experiments multiply rapidly. National variations with the classic experiences of industrialization, migration, urbanization, race problems, and labor relations are numerous. These subjects lend themselves to quantified study and are more amenable to the methods of the social sciences. An affinity between comparative history and social science will naturally encourage additional experiments of comparison among historians of these fields. As for historians who cope with the period after America moves out of isolation into involvement in world politics and world wars, they are likely to regard comparative exercises as more of a necessity than a diversion.

There is a tradition in the historical guild and an instinctive aversion among its votaries against the abstract. In every true historian there is still a humanist with a profound respect for the varied particularity of human experience and a jealous regard for the precise integrity of time and place in the remembrance of things past. These instincts inevitably create tension between the historian and the social scientist, who deals freely with categories, prototypes, and statistical variables that override limits of space and time and lend themselves to comparisons. When the historian combines the instincts of his guild with a conviction about the distinctiveness and uniqueness of the national experience he studies, he is likely to be skeptical about experiments with comparative analysis.

Marc Bloch, the brilliant French comparative historian, with all his devotion to the unique and the particular, could boast with impunity, "I have used a powerful magic wand, namely, the comparative method." If the sorcerer's apprentices use the wand with the master's regard for particularity and uniqueness, the consequences need not be disastrous and the magic may continue to work.

8

Emancipations
and Reconstructions:
A Comparative Study

In its original form the following essay was presented in Moscow in 1970 at the XIII International Congress of Historical Sciences under the title, "Emancipations & Reconstructions: A Comparative Study." It drew criticism from the Russian historians who commented on the paper, one of whom pronounced it another example of "American exceptionalism." Others joined in the discussion, some to defend my position, others to suggest further comparisons.

COMPARISONS ARE ESSENTIAL TO ALL HISTORICAL UNDERSTANDING. American understanding of freedom and of the price the nation paid for it has suffered from lack of comparative reference. In proposing such an approach to the study of emancipation and Reconstruction history, I am of course conscious of the recent outburst of interest in the comparative history of slavery and the light it has shed on an American institution that was thereby rendered less peculiar and more understandable.

Comparative studies might also help understand what followed slavery. But, though the literature on comparative slavery has reached impressive proportions, very little has been written so far on the comparative history of emancipations and reconstructions. Yet there have been as many emancipations as there have been slavery systems, and we might presume that as much light could be shed upon the American experience by the comparative study of the one as of the other.

The nineteenth century was preeminently the century of emancipations, the period, as Victor Hugo said, of an idea whose time had come. Its time came relatively late in the United States of America, for on the world stage more emancipation dramas were enacted before than after that of 1865. The great age of emancipations was the half-century from 1833 when the British opened it, to 1888, when Brazil (and two years earlier Cuba) belatedly closed it. Earlier small-scale abolitions in the newly independent northern states of British North America were somewhat similar to those of the newly independent states of Spanish South America in that they involved relatively few slaves and in that slavery was comparatively unimportant to their economies. The abolitions and reconstructions of the great age of emancipations were primarily those of plantation America, scattered southward from Virginia to southern Brazil and spread eastward from Texas along the Gulf and through the Caribbean to Barbados. I shall confine this paper to that scope, omitting other areas. This vast area of maritime and continental provinces and nations possessed enough common features and similarities, together with enough differences and cultural variables, to make plantation America, as Charles Wagley says, "a magnificent laboratory for the comparative approach."[1] To explore the opportunities of comparative analysis would require a book. All I can attempt here is to suggest some possibilities and outline the framework of comparison.

Among the common features of the plantation America to which the American South belonged were a one-crop agriculture

[1] Charles Wagley, "Plantation-America: A Culture Sphere," *Caribbean Studies*, IV (1964), 12.

under the plantation system, a climate suitable for such a system, a background of slavery, a multiracial society, and a large population of African origin. Much more numerous than the common characteristics were the differences that distinguished the component parts. Six imperial powers controlled or had possessed parts of the area—the Spanish, Portuguese, English, French, Dutch, and Danish—not to mention the independent emancipating republics of Haiti, Brazil, and the United States. These powers were broadly divided in religious traditions between Catholics and Protestants, and their colonies and provinces differed among themselves in the crops they grew, the health and stage of development in their economies, in man-land ratios, and in racial, cultural, and political variables of bewildering complexity. Each of the many emancipations and readjustments involved was a unique historical event, and any valid comparative study will scrupulously respect the integrity of each and avoid facile generalizations. The most natural opportunity for comparison with the experience of the United States, and the one that will most often recur, is that presented by the British West Indies. Most of these colonies shared with the older slave states of the eastern seaboard a history of seventeenth- and eighteenth-century British rule and of populations with similar origins on the black and white sides, together with a common language and many common institutions. Yet, profound differences existed between the society of the island colonies and that of the continental states. Not only that, but probably as many differences existed among the fifteen island colonies that stretched from Jamaica to Trinidad as existed among the fifteen slave states that stretched from Delaware to Texas. The old sugar culture in Barbados, like the old tobacco culture in Virginia, went back to seventeenth-century origins, and, though Guiana and Trinidad were not so new and booming as Louisiana and Mississippi at the time of emancipation, they presented sharp contrasts to the older colonies within the empire. All these differences must be kept in mind when comparisons are ventured.

Since the experience of the United States is central to our concern and its illumination the main purpose of these comparisons, it is well to define first the unique character of its history. In all, some six million slaves were manumitted by the various abolitions of slavery in plantation America between 1834 and 1888. The slave states of the South accounted for four million of them, or about two-thirds of the total. The number liberated in the South was about five times that on the slave rolls of all the British West Indies in 1834 and eight times that of Brazil in 1888 at the times of abolition. In all the Latin American societies, of course, much liberation preceded abolition. Outside the South the slaves of the British West Indies and Brazil made up the two largest single liberated populations. The emancipation experience of the South therefore dwarfs all others in scale and magnitude.

Another unique feature of the southern experience was the high ratio of whites to blacks. In spite of the enormous number of slaves involved, the white population of the South outnumbered the black two to one. It is true that in two states the freedmen were in the majority and in one approached numerical equality, but nowhere save in isolated spots like the South Carolina Sea Islands did blacks reach such overwhelming preponderance as they did in the Caribbean islands, where ratios reached ten to one, though varying greatly. Three-quarters of the southern whites in 1860 did not belong to slaveholding families, and in them the freedmen faced competition and resistance to their aspirations that they faced nowhere else in plantation America. In all other parts of that great area save Brazil (with many uniquenesses of its own), the dominant cultural tradition was that of a small white minority wielding power over the vast black majority; in the South (and even more in the United States as a whole), the culturally dominant tradition was that of the overwhelming white majority.

Of comparable importance is a third circumstance (among many others) that added vastly to the uniqueness of the South's experience. This was the terrible war that brought about the end of slavery. Wars were not without influence on the weakening of the institution elsewhere, for example in Haiti, Cuba, and Barzil. But nowhere else did a slave society wage a life-and-death struggle for its existence with abolition at stake. And no other war in the Western world between those of Napoleon and the two world wars compares with the Civil War in bloodshed—one life for every six slaves freed and almost as many lives sacrificed in America as there were slaves liberated in the British West Indies without any bloodshed. The end of slavery in the South can be described as the death of a society, though elsewhere it could more reasonably be characterized as the liquidation of an investment. Of the numerous peculiarities that set apart the South's experience with abolition, then, these three claim special consideration: the magnitude of emancipation, the preponderance of whites, and the association with a terrible war.

Neither in Brazil nor in Cuba is the phenomenon of emancipation related to formal abolition in the way emancipation and abolition are related in the colonies of north European powers— much less in the American South. In the latter areas the slave population generally increased in absolute numbers and usually in proportion to the free population right up to the time of abolition. Then, after periods of "apprenticeship" or semislavery (except in the South), all were simultaneously and legally freed. The situation was strikingly different in Cuba and Brazil. The slave population in Cuba reached its peak forty-five years, and in Brazil thirty-eight years, before formal abolition. The number as well as the proportion of slaves in the total population had been declining in Cuba since 1841, when there were 421,649 slaves, or a third of the total population. During the 1880s they dwindled from some 200,000 to fewer than 30,000 before abolition.[2] The slave population of Brazil reached its peak in 1850, when 2,500,000 constituted about 30 percent of the total population, and before abolition in 1888 the number had declined to 500,000 and the percentage to less than 3.[3]

It is clear that Cuba and Brazil present special problems for

[2] Herbert S. Klein, *Slavery in the Americas: A Comparative Study of Virginia and Cuba* (Chicago, 1967), 123, 202; Arthur F. Corwin, *Spain and the Abolition of Slavery in Cuba, 1817–1886* (Austin and London, 1967), 146.

[3] Stanley Stein, *Vassouras: A Brazilian Coffee Country, 1850–1900* (Cambridge, Mass., 1957), 294.

the comparative study of emancipations and reconstructions. The most elementary and baffling one is to locate these phenomena in time. It is not a simple choice such as that between 1834 and 1838 as in the case of British emancipation, or between 1863 and 1865 as in the United States. Slavery began to decline in both Cuba and Brazil before the period of abolition laws began, and emancipation had largely run its course before slavery was abolished. In the history of neither of these countries was there any phenomenon like the total emancipation of four millions coinciding with the abolition of slavery that occurred in the American South. Or even the smaller and more gradual process that occurred in the West Indies.

One instance of emancipation remains to be accounted for—one that is an exception to all the others and preceded all the others—that of Haiti, which became the first Negro republic in Western history and the second independent state in the New World. Both emancipation and independence were the products of slave rebellion during the French Revolution, the most successful and the bloodiest slave revolt of modern history. After massacring or driving out all whites, the rulers imposed a tight military control over black labor, dividing all men into laborers or soldiers, making all women laborers, and using the soldiers to impose an iron discipline on workers. With no commitment to tradition and no obligation to foreign white powers, the rulers held a carte blanche for the creation of a new black society and economy. And this is what they created.[4] Emancipation and reconstruction in Haiti involved so many unique circumstances as to make comparisons with its experience of doubtful value.

Statistics on the Atlantic slave trade by Philip D. Curtin illuminate and enrich the comparative study of emancipations and reconstructions. During the whole period of the Atlantic slave trade, legal and illegal, British North America (including Louisiana) received 427,000 or only 4.5 percent of the total imports. This is compared with 4,040,000 or 42.2 percent imported in the Caribbean islands and 3,647,000 or 38.1 percent imported by

[4] James G. Leyburn, *The Haitian People* (New Haven, 1941), 20–93; C. L. R. James, *The Black Jacobins* (New York, 1963).

Brazil.[5] The disparities in imports, especially in view of later slave and Negro populations of the United States and elsewhere, are quite startling.[6] The period of importation is as important for the comparative study of emancipations as the numbers and proportions. For British and North American territory, the legal slave trade ended in 1808. The last years of the trade were the heaviest for many islands, Jamaica importing 63,000 in the last seven years. Illegal trade continued to the United States but added only about 51,000 slaves after 1808. On the other hand, Cuba imported 570,000 between 1808 and 1865. That was 143,000 more than Brtish North America had imported between 1619 and 1860, and it was 80 percent of the total Cuba had imported since the time of Columbus. From 1811 to 1860, Brazil took in 1,145,400 slaves, or nearly a third of its total importation since the sixteenth century and more than three times the number imported by the United States before the legal trade ended in 1808.[7]

Curtin's statistics add a neglected set of variables to the comparative equation and point up additional aspects of uniqueness in the American experience. The 4,000,000 manumitted American slaves of 1865, as well as the 500,000 free blacks, were descendants of 427,000 Africans. The great majority of them were descended from seventeenth- and eighteenth-century stock (mainly the latter), as are their 20,000,000 or so descendants who are our contemporaries. All but a few were at least two generations removed from their African origins at the time of emancipation, and most of them were more than two generations. They were therefore further removed than any other emancipated population of the New World, and they had been through

[5] Philip D. Curtin, *The Atlantic Slave Trade: A Census* (Madison, Wis., 1969), 88–89, Table 24.

[6] Haiti, for example, imported 864,000, 9 percent of the total, or more than twice as many slaves as the whole United States. Jamaica imported 748,000, nearly twice America's total, and held only 311,070 in 1834. The tiny island of Barbados took in 387,000 or 4 percent of the total, against 4.5 percent for the continental United States. The French colonies of Martinique and Guadaloupe received 657,000 or 6.8 percent, and Cuba imported 702,000 or 7.3 percent. *Ibid.*

[7] *Ibid.*, 40, Table 9 B; 46, Table 11; 268, Table 77.

a longer period of adjustment, accommodation, and acculturation to America and to slavery than any other slave population at the time of abolition. It is true that abolition came a generation later in Cuba and Brazil and that slavery began earlier and lasted longer in both countries. But Cuba imported more than four-fifths of its total in the nineteenth century and, according to Fernando Ortiz, continued to import them up to six years before final abolition. For all of the 3,647,000 slaves landed in Brazil over the centuries, the maximum number of 2,500,000 on the slave rolls at any time was reached in 1850 and declined steadily thereafter. Yet nearly half the latter number were purchased after 1810, and only 500,000 remained on the rolls in 1888.

Of all the numerous components of plantation America, therefore, the American South seems to have had a slave population at the time of abolition that was unique in many respects. Not only was it by far the largest population, but it was derived from the smallest imports in proportion to the number emancipated or to the total black population; it was the furthest removed from African origins; and it had the longest exposure to slave discipline in large numbers. It is difficult to imagine any other slave powers, given the origins and circumstances of their slaves, attempting a simultaneous and total emancipation of their slave populations without periods of apprenticeship or other gradualist devices. At any rate, none of them made the attempt. This is not to suggest that the United States itself was prepared for the bold experiment or that the experiment was a success, but merely that this country was the only one that tried and that, though badly prepared, it was still better prepared in at least some respects than were older countries and colonies.

One of the most distinguished minds ever addressed to the problem of the transition from slavery to freedom was that of Alexis de Tocqueville. In July, 1839, he published a report he made to the French Chamber of Deputies on the abolition of slavery in the French colonies. Tocqueville proposed "an intermediate and transitory state between slavery and liberty," which would serve as "a time of trial, during which the Negroes, already possessing many of the privileges of free men, are still compelled to labor." The transition period he thought to be "indispensable to accustom the planters to the effects of emancipation" and "not less necessary to advance the education of the black population, and to prepare them for liberty." This was, he thought, "the most favorable moment to found that empire over the minds and the habits of the black population." Since Tocqueville believed that "only experience of liberty, liberty long possessed," could prepare a man to be "a citizen of a free country," he thought of the basic issue of reconstruction as a cruel dilemma. In words with universal application for our problem, he wrote "The period which follows the abolition of slavery has therefore always been a time of uneasiness and social difficulty. This is an inevitable evil; we must resolve to meet it, or make slavery eternal." Tocqueville resolved his dilemma with a classic paradox: we must, he declared, "if necessary, compel the laborious and manly habits of liberty."[8] Compelling people to be free raised the ancient problem of reconciling force with freedom, its opposite, and that paradox lay at the heart of the problem of emancipations and reconstructions everywhere in the world.

One precedent for our comparative study is a monograph by a Dutch scholar, Wilhelmina Kloosterboer. In *Involuntary Servitude Since the Abolition of Slavery,* she extends her survey beyond plantation America, to which we are mainly limited, and takes in Africa, Asia, and Oceania. She concludes that some system of involuntary or forced labor almost invariably replaced slavery after abolition in all parts of the world. "Where slavery had been widespread," she writes, "emancipation was followed by the imposition of drastic measures to retain a labour force. Apart from other stipulations there was almost in all cases a decree against 'vagrancy' (Jamaica, Mauritius, South Africa, the United States, the Portuguese Colonies, etc.) which in effect always amounted to compulsory labour when strictly applied." The experience of remote and exotic countries will have a famil-

8 Alexis de Tocqueville, *Report Made to the Chamber of Deputies on the Abolition of Slavery in the French Colonies* (Boston, 1841), 9–10, 16, 26–27, 46–50; Seymour Druscher (ed.), *Tocqueville and Beaumont on Social Reform* (New York, 1968), 98–173.

iar ring to those who know the history of Reconstruction in the South. "The harshness of the measures taken in many countries directly after abolition is not surprising since . . . where the use of Negro slaves was widespread and almost essential for the economy, the direct result of abolition was chaos. The Negroes wanted to get away from their old work on the plantation, for to their minds it was slavery under any name; and the climate in most areas concerned was such as to make it possible for them, at least for a while, to live without having to work at all." Freedmen, under whatever flag and of whatever color, resisted signing labor contracts and sought land for themselves. Forceable measures all had the same purpose: to get the freedmen back to the fields—cotton fields, tobacco fields, sugar fields, coffee fields, all kinds of fields—and mines as well. Whether political control was in the hands of an imperial government or a federal government, it is remarkable how little restraint such authority actually exerted in protecting the lives, civil rights, and human rights of the exploited.[9]

One purpose of this study is to test the validity of this thesis and of Tocqueville's speculations and to see what light they throw on the American experience. When Tocqueville made his report to the Chamber of Deputies in 1839, he had foremost in mind, as he said, "the events which are happening in the British colonies surrounding our own." The previous year the British West Indies had prematurely ended their unhappy experiment with apprenticeship as a sequel to abolition. It had displeased all parties—planters, apprentices, and abolitionists. For all the indulgence, which was beyond the wildest dreams of South Carolina and Mississippi planters who formed the black codes of 1865,[10] the West Indian masters behaved remarkably like their continental cousins thirty years later. Like them the islanders complained when their servants retained the work ethic they had learned as slaves: lying, stealing, malingering, laziness, gross carelessness,

[9] Wilhelmina Kloosterboer, *Involuntary Servitude Since the Abolition of Slavery: A Survey of Compulsory Labour Throughout the World* (Leiden, 1960), 191–203.

[10] Theodore B. Wilson, *The Black Codes of the South* (University, Ala., 1965).

and wastefulness. Masters alone knew the Negro character, they declared, and looked back to the old regime for model and techniques of discipline. Given the deferred promise of freedom, great tact was required to get freedmen back to work, but tact was not a pair of the average overseer's training. He had been schooled, as the governor of Jamaica remarked, in "the diplomacy of the lash," not in the arts of persuasion.[11]

Colonial legislatures framed black codes that put the later southern state legislatures to shame. Jamaican lawmakers made an undefined crime of "insubordination" punishable by thirty-nine lashes or two weeks on the chain gang and defined "vagrancy" as "threatening" to run away from one's family. A police officer could break up any meeting that he had "reasonable cause" to think would stir up insubordination. On that island an apprentice who absented himself from work for two days in a fortnight was subject to a week on the chain gang or twenty lashes.[12] In legislative initiative and defiance, Jamaica was the Mississippi of the Caribbean on matters concerning Negroes, and other islands often followed its example as closely as they dared. The island legislatures displayed all the ingenuity and determination, for which their southern counterparts later became famous, in subverting the purposes of the abolitionists and recapturing their old powers. In this game of defying the Colonial Office of the home government, the colonial governors were thrust into the unhappy role played by the military governors and carpetbag administrators of the southern states. Complaints of the "sullen intractableness" of West Indian assemblies filed with the Colonial Office would have seemed quite familiar in the Washington, D.C., of the 1860s.[13]

Four years of experience with the apprenticeship system brought it into disrepute in many quarters. Dissatisfaction varied from colony to colony, but it was generally argued that relations

[11] W. L. Burn, *Emancipation and Apprenticeship in the British West Indies* (London, 1937), 176–79.

[12] *Ibid.*, 166n–67n.

[13] Paul Knaplund, *James Stephens and the British Colonial System, 1813–1847* (Madison, Wis., 1953), 107–16; W. L. Mathieson, *British Slave Emancipation, 1838–1849* (London, 1932), 60–61, 73.

between labor and planter had deteriorated and that the system had generated bitter new frictions. Negroes complained endlessly about hours of work, mistreatment, and punishment. Their friends reiterated again and again that apprenticeship was only a modified slavery. About the only modification visible in most instances was the removal of the whip, legally at least, from the hands of the overseer—though that did not put an end to flogging. The special magistrates intervened to order flogging done in the workhouses, which was often done with excesses of brutality and bloodiness that were shocking even in a time when corporal punishment was still widely used. A series of books exposing such atrocities appeared in 1837, arousing special horror over the flogging and torture of women on treadmills. British humanitarians convinced people at home that they had been cheated and swindled into paying compensation for slaves who continued under a more brutal slavery. As a training for freedom, apprenticeship had consigned the freedman to compulsory labor that provided no experience of freedom. Returning to the battle, English abolitionists and humanitarians marshaled their forces to put an end to apprenticeship and declare full freedom, which was done in 1838.[14]

Getting wind of Parliament's intentions, the assemblies of the self-governing colonies anticipated the move by abolishing the apprenticeship system themselves as of August 1, 1838, rather than acknowledged British dictation. They accompanied this act with stiff and sullen assertions of their right of self-government, "confirmed by time, usage, and law," in matters of taxation, police laws, and local affairs. Their purpose was to retain control over black labor and in effect subvert the humanitarian revolution of civil rights the home government sought to impose. The English Radicals rebelled, but the newly crowned queen intervened, and the government bowed to the defiant colonial assemblies. The Radicals and humanitarians got their abolition law

[14] Burn, *Emancipation and Apprenticeship*, 340–57, 364–71; Philip D. Curtin, *The Two Jamaicas: The Role of Ideas in a Tropical Colony, 1830–1865* (Cambridge, Mass., 1955), 94–95; W. L. Mathieson, *British Slavery and its Abolition, 1823–1838* (London, 1926), 271; Mathieson, *British Slave Emancipation*, 40.

and civil rights laws, but the local control remained in the hands of the small ruling class of masters, who had ruled under slavery.

William R. Brock, an English historian, has suggested in a book on Reconstruction that one root of America's trouble in enforcing the law in the South lay in the national commitment to an outmoded eighteenth-century Constitution with archaic checks and balances, states' rights, and other inhibitions on majority rule and national authority. These restraints, he points out, shielded the southern states from Radical reform and encouraged them to resist northern terms. In his opinion, "a drastic solution imposed by a simple majority unhampered by checks and balances"—in other words, a proper English parliamentary procedure—would have prevented failure.[15] Perhaps. But Britain's own experience with enforcing Radical parliamentary rule in the West Indies does not strengthen this argument. Parliament, like Congress, was faced with a states' rights and home rule crisis, and the Radicals of Parliament gave in quicker than the Radicals of Congress. In effect, Jamaica got home rule before being subjected to radical reconstruction, instead of afterward as was the case of most southern states. The Jamaicans and Barbadians won their struggle in the short run more completely than the Alabamians and Louisianians won theirs, but did not retain the fruits of victory so long.

Monopoly of political power enabled masters to extend their control over labor by legislation. Coercive purposes were concealed in "innocent looking" enactments, such as a police act prohibiting persons from transporting produce without written permission from the owner of the land, which could easily be used to prevent illiterate settlers from marketing their crops. Other laws were more forthright in purpose. Stringent vagrancy acts permitted "anyone," that is, any white person or his agent, in the absence of police to arrest a vagrant; another law made workmen liable to three months' imprisonment with hard labor "for any misconduct whatever." The special magistrates used under apprenticeship were retained, and a new law declared

[15] W. R. Brock, *An American Crisis: Congress and Reconstruction, 1865–1867* (London, 1963), 272–73.

that their "authority over the manual laborers of Jamaica will be peremptory and unlimited in the highest degree."[16]

The failure of these efforts at full labor control in some islands, such as Jamaica and especially Trinidad and Guiana, was associated with two interrelated conditions: the decline in production and prosperity of the sugar plantations and an abundance of uncultivated land. The first demand of emancipated slaves was always for land. It was so among those of the southern states in 1865, but there the solution more nearly approximated that of Antigua, Barbados, and the Lesser Antilles. In islands with no extra land, the freedmen had little choice to return to work for the white man. There was extra land in the South, but that which was most available was quickly snatched from their grasp by the frustration of the Freedmen's Bureau plans for distributing abandoned lands, and the less available land was beyond their reach for lack of capital.[17] In Jamaica little more than a third of the arable land was under cultivation at the time of emancipation, and the number of uncultivated acres was annually increased by bankruptcies and the abandonment of plantations. Freedmen could not be kept off these lands, either by law or private agreement. Over the years a substantial independent black peasantry of small landholders developed. The same thing occurred in Trinidad and British Guiana, where even more land was available. All these movements diminished planter control over the blacks.[18]

In colonies where this occurred, planters regularly resorted to large-scale importations of contract coolie labor from the Orient. The history of coolie labor comes near to matching the history of slavery in human exploitation, misery, and degradation. Often transported farther from their native land than the Africans had been and in much the same manner, the Orientals

---

[16] Curtin, *Two Jamaicas*, 95–98; Burn, *Emancipation and Apprenticeship*, 360–61.

[17] William S. McFeely, *Yankee Stepfather: General O. O. Howard and the Freedmen* (New Haven, 1968).

[18] W. L. Mathieson, *The Sugar Colonies and Governor Eyre, 1849–1866* (London, 1936), 3, 72; Curtin, *Two Jamaicas*, 106–109.

were dumped in environments often more hostile to them than to Africans and without such minimal protection as was afforded by an owner with an investment to safeguard or missionaries with consciences to serve. They were sometimes advertised, sold, and treated like cattle. Slavery had given way to forced labor under a new guise, with different races under the yoke. Before the British stopped the immigration of contract labor in 1917, Guiana imported 239,000 East Indians and 14,000 Chinese, and Trinidad took in 135,000 East Indians. Other colonies made smaller imports. The French imported about 65,000 East Indians for their Caribbean colonies, and the Dutch took in at their colony of Surinam 34,848 East Indians and 30,905 Javanese over a long period.[19]

Nothing in the southern experience compares with the coolie labor solution. It is not that southern planters were indifferent to Caribbean experiments with coolies. They were extremely interested. They were as sure as their West Indian counterparts that freedmen would not work the plantation without compulsion, and they sought substitutes. They organized companies, held conventions, even sent an agent to China to promote coolie imports, but the federal government frowned on the idea, the planters lacked capital, and only a handful of coolies actually turned up in Dixie.[20] This made a great deal of difference in the distinctive adjustment the South made to free labor. The Dutch, for example, imported twice as many East Indians and Javanese as they emancipated Africans in Surinam, and between them Trinidad and Guiana imported as many coolies as the United States imported African slaves in its whole history. The Mauritian planters, as one historian puts it, solved "the industrial problem of emancipation . . . by the elimination of the negroes" and

---

[19] Mathieson, *The Sugar Colonies*, 4–5, 51–52, 77; Donald Wood, *Trinidad in Transition: The Years After Slavery* (London and New York, 1968), 130–31, 136–37, 158; Leo A. Despres, *Cultural Pluralism and Nationalist Politics in British Guiana* (Chicago, 1967), 56.

[20] Vernon L. Wharton, *The Negro in Mississippi, 1865–1890* (Chapel Hill, 1947), 97–103; Robert S. Henry, *The Story of Reconstruction* (New York, 1938), 364.

were thus able "to escape from the task of converting slaves into free laborers."[21] This escape from the basic problem of emancipation and readjustment was only partially available to planters in the Caribbean and not at all to planters in the American South.

Cuban planters anticipated the abolition of slavery by four decades in their use of coolie labor both as a supplement to and a substitute for slave labor. Beginning in 1847 great numbers of Chinese coolies were imported, sold, bought, transferred, and worked in the manner of slaves, though nominally they were "voluntarily obligated" by eight-year contracts. Official regulations of 1849 authorized the use of whips, irons, and imprisonment for coolies who resisted labor or disobeyed orders. They died in great numbers and suicides were frequent, yet over the next quarter of a century more than 124,000 coolies reached Cuba. These were also years of the heaviest imports of African slaves.[22]

The new masters of post-abolition Brazil, with a coffee boom and an industrial expansion on their hands, had taken drastic measures to anticipate the shortage of labor. Using state subsidies, they recruited nearly a million European immigrants, most of them on a contract-labor basis, in the 1880s and 1890s. Coffee planters and industrialists drove their immigrant labor, the majority of them Italian peasants, as ruthlessly as they had driven slaves until a renewed labor shortage forced them to relent.[23]

Much has been made of benevolent Iberian slavery and race relations during slavery as a superior preparation for freedom. Whatever restraint Spain had exerted over Cuban labor policy to protect the blacks came to an end twelve years after abolition, when Cuba won its independence. In effect Cuba won home rule, not so quickly as Jamaica but at precisely the interval after abolition as South Carolina and Louisiana. Home rule in Cuba meant much the same as home rule in Jamaica and Mississippi: the rule of the whites and the exclusion of the blacks. At least the two dominant political parties of independent Cuba pro-

---

[21] Mathieson, *British Slave Emancipation*, 238.
[22] Corwin, *Spain and the Abolition of Slavery*, 109–10, 135–36.
[23] Stein, *Vassouras*.

claimed that to be their purpose. Both came out squarely for white supremacy and agreed that Negroes "constitute a depraved and inferior race which must be kept in its proper place in a white man's society."[24]

Brazilians are especially noted for their claims of racial felicity and patriarchal benevolence. One Brazilian historian maintains that "there was nothing [in Brazil] which can be compared with the period of Reconstruction in the United States." Certainly there were differences, but anyone acquainted with Reconstruction in the South will find in post-abolition Brazil much that is comparable. The familiar "mass exodus from the plantations" occurred on schedule. There were the standard days of jubilation and the usual pictures of former slaves "wandering in groups along the roads with no destination," changing plantations, seeking lost relatives and of the old and decrepit, to whom freedom "brought hunger and death" and abandonment by their masters. In the early days the freedmen appeared "disoriented, not knowing what to do with their freedom," many of them "dazed by the rapidity of the transformation." Where possible, planters clung to the old plantation routine. A rumor spread among freedmen that a small plot of land was to be granted each former slave, but nothing came of it. Like southern planters, Brazilians complained that freedmen confused freedom with laziness. Like them too, Brazilian planters avoided creating a black peasantry by refusing to sell them land. Like southerners, they tried the wage system, gave it up, and turned their labor force into sharecroppers under the lien system while planters became supply merchant—the Brazilian-southern escape by compromise from the classic problem of "converting slaves into free laborers."[25] Few know what went on in the backcountry, the depressed sugar country of the northeast, Brazil's counterpart of the American South. A modern writer asks whether slaves there were "really emancipated or

[24] Philip Foner, *A History of Cuba and Its Relations with the United States* (New York, 1963), II, 293.

[25] Stein, *Vassouras*, 250–72; Florestan Fernandes, *The Negro in Brazilian Society*, trans. Jacqueline D. Skiles and Burnel and Arthur Rothwell; ed. Phillis B. Evelett (New York, 1969), 1–4, 7, 14–16, 18–19, 23, 35, 42, 48, 50, 54–56, 135–37, 183.

merely freed from the name of slave? The fact is that whether he was slave or serf, farmhand, sharecropper or leaseholder, the Brazilian peasant, at least in the Northeast, has always been accustomed to forced labor, hunger, and misery."[26] The long legacy of slavery was much the same here as elsewhere.

There is no space here for comparative analysis of the political adjustment to freedom, but it would be more a study of contrast than comparison. For nowhere in plantation America during the nineteenth century, with the partial exception of the French possessions, did the white man share with black freedmen the range of political power and office that the southern whites were forced to share briefly with their freedmen. Not even in the British West Indies, with their overwhelming preponderance of blacks, was there anything that could be described as "Black Reconstruction." In effect the blacks, though nominally emancipated, were quickly eliminated from politics. It is true that a class of "browns" or "coloreds" did gain a share of office and political power, but that is another story.[27]

This introduces the infinitely complicated subject of comparative race relations. To do it justice would require a whole book, but some notice of it is essential and I shall have to oversimplify. In general, I believe race prejudice and discrimination were universal in plantation America. I find very helpful a distinction that a Brazilian scholar, Oracy Nogueira, has drawn between two models of prejudice, "prejudice of mark" and "prejudice of origin." The latter type, prejudice of origin, in its pure form is peculiar to the United States. It is directed at anyone, regardless of physical appearance or personal attribute, known to be in any degree of African origin. This peculiar white myth of what constitutes a "black" is so universal in the United States as to be accepted by so-called black nationalists. Elsewhere, particularly in Latin America, prejudice varies according to "mark,"

[26] Josué de Castros, *Death in the Northeast* (New York, 1966), 9.
[27] H. A. Wyndham, *The Atlantic and Emancipation* (London, 1937), 120–21, 124, 130; W. G. Sewell, *The Ordeal of Free Labor in the West Indies* (New York, 1861), 37–38, 258; W. P. Livingstone, *Black Jamaica* (London, 1899), 58–61.

physical or otherwise, and discriminates fastidiously among all the infinite varieties, as well as personal attributes and attainments, that amalgamations between Africans and other races can produce. In that sense, prejudice of mark is literally more discriminating than prejudice of origin, though the pure black appears to suffer as much exclusion from the one as from the other type.[28]

The British West Indies fall somewhere between the two models in their recognition of a separate caste of "coloreds" or "browns" between whites and blacks, sharing some of the privileges of the former and some of the penalties of the latter. During the thirty years after abolition, whites and blacks drifted farther and farther apart into separate cultures, economies, and religions. The coloreds were no help in mediating between races, for their relations with blacks were worse than those between whites and blacks. The browns renounced their black heritage and identified with the whites. The early 1860s were a time of social tension, economic depression, and natural disasters in Jamaica. The contrast between their former glory and wealth and their current poverty and misery sent whites in search of scapegoats. In this search white Jamaicans anticipated the whole demonology of Reconstruction among southern whites, with their own varieties of carpetbagger, scalawag, missionary, Radical, Freedmen's Bureau, and most of all the Negro—the lazy good-for-nothing Quashee of the classic stereotype, to which Thomas Carlyle lent his famous name. The old paternalistic ambivalence of slavery days toward blacks, half genial, half contemptuous, gave way to feelings of insecurity, fear, and withdrawal. One source of this was a steady decline in the number of whites, both absolutely and relatively. By 1861 whites had dropped to 14,000 out of 441,000, only 3.1 percent, and the blacks were rapidly increasing. "In Jamaica," writes Philip Curtin, "the race question was often hidden behind other issues, while in the American South other issues tended to hide behind racial con-

[28] Oracy Nogueira, "Skin Color and Social Class," in *Plantation Systems of the New World* (Washington, D.C., 1959), 169.

flict." The blacks of Jamaica seemed stronger and more suspicious in the mid-sixties. A weird religious revival seized them, mixed with economic discontent and protest.[29]

There had been other local riots, bloodshed, and lootings since abolition, but the Morant Bay riot of October, 1865, came in a time of great distress and social tension. It sprang from no revolutionary ideology and was over in two days of sporadic violence that took the lives of 22 and left 34 wounded, some shops looted, and 5 buildings burned—nearly all confined to one parish. But a hysterical governor declared it island-wide, conspiratorial, and insurrectionary and released uninstructed soldiers and colored maroons upon the people. In all they killed 439, many with excessive brutality; flogged 600 men and women with fifty to a hundred lashes, often with cruelly wired whips; and burned 1,000 huts, cottages, and buildings, most of them belonging to the poorest blacks. And then in the ensuing panic the whites voted to abandon what they had held for thirty years essential to their very existence—home rule and self-government—and the Colonial Office, swayed by stories of Negro fiendishness, approved the end of representative government and took over from the frightened planters.[30]

Southerners were destined to repeat many of the errors of Jamaica, but not in their wildest excesses, not even those of New Orleans and Memphis in 1866, did they come near approximating the bloodbath of Morant Bay. The garbled and exaggerated account of the Jamaican tragedy that southern whites read in their newspapers opened an appalling vision of the future. In October, 1865, the whites of the crushed and defeated Confederacy faced with anxiety most of the uncertainties and terrors of their own ordeal of free labor and Negro equality. Would freed-

[29] Curtin, *Two Jamaicas*, 106–109, 116, 146–48, 168–77; Douglas Hall, *Free Jamaica, 1838–1865: An Economic History* (New Haven, 1959), 157–63; Lord Oliver, *The Myth of Governor Eyre* (London, 1935), 53–187; Graham Knox, "British Colonial Policy and the Problem of Establishing Free Society in Jamaica, 1838–1865," *Caribbean Studies*, II (January, 1863), 3–13.

[30] Hall, *Free Jamaica*, 245–64; Livingstone, *Black Jamaica*, 58–81; Bernard Semmel, *The Governor Eyre Controversy* (London, 1962).

men work without compulsion? Were they prepared for freedom and self-government? Was race war inevitable? For thirty years they had debated with American abolitionists the success of emancipation in the West Indies. The abolitionists felt they had the better of the old argument. But the news from Jamaica in the fall of 1865 seemed to southerners the final word in the old debate, the confirmation of their views: freedom was a failure in the West Indies.[31]

And so it was, in a manner of speaking. And so would the southerners' own more gigantic experiment with freedom fail. And they might have gone further and pointed out its failure throughout plantation America. But failure, like most human experience, is relative. It depends on expectations and promises, on commitments and capabilities. One man's failure is another man's success. And in a way the American failure was the greatest of all. For in 1865 the democratic colossus of the New World stood triumphant, flushed with the terrible victories at Gettysburg, Vicksburg, and Appomattox. Its crusade for freedom had vindicated the blood shed by its sons, and in the full flush of power and victory and righteousness its leaders solemnly pledged the nation to fulfill its promises, not only of freedom but also the full measure of democracy and racial equality. The powers of fulfillment, sealed by the sacrifices of a victorious war, were seemingly unlimited, though of course they were not. At least the federal government was no remote transatlantic metropolitan parliament on the banks of the Thames or the Seine. It sat on the Potomac, with General Robert E. Lee's Arlington mansion in full view of the White House windows across the river, and its armies garrisoned the defeated states.

Yet we know that, although the North won its four-year war against a fully armed, mobilized, and determined South when the issue was slavery, it very quickly lost its crusade against a disarmed, defeated, and impoverished South when the issue was

[31] James M. McPherson, "Was West Indian Emancipation a Success? The Abolitionist Argument During the American Civil War," *Caribbean Studies,* IV (July, 1964), 28–34.

equality. For on this issue the South was united as it had not been on slavery. And the North was even more divided on the issue of equality than it had been on slavery. In fact, when the chips were down, the preponderant views of the North on that issue were in no important respect different from those of the South—and never had been.

9

The Lash
and the Knout

When the preceding paper comparing emancipations in the New World came under attack at the Congress of Historians at Moscow, a Polish delegate came to my defense from the floor. He not only praised my experiment in New World comparisons but urged that a comparative study of Russian serfdom and American slavery be undertaken. I applauded the proposal, but it was seventeen years before the idea came to fruition in Peter Kolchin's book, Unfree Labor: American Slavery and Russian Serfdom. *The following is a review essay on that work.*

Writing about the family of Mary Chesnut, the South Carolina writer, Edmund Wilson remarked that "comparisons with Russia seem inevitable when one is writing about the old South."[1] Russian serfdom and American slavery present a challenge to historical comparison that would seem all but irresistible. Yet the challenge has been around a long time without attracting

[1] Edmund Wilson, *Patriotic Gore: Studies in the Literature of the American Civil War* (New York, 1962), p. 288.

a taker. Alexis de Tocqueville should have been the one to start
the ball rolling a century and a half ago. He was one of the first
to recognize the significant comparability of the two nations, the
one marching east, the other west, each fated, he wrote in 1835,
"to sway the destinies of half the globe." Tocqueville was also
keenly interested in slavery, yet he never compared the systems
of servitude in the two countries in *Democracy in America* except to say, somewhat inaccurately, that in the American and
Russian conquests of expansion, "the principal instrument of the
former is freedom; of the latter servitude."[2] Of course Tocqueville
could not have foreseen the almost simultaneous abolition of
Russian serfdom and American slavery in the 1860s, events that
drew attention to their parallel histories. But even that riveting
coincidence failed, for all the attention it got, to evoke the comparative study by historians that might have been reasonably
expected.

Modern historians have to some extent broken out of the
national boundaries traditionally set for the study of American
slavery and produced a number of works comparing it with
bondage elsewhere. But the partners chosen to be compared have
so far been confined largely to New World slave societies or
South Africa. Among causes inhibiting comparisons of American
slavery with Russian serfdom, the forbidding differences between
the two countries probably figured most prominently. Not only
were there the formidable differences between an imperial monarchy and a federal democracy, but marked differences in religion, race, and demography, and those between masters as well
as between bondsmen of the two societies that seemed to stand
in the way.

Marc Bloch, the French historian and pioneer of the comparative method, once remarked, "It is often supposed that the
method has no other purpose than hunting out resemblances."
But, he pointed out, "correctly understood, the primary interest

---

[2] Alexis de Tocqueville, *Democracy in America*, Vol. 1, Phillips Bradley,
ed. (New York, 1972), p. 434 for Russo-American comparison; pp. 333–379
on slavery.

of the comparative method is, on the contrary, the observation of differences."[3] Bloch would agree that well-paired subjects for comparison require similarities as well as differences. Given the rich endowment of differences in the Russo-American pair, the number of resemblances that turn up is all the more remarkable. But it was the differences that had the more inhibiting influence on historians.

In addition to the intricate problems of pairing, American historians face special impediments to comparative studies. One is the myth of American exceptionalism, a myth with more substance for support in the North than in the South, which shares so many historical misfortunes with the rest of the world as to invite comparisons promiscuously. Other common blocks to comparative history are the result of professional specialization within national borders, which often leads to spotty command of the other nation's history, and incidentally to unreliable command of needed languages.

All these difficulties are handsomely overcome in *Unfree Labor: American Slavery and Russian Serfdom* by Professor Peter Kolchin of the University of Delaware. His first book was an account of the response of slaves to emancipation and reconstruction in Alabama, a work that demonstrated his mastery of the sources and of the scholarly literature on the American side.[4] On the Russian side, it is evident that Kolchin is at home with the language and has made wide use of both source material and scholarship, in Russian and other languages. Full evaluation of his scholarship on the Russian side must be left to critics better qualified than the reviewer. It will be clear to any discerning reader, however, that *Unfree Labor* is a learned and sophisticated book in the tradition of high scholarship, as well as a book written to be read and enjoyed. Those who share a taste for comparative history will be taken with the author's spirit of play, his readiness to ask "what if," and his zest for experiment and dis-

[3] Marc Bloch, "Toward a Comparative History of European Societies" (1928) in Frederic C. Lane and J. C. Riemersma, eds., *Enterprise and Secular Change: Readings in Economic History* (Chicago, 1953), pp. 494–521.
[4] Peter Kolchin, *First Freedom: The Response of Alabama's Blacks to Emancipation and Reconstruction* (Westport, Conn., 1972).

covery. (Discovery by comparative study? Yes. For example, the tripling of the American slave population after importation had ceased held no particular significance until it was discovered that the slave population of no other New World slave society grew at all after the slave trade ended, and that of many declined.)

Undaunted by differences, Kolchin holds that it is just because of their "strikingly different historical environments" and because Russian serfdom and American slavery were "in many ways fundamentally unlike," that comparison of the two "proves especially revealing." Not only does he expand the geographical scope of comparative studies but the temporal span as well, reaching back to the seventeenth century and demonstrating that serfdom and slavery evolved and changed significantly over time. Another departure from much previous comparative history is his avoidance of writing parallel histories that leave comparisons to the conclusion, or even to the reader, and his practice of interweaving history with comparison and making each chapter comparative. After an introduction setting forth the origins and development of bondage in the two countries down to the mid-eighteenth century, the book consists of two parts, the first treating the world of the master, the second that of the bondsman. There follows a brief epilogue drawing together the main themes and comparing the crises faced by the two societies in the mid-nineteenth century that led to emancipation.

The two systems of bondage emerged on Europe's eastern and western borders at about the same time, both in order to provide by compulsion agricultural labor that could not be obtained by other means. In Russia enserfment of the peasants developed gradually until, by the beginning of the seventeenth century, they rather suddenly lost their right to move, began their decline to a status resembling chattel slavery, and merged eventually with a slave minority that had existed prior to serfdom. The serfs were subject to the authority, and bound to the land, of their landlords, who became for all practical purposes their owners. Also plagued by the shortage of labor, one that white indentured servants could no longer meet, English settlers in the American colonies increasingly resorted to enslaved Africans, and Britain became the foremost slave-trading country in the world in the late seventeenth century. By the middle of the eighteenth century black slaves, like white serfs, "appeared part of the natural order, as God-given as government or agriculture itself," and among Americans as among Russians "the notion that it was wrong for some to live off the labor of others—even under physical compulsion—was virtually nonexistent."

Kolchin agrees with the current consensus of historians that for more than a hundred years before emancipation, the status of serfs was virtually indistinguishable from that of slaves, and that Russian serfdom was a kind of slavery. He emphasizes, however, that serfdom took a form that differed in two ways from the form slavery took in the American South. One was that American slaves were taken from Africa against their will and sold to people of different nationality, language, race, and culture, and remained in many ways aliens in a white America. In Russia serfs and masters were nearly always of the same nationality, language, and religion. Serfs were the lowest class of their own society, but the peasants, about one half of whom were serfs, were the essence of Russia and not outsiders as blacks in America were. The Russian example confutes the notion that no people would enslave their own compatriots. Nevertheless, noblemen and peasants came to seem as different from each other as blacks and whites, Africans and Europeans, in America.

The second important difference between slavery and serfdom followed from the first: the role of tradition in limiting the control of master over bondsman was greater in Russia than in America. Slaves worked for their masters all the time and received maintenance, while most serfs worked part-time for owners and got little if any support from them. They maintained themselves off their land allotments. Tradition and custom had less weight in America, where both slaves and masters were relative newcomers, and bondsmen could not claim as much independence.

While bondsmen made up roughly similar proportions of the total population—about one-third in the South and one-half in Russia—the proportion of owners to bondsmen differed widely. Noblemen serf owners were only a tiny percent of the population, while in the South about a quarter of all whites were members of slave-owning families. Russian noblemen lived in an overwhelmingly serf or peasant world, and serfs were held in far larger units than American slaves. In 1860 only one American slave owner held more than a thousand slaves as compared with 3,358 such Russian serf owners. Most serfs belonged to noblemen owning more than two hundred, and nearly half to those owning more than one thousand. In striking contrast, almost half of American slaves were held by owners with fewer than twenty, and three-quarters by those with fewer than fifty. In the South only 2.4 percent of the slaves had owners with more than two hundred bondsmen; in Russia 80.8 percent of the serfs had such owners. Holdings of some noble families exceeded 10,000 souls, and were distributed among many estates across numerous provinces. In both countries there were great regional variations in size of holdings and proportion of bondsmen and owners in the population.[5]

Important differences in human relations and labor management followed from these statistics. Most serfs rarely saw their owners, who remained remote, faceless figures to be dreaded or appealed to mainly in crises. On the other hand, slaves typically dealt with their owners regularly, and slave owners, for better or worse, knew them personally and took a lively interest in them. Absenteeism was the rule among Russian owners, the exception among Southern planters, most of whom lived on the plantation. Serf owners relied on intermediaries, the wealthiest on administrative bureaucracies, to run their estates and exact from the serfs the labor or payment in kind and money due them. A few rich slave owners had managers, but most large plantations got along with an overseer who worked through slave drivers.

Noblemen as well as planters, in seeking to prevent unex-

---

[5] Russian figures are usually males only, hence I have doubled them.

cused absences and discourage fugitives, required passes to leave the estate, used patrols or guards, and punished offenders. Other management problems common to masters of slaves and serfs were those of morals and marriage, particularly marriage off the estate. Comparison indicates far greater emphasis in America than in Russia on the protection and care of the slaves. Partly this reflects the difference between a system in which the master fed, housed, and clothed his slaves and one in which the serfs fended for themselves. The absentee mentality of the noblemen and the residential paternalism of the planters also played a part, as did the white conviction that blacks were, like children, unable to care for themselves. That conviction fit in perfectly with the planters' policy of maximizing dependency and fostering the dependent nature of slaves. The effect of these differences was to produce

> a Russian master class that looked to their estates primarily for the income they generated, and a southern master class that, although not negligent of the financial benefits their holdings produced, regarded slaveholding as a way of life with nonpecuniary rewards of its own.

The contrast in the way masters lived had significant implications for the treatment serfs and slaves received. Both subject classes were accustomed to long hours and backbreaking work as their normal lot, but both resented the injustice of exploitation, compulsion, and denial of freedom. It was the compulsions that accompanied their work, including punishment and interference with their family life, that caused the bitterest resentment. In both countries masters held the power to compel or deny marriage and forbid the taking of partners from outside. Admitting that evidence of sexual relations between the classes is scarce, Kolchin nevertheless holds that "there can be no doubt that such relations occurred far more frequently in the United States South than in Russia." That view is certainly encouraged by circumstances: the master in residence and the small size of holdings in the South increased the chances of contact, whereas absenteeism and large holdings in Russia diminished those chances.

Forced separation of families by masters presents another contrast between the two systems. Though such separations occurred in Russia, they were less common than in the South. For one thing slave marriages had no standing in law, whereas serf marriages had full legal recognition and were sanctified by the Church; family bonds were taken much more seriously in Russia. Although the law was often violated, imperial decrees forbade selling family members apart and selling unmarried children. Separation of families was more frequent in the South than in Russia, not so much because of different moral standards as because of different historical experiences. Slavery started with forced family separation in Africa, and slaves for a long time continued to be devoid of any rights society was bound to respect. They lacked many rights in law and tradition that serfs never lost in their own country.

Physical punishment was a regular cause of bitterness in both societies, and in both was more casual and frequent in the seventeenth and eighteenth centuries than in the nineteenth century, though bad enough then. In the South a few masters spared the lash, and a few inflicted sadistic tortures (both extremes drawing community criticism), but most stayed well between these extremes. Spotty evidence suggests that while most slaves were not punished often, most masters did often resort to the whip. The primary purpose of punishment among slave owners was to influence future behavior, and with serf owners brutal retribution was intended to serve as an object lesson. Slaves were punished more often but less severely than serfs, who stood in dread of the cruel knout.

The spread of humanitarianism, together with the end of imports and the rise in the price of slaves, encouraged more humane treatment of human property by planters during the nineteenth century. Slaves became their "people" rather than simply an investment, and gestures of concern for slave welfare a means of strengthening the institution against abolitionist attacks. Standards of housing, diet, medical attention, and life expectancy exceeded those in the Caribbean as well as those in Russia. The intense relationship between master and slave under residential paternalism, while not necessarily a "better" bondage, produced not only fear, hatred, and unwelcome interference in their personal lives, but sometimes respect and affection as well. In Russia the government took steps toward amelioration of serfdom, and some serfs were freed before abolition, but in the main they perceived no improvement in their treatment or living standards, and few masters cultivated a paternalistic ethic. In addition to a harsher climate, poorer soil, and an appalling death rate (more than one-third higher than that of southern slaves), Russian serfs also faced a more callous disregard for their humanity on the part of absentee masters. As Nicholas Turgenev, a relative of the novelist, put it bluntly, *"En Russie noblesse n'oblige pas."*

In spite of numerous differences, the master classes of Russia and the South shared many similar views. Both expressed aristocratic pretentions and ideals, including honor, duty, courage, and courtesy, and in both aristocracies many failed to live up to their ideals. Along with all this went the habit of command, pride of rank and lineage, and a style of living that ran to luxury and display. In both aristocracies were many newcomers of humble origins, comparative beginners at the grand style, most of them unable to rise to it. With their greater wealth, Russian noblemen could outdo southern aristocrats in display and luxury, especially in numbers of domestic servants. Few southern planters had the means, and the style of those who did was often cramped by the rise of democracy in America. In spite of all that, the planter aristocracy was clearly the stronger of the two. Real power in Russia rested in the czar and his bureaucracy, for the nobility lacked the political roots and local power that normally go with landed wealth. "In a curious way," writes Kolchin, "Russian noblemen were less aristocratic than American planters, and their sway over society was considerably less extensive as well." The Southerners were able to build a much more secure and defensible existence than their Russian counterparts.

Awareness of concerns and ideas common to both aristocracies occasionally comes to light among contemporaries, as in the observation by T. R. R. Cobb of Georgia in 1858 that Russian serfs "are contented with their lot and seek no change. They are indolent, . . . mendacious, beyond the negro perhaps, and feel no shame at detection." Defenders of serfdom and slavery used strikingly similar arguments, including racial theories. The latter were less elaborately buttressed with biological and scientific arguments by the Russians (though some noblemen claimed that whereas their bones were white those of peasants were black) and most serf owners held that peasants were as innately inferior, lazy, and childlike as slave owners claimed blacks to be. Realizing that most slave systems were not based on racial distinctions, Southerners like George Fitzhugh and others downplayed racial justification in favor of claims for the superiority of the slave system regardless of race. Muscovites as well as Confederates used religious, economic, and sociological defenses of bondage and made invidious comparisons between the security and harmony of their labor system and the horrors of wage slavery. The pro-serfdom argument, however, was never elaborated with anything like the force, sophistication, boldness, and volume of the proslavery argument. "The major difference was not so much in the arguments used as in their tone, depth, and subtlety," in all of which Southerners surpassed Russians.

On the way from the view that slavery was a regrettable evil to the doctrine that is was a "positive good," the planters gained momentum and solidarity while during the same period the noblemen were losing conviction and public support. Whereas the Russian intelligentsia, many government officials, and even some serf owners themselves were abandoning or attacking the cuase of serfdom, popular opinion in the South rallied strongly to the defense of slavery. One reason for the difference was that the attack on slavery and planter morality, unlike the attack on serfdom, came from outside, and the abolitionist assault on slavery seemed to be an attack on the South itself. Moreover, in Russia emancipation threatened only the livelihood of the masters, while in America it threatened their lives and their way of life as well as the life of an entire society. Defenders of that society were autonomous and dominant, politically as well as culturally, while the noblemen were politically dependent and weak. And even if they had had a strong case to make there was no free press to propagate it and no "public" to respond in Russia.

To return to the controversial importance of race in this equation, it is clear that serfdom was unusual in lacking an ethnic or racial base for social distance between master and bondsman to legitimize servitude. In America, on the other hand, the confusion of race with class made race an essential element of slavery. Although Russians employed the same stereotypes about white serfs that Americans used about blacks, and although it is evident that "race" is largely a subjective concept, more a creature of culture than of nature, nevertheless race became so identified with slavery in the South and in the minds of whites that it gave slavery much of its distinctive character in the South. It facilitated the paternalistic role of planters, accentuated the perception of slaves as outsiders without claim to rights as members of the body politic, and, in conjunction with democracy, strengthened support of slavery from nonslaveholders. It also supported the conviction that all blacks, free as well as slave, were outsiders in their own country.

Slaves as well as serfs were able to gain a measure of autonomy in communities making up slave quarters and peasant villages, but the degree and nature of independence differed in the two countries. Serfs spent their lives in their peasant commune, or "mir." A world apart from the rest of Russia, consisting almost entirely of peasants, the mir and its deliberative body had broad authority over village affairs and provided a communal mentality. Unlike serfs, slaves were not "at home" in a traditional world with customs of centuries slow to change, but were of foreign origin, different race, and different culture. African gods and languages died more quickly in the United States than in the Caribbean and Brazil, and the slave's experience was as subject to change as that of other Americans. With less isolation from masters than the mir, the slave quarters still afforded the slaves a measure of independence "from sundown to sunup," a limited breathing space in which to live their own lives, a refuge from constant interference by whites.

Another refuge for bondsmen of both societies was the family, though interference by owners in family life was more pervasave in the South than in Russia. In this as in many other differences, absentee and residential mentalities, along with persistence and absence of sheltering tradition and custom, figured prominently. Unless broken by sale, slave families of the South were large, nuclear, prolific, long lasting, and typically had two parents of durable union present. A predominantly Creole slave population with even sex ratios and a high reproductive rate explains the stability, the anguish at forced separation, and the importance of black families to slave life. They were female-centered families with women having positions quite different from those of white women. Not subject to the control that property ownership gave men in the white world, and doing the same work as their men, women had unusual authority in the slave family during an era that took male dominance for granted. By contrast, the male heads of serf families ruled their brood with an iron hand, tyrannized their wives, and meted out physical punishment to wives, sons, and daughters who displeased them. Enmeshed in many generations of tradition and much freer from interference, serf families differed in structure and character from their slave counterparts.

For lack of other institutional outlets, religion had a central place in the slave community, usually becoming the very heart of it. Quite different from values preached to them by whites, those of black preachers were charged with intensity and demonstrative emotionalism. The black preachers were seen as leaders before and after emancipation. For Russian peasants religion was only one of a multitude of cultural forms, beliefs, values, and traditions that custom preserved from early times, and were lost to slaves. With the peasants, religion was more ritualistic than enthusiastic, and priests were often held in suspicion or antagonism rather than hailed as leaders. Sorcery, magic, spirits, and witches pervaded the beliefs of both classes, those of the Russian peasants even more than the American slaves. Peasant folk tales performed many of the same functions as slave tales, and some were virtually identical with the American variety.

Examining the resistance to their bondage by the bondsmen is one of the best means of clarifying their views of themselves and their world. Both serfs and slaves engaged in a wide variety of rebellious activity, much of it short of outright rebellion. Of the latter, silent sabotage, such as malingering and stealing, was often so ambiguous as to make it hard to tell when it actually constituted resistance. Not so with the opposite extreme of organized armed rebellion, the most dramatic form of resistance and one peculiarly characteristic of Russia. At roughly fifty-year intervals in the seventeenth and eighteenth centuries four great wars, called "peasant wars" by Soviet historians, swept across Russia. Part uprisings and part civil war, they were not composed entirely of peasants or serfs. Each leader professed to be fighting in support of monarchy, but nevertheless had revolutionary goals. The last of these, the bloodiest uprising in Russian history, in 1773 and 1774, enlisted millions of peasants in an attempt to overthrow the nobility.

Nothing remotely like this occurred in the American South. The Seminole Indian wars in the first half of the nineteenth century were the closest approximations, and slaves joined the Indians only in hundreds, not in millions. Herbert Aptheker is quite misleading in reporting 250 "revolts and conspiracies in the history of American Negro slavery" involving at least ten slaves.[7] As Kolchin says, "Most of these were minor incidents of unrest that were quickly put down . . . before they even occurred." Of the handful that reached more than tiny proportions, two occurred in colonial New York and were readily suppressed. The bloodiest in the South was that of Nat Turner in 1831, consisting of seventy slaves and lasting less than two days. Factors conducive to rebellion, such as absentee owners, large units of bondsmen, and their predominance in the population, were much more prevalent in Russia than in the South. The wonder is that slaves attempted

[7] Herbert Aptheker, *American Negro Slave Revolts* (International Publishers, 1963), p. 162. Eugene D. Genovese, on the contrary, emphasizes "the weakness and limited extent of the revolts" (*Roll, Jordan, Roll: The World the Slaves Made,* Pantheon Books, 1974, p. 588). An exchange on this point between Aptheker and Woodward is in *The New York Review of Books,* Letters to the Editor, March 3, 1988.

revolts at all, and even in Russia none of the great uprisings occurred after 1774.

More common and more significant were smaller acts of defiance. Russians used a collective form of resistance called the *volnenie,* for which there was no exact American equivalent. A *volnenie* typically started with a group of serfs who complained of grievances by petition, resisted owner authority, and went out on strike. The confrontations could involve hundreds, last for months, even years, and result in gains for the serfs. More often they ended in harsh punishments, savage beatings, and exile for penal servitude. Confrontations between slaves and plantation authorities were also common, but they usually took the form of individual slaves standing up to whites, and abundant records of such conflicts exist. The main difference between the Russian and the American confrontations was that the former were overwhelmingly collective and the latter individual.

Both serfs and slaves expressed resistance in the form of flight, and again the Russians and Americans differed. The serfs usually fled in families but also in larger groups of hundreds and even thousands, using collective strategy in times of crises. In America slaves escaped by the hundreds to Spanish Florida, and during the Revolutionary War thousands fled to the British forces, who encouraged defection from masters. Predominantly, however, slave flight was individual, local, and temporary. While the fugitives got help at times from other blacks, they had to flee through a vigilant white world, whereas the escaped serfs moved more securely through a peasant world. Slaves, like serfs, resorted to flight or resistance when authorities breached their notion of what they had a right to expect.

Bondsmen of both countries developed cultures distinctive from those of their owners. The cultures that serfs and slaves developed differed in the degree they were defined by class or caste. In general the life of a southern slave was shaped by slavery more than that of a Russian serf was by serfdom. All but a few blacks in the South were slaves. Only about half the peasants were privately held serfs, but most of the remainder were state peasants, who had no immediate owner and therefore enjoyed greater personal freedom than the serfs. Thus slave culture appeared almost identical with black culture, whereas in Russia the bondsman's culture was about as much peasant as serf. The mir was an institution of both state peasants and serfs, in which they enjoyed a continuity of culture and less interference from owners. Racial identity and loyalty were stronger than class identity and loyalty among slaves. Serfs felt identity with peasants, but their primary loyalty was to their village or commune rather than to class or caste. A sense of unity existed among both, but serf attachment was chiefly local, and slaves felt oneness with blacks in general. Class stratification, limited among both, was less marked among American slaves than among Russian serfs.

As survivals from an archaic order, serfdom and slavery had common conflicts with a modern world of nineteenth-century capitalism and simultaneously faced crises that ended with abolition of the two systems. But they faced their mid-century crises in very different ways. Both systems embodied contradictions between the market mentality of the masters in the distribution of their product and the noncapitalistic nature of its production. The southern masters were more commercial in their behavior than were the Russian, but it was the mode of production by slave labor more than that of distribution that was influential in shaping the societies and the way they met their crises. Southern slavery was uniquely suffused with a paternalistic ethos and the nonmarket relationship between resident masters and their slaves. Between noblemen and serfs relations were more shaped by market forces.

Southern slaveholders developed a far more cohesive world and much more power over it than did the noblemen in their world. By mid-century slavery was flourishing as never before, and serfdom was staggering toward bankruptcy. The aggressive vitality of the planter aristocrats in defense of their society and their spirited commitment to slavery as a way of life contrasted sharply with the submissiveness and withering support of serfdom on the part of the Russian nobility. The southern planters were the only masters of unfree labor in the nineteenth-century world who carried resistance to the extreme of an all-out show-down in civil war. In Russia emancipation was the decision of Czar Alexander II, and it was carried out peacefully with no threat of forceful resistance and only cooperation or impotent grumbling from noblemen. The owners were compensated for their loss, and emancipation was effected in their interest. With them as with all slaveholders in the New World apart from those of Saint Domingue and the South, abolition was the liquidation of an investment rather than the end of a society. Slavery ended violently in the South as the result of defeat in a rebellion on which the planters staked everything and lost. They were the only owners of human property in their time except those of Brazil to suffer emancipation without compensation and the only ones, save for the French colonists in Guadeloupe and Martinique in 1848, to endure radical efforts to bring the emancipated to equality and franchise as well as freedom. What they experienced was not only the overthrow of slavery but a revolution and the end of a society.

More than once in this fascinating study in comparative history there are hints of the intention of illuminate more than the past, and indeed the book concludes with a sentence containing the explicit suggestion that "it is well to remember the extent to which that earlier world has shaped our own." When we think of the century since these archaic systems of unfree labor were abolished by the two nations—one that enchained its own people and one that enslaved people of alien culture and different color—the comparison of past societies gains significance for contrasts in the present. This makes all the more welcome the author's promise of "a sequel in which I will examine the abolition of bondage in the United States and Russia." Readers won by the comparison of serfdom and slavery will await comparison of the consequences of their abolition with all the more interest.

10

Reconstruction:
A Counterfactual
Playback

Some comparisons are not readily recognizable as such. Thus when historians speak of what might have been or enumerate counterfactual outcomes of events, as they frequently and often quite legitimately do, they are actually comparing what did happen with what might have happened. Or when they place an event in a familiar category, such as renaissance, revolution, or restoration, they are suggesting comparison with other historic events so categorized. These types of comparative history can be as illuminating as the more conscious or formal ones. In the following essay some of these more informal comparisons are employed to cast light on the outcome of American Reconstruction.

THE RUINS OF TWO GREAT FAILURES dominate the landscape of
American history. They stand close together in the middle distance, back to back, but separate and distinct. One is the ruins
of the Confederacy, the South's failure to gain independence.
The other is the ruins of Reconstruction, the North's failure to
solve the problem of the black people's place in American life.
The South's failure was the North's success and vice versa. Each
can be and, of course, has been described by its opponents as
simply the wreckage wrought in preventing acknowledged wrong.
But from the standpoint of their supporters and champions there
can be no doubt that each of these ruins represents a great Amer-
can failure.

They stand out all the more conspicuously on the historical
landscape because of their unique character. Failures and defeats
on the grand scale are notoriously exceptional and uncharacteris-
tic in the American experience. And so far, at least until very
recent years, these two stand as the only instances of striking
significance. They are surrounded by monuments of success, victory, and continuity, features far more familiar to the American
eye. Some of these monuments—the Revolution, the Constitution, the two-party system, the parties themselves, the basic economic institutions, all still live and going concerns—are much
older than the two historic ruins. This side of them in the fore-
ground of American history stand more recent monuments in the
traditional success style of the American Way, marred only somewhat by late twentieth-century exceptions. But the middle distance is still dominated by the two great historic failures.

The unavoidable responsibility of the historian is to explain
these failures. But the strangeness and un-American character of
failure seems to have inhibited or warped the fulfillment of the
task. One evasive strategy of historians of the Confederacy has
been first to acknowledge more or less candidly that the movement was misguided and perhaps destined to fail from the start
and even to admit tacitly that it was best for all concerned in the
long run that it did fail. But then to dwell at length on the high
moments, the ephemeral triumphs, the selfless devotion, the

nobility of leadership, and the hardships and suffering of the participants. Essentially romantic, the lost-cause approach emphasized the glory and tragedy without too much attention to causes and consequences. Recent historians of the Confederacy have been addressing themselves more and more to the causes of failure and less to the epheremal triumphs. But for a long time the South's refusal to face up to its own defeat contributed to the North's failure in accounting for the sequel to Appomattax.

Historians of Reconstruction have played variations on these Confederate themes without exactly duplicating the order or the mood. For a long time they too started with the assumption that the movement was misconceived and doomed to failure from inception and that, all things considered, it was just as well that it did fail. Since failure was regarded as both inevitable and fortunate, the problem of explaining it did not appear very challenging. With these more or less common assumptions, historians of the old school divided mainly on how they distributed their sympathy and admiration among the victims—the humble freedmen, the misguided idealists, the bumbling Presidents, or the long-suffering Southern whites—and on their distribution of blame among villains—Radical Republicans, Carpetbaggers, Scalawags, or black freedmen. They were in substantial agreement, however, in their homage to the tragic muse. Whether the spotlight was focused on the victims or the villains, the overriding preoccupation was with tragedy. The best seller on the subject was entitled *The Tragic Era,* by Claude Bowers. But whether as a cause for satisfaction or lament, there was little equivocation about the verdict of failure.

In the last few decades a shift has occurred in the common assumptions and preoccupations about Reconstruction historians. Failure is no longer regarded as inevitable or complete, the movement as misconceived, or the outcome as fortunate. On all these matters there has occurred a reversal of attitude. The treatment is still fundamentally tragic, but the reading of the tragedy has changed. The tragedy was not that a misguided movement had caused so much unnecessary suffering, but that a noble experiment had come so near fulfillment and failed. Furthermore, the impact of failure itself has been blunted and the historical problem of explanation shelved by a new emphasis on the positive accomplishments of Reconstruction.

Much of the attention of revisionists has been focused on correcting the excessively negative picture painted by the old school and exposing the injustice and cruidity of the stereotypes. New studies have pictured the old abolitionists as persevering champions of the freedmen. The collective portrait of the Radical Republican congressmen that emerges from revisionist biographies and monographs is one of high-minded idealists who rose above selfish political and economic interests. Studies of Northern teachers and preachers who went to the South on missionary enterprises stress their seriousness of purpose and the devotion and fearless dedication of their service. Carpetbaggers of vision and courageous statesmanship have been sympathetically portrayed. Scalawags of the new historiography appear to derive either from wealthy Southern aristocrats or from sturdy Jacksonian yeomen, depending on one's school of revisionism or one's technique of quantification. Among black leaders and statesmen revisionists have discovered a gratifying amount of talent, ability, and vision. Swindlers, grafters, and corruption have been discounted by comparison with contemporaneous fraud and graft in Northern states. The result of all this has been a wholesale decimation of stock figures in the demonology of Reconstruction.

Praiseworthy achievements of Radical Reconstruction include not only the legislative and constitutional foundations for black citizenship, franchise, and civil rights, but the training and preparation of freedmen for political action. Radical state governments are also justly credited with framing laudable and often durable state constitutions and law codes, with providing relief and welfare for the distressed, with establishing public schools, and with inaugurating new public services. Scholars have pronounced the freedmen's economic progress during Reconstruction, given their low starting point, a tremendous success and enumerated with pride their gains in land and capital. Others have pointed out the general progress of the South in economic recuperation and growth. The emphasis here, as in so many other areas of revisionist history, is not on failures but on the successes of Reconstruction.

For this and other services of the revisionists we should be duly grateful. So successful have the revisionists of the 1960s and their followers been that they have virtually wiped the revisions of the 1900s and 1930s off the map. This is progress, as progress is measured in historiography, but a little more of it and we will arrive back at that tragic spring when lilacs last in dooryard bloomed—April, 1865.

The achievements of the revisionists are impressive. But as a contribution to explaining the failure of Reconstruction they tend rather to complicate than to solve the enigma. For if, as they have demonstrated, the statesmanship of the Radicals was all that inspired and their motivation all that pure, if the freedmen were so responsive and capably led, if government by the Scalawag-Carpetbagger-freedmen coalition was all that constructive, and if the opposition were indeed headed by a misfit in the White House who was out of touch with the electorate, then success would seem more indicated than failure. The paradox reminds me of the first historical problem I confronted as a boy. It went something like this: If Marse Robert was all that noble and intrepid, if Stonewall was all that indomitable and fast on his feet, if Jeb Stuart was all that gallant and dashing, and if God was on our side, then why the hell did we *lose* that war?

This is not to write off the accomplishments of the revisionists. I hope the record is clear that I have aided and abetted and egged them on, presumed to teach some of them, read many of their manuscripts and all their monographs, praised what I could and encouraged when I could. What they did in the main much needed doing. I do believe that they have produced many works with better prospects of durability than the school of the 1900s or that of the 1930s.

I am more interested in what comes next and what problems remain unsolved. This brings me back to the old problem of failure. As I have remarked earlier, Americans have rather a thing about failure—about confronting it, confessing it, and accepting it, as well as about explaining it. It is noteworthy that the great bulk of work done by the revisionists has been on Andrew Johnson's administration, not on the two Grant administrations, that is, on the period where, paradoxically, the ephemeral successes and triumphs multiplied, not the period of twice that length when the failures piled up or became unavoidably conspicuous. This may be mere coincidence, but my guess is that it is more than that. Another tendency might be called the deferred success approach, the justification (or dismissal) of failure in the First Reconstruction on the ground that it prepared the way for success in the Second Reconstruction, or maybe a Third yet to come. Thus one historian writes that the failures of the First Reconstruction diminish to insignificance in comparison with successes of the Second in advancing equal civil and political rights for blacks and promise of further progress to come. This is a generational shift of the burden of responsibility. But it must be recognized as essentially another strategy of evasion.

One habit of mind that has complicated American ways of dealing with failure, apart from a relative unfamiliarity with the experience, has been the isolation of American history from comparative reference. Comparisons have indeed been used with regard to Reconstruction, but they have been internalized. Lacking foreign comparisons, or indifferent to them, Americans have turned inward to compare professed ideals with actual practice. This has encouraged a strong moralistic tendenry in our historiral writing and controversy. Since the nation has advertised a commitment to some very lofty ideals and principles, the contrast between performance and principle has always been painful, and the application of absolute and abstract standards of judgment often sets up moral disturbance that clouds issues and distorts perspectives.

For more realistic perspective on the American experience of Reconstruction we need to turn to comparison with foreign experiences, including but not limited to those of the other twenty-odd slave societies in the New World that went through the post-emancipation ordeal. To avoid repetition, since I have sampled those comparisons before, I must be content with summarizing conclusions of the best informed authorities. The most important finding is that wherever slavery was widespread, emancipation was invariably followed by resort to drastic measures, including use of force, to put the freedmen back to work. The old masters of the American South were by no means alone in resorting to black codes and chain gangs. Old masters everywhere—West Indies, Latin America, Africa, Asia—took forceable steps to drive the freedmen back to work.

Furthermore, in those lands undergoing emancipation where the process of reconstruction was subject to outside control or supervision, whether from the crown, the mother country, an imperial or metropolitan administration, or as in the South the federal government under Northern control, such authorities proved quite ineffective in protecting the lives and rights of the emancipated. The universality of failure by authorities and oppression by old masters does not excuse or justify either the governments or the masters anywhere—especially not a government that had just fought a bloody civil war in the name of freedom. Reconstruction left a lasting blot on the American conscience and national history and continues to breed moral recrimination between regions and races. But at least the comparative context removes the stigma of uniqueness and places moral issues in a broader setting. That, I believe, is a legitimate use of history—not only to recover the past but to enable us to live with it.

Another type of comparison has often been used in interpreting Reconstruction, but not always with sufficient caution. To place a historical event in a category of events is to make a comparison. Thus, when Reconstruction is spoken of as a revolution, we are compelled to think of it in comparison with other revolutions. If we reserve the term "revolution" for the classic phenomena of England in the seventeenth century, America and France in the eighteenth century, and Russia and China in the twentieth century, then it is certainly misused when applied to the American Reconstruction of the nineteenth century. For in the last instance there were no mass executions, no class liquidations. No heads rolled. There were constitutional changes, to be sure, but they were insignificant compared with those in England, France, Russia, and China, and they were mainly effected through constitutional forms. The South's so-called Bourbons or Redeemers did not become proscribed and outlawed émigrés. They remained at home, retained their estates, took over from the ephemeral radical governments, and after their so-called counter-revolution they did not find it necessary to make very drastic changes in the system left them by the so-called revolution. All things considered, it would be better to abandon both the concept of revolution and that of counter-revolution in writing of Reconstruction as it *was*.

But in writing of what it *might* have been, what many hoped it would be, and of why Reconstruction failed, the concept of revolution seems indispensable. It should be fairly obvious that in order to succeed with the professed aims of full civil rights, equality, and justice for the freedmen, Reconstruction would have had to go much further in the way of revolutionary measures than it ever did. Even then it might have failed, for revolutions are not invariably successful nor are their innovations always lasting. It is not very helpful to prescribe revolution in the abstract without specifying the revolutionary program. Nor is it very realistic to imagine a revolutionary program without regard to the nature of the party and the people who would carry it out and the historical context in which they would have worked. Only by that means can we test the hypothesis that the failure of Reconstruction is to be explained by the lack of revolutionary measures.

One revolutionary measure, a favorite for the speculation over a century, is the confiscation of rebel estates and redistribution of them among the freedmen. This deserves serious consideration for a number of reasons. In the first place such a proposal was seriously made and had an able and powerful advocate in Thaddeus Stevens. The Stevens plan called for the confiscation of all rebel estates over $10,000 or over 200 acres. He estimated that this would result in the taking over of some 394 million out of 465 million acres in the rebel states. The redistribution would give 40 acres to each adult male freedman. This would take 40 million acres, and the remaining 254 million would be sold to the highest bidder and the proceeds allocated to pensions for Union veterans, damages and reparations, and enough left to retire three-quarters of the national debt. The plan was defeated, of course, but it has had later advocates such as W. E. B. Du Bois and various other Marxists.

Americans need no Marxist precedents, however, for there was ample precedent for the wholesale confiscation of the estates of disloyal elements of the population in the treatment of Tories during the American Revolution, and there was a spectacular contemporary example abroad in the distribution of some of the confiscated lands to emancipated serfs by the Czar of All the Russias in 1861. The American freedmen surely had as great a moral claim on the land on which they had toiled for 250 years. Furthermore if the federal government could overcome the legal and constitutional problems of confiscating the slave property of the planters, it surely could have justified confiscating their landed property as well. The planters would have objected strenuously, of course, but they would have been powerless to prevent the action had Congress been determined. Let us assume, then, that the Stevens Land Confiscation Bill actually passed, that President Ben Wade signed it in the White House after President Johnson's removal by successful impeachment, and that the Fortieth Congress then brought to bear all its experience and wisdom in refining the legislation and President Wade marshalled the best talents for administering the land act. What would have been the consequences for the outcome of Reconstruction? Would this have converted a failure into a reasonable success?

No one can possibly say for sure, of course. What one *can* describe with some assurance, however, is the record of the same federal government, the same Congresses under the control of the same party in administering and distributing public lands elsewhere. Again we resort to the comparative approach, though this time the comparisons are drawn from domestic rather than foreign instances. The Reconstruction period coincided with the great era of public land distribution by the federal government according to the provisions of the Homestead Act of 1862 and other federal land laws placed on the books between 1862 and 1878. The public domain available for distribution under the Homestead and subsequent acts amounted to some 1,048,000,000 acres, more than half the total area of the nation and more than two and a half times the 394 million acres of confiscated rebel estates that would have been added to the public domain by the Stevens Act. This fabulous opportunity, without precedent in history, appeared to be the fruition of the American dream, the most cherished dream of reformers—free land for those who tilled the land.

What came of that dream in the administration of the Homestead Act is a matter of public record. We know that as things turned out the homesteaders got short shrift and proved to be the least favored of the various groups attracted to the western lands. The land-grant railroads alone got four times as much land as the homesteaders in the first four decades of the Homestead Act. In that period 84 percent of the new farms brought under cultivation were purchased or subdivided from larger holdings. Of the patents actually granted to homesteaders a great number were handed to pawns of speculators and monopolists, so that in all probability little more than one-tenth of the new farms were free in the homestead sense. Furthermore, the bona fide homesteader was typically shunted off into the poorest land and least desirable tracts, while the speculators pre-empted tracts closest to settlement and transportation and held them for resale at prices beyond the means of the class the Homestead Act was presumably designed to help. It is the opinion of Fred Shannon that, "In its operation the Homestead Act could hardly have defeated the hopes of the [land-reform] enthusiasts . . . more completely if the makers had drafted it with that purpose uppermost in mind."

While many of the same people who drafted and administered the Homestead Act for the West would in all probability have drafted and administered the Stevens Act for the South, it is only fair to remember that the Western land problem was complicated by variables absent from the Southern picture— granting that the latter had its own complications. But at least the South lay within the humid, forested longitudes, conditions that were far more familiar to Eastern lawmakers than Walter Webb's Great Plains, and also the rebel estates provided a larger proportion of arable land, much more conveniently located in relation to the prospective homesteaders. Because of these advantages and the idealism said to have motivated Radicals in their dealings with freedmen (however inoperative it was in the same men's dealings with Western homesteaders) it is possible that the Stevens Act would have had a happier history than the Homestead Act and that the black freedmen would have actually entered into the promised land, peacefully and cheerfully, each one secure in the possession of his forty acres. And let us throw in an army mule apiece for good measure.

That outcome is conceivable and one would hope even probable. But in calculating the degree of probability one is forced to take into account certain other conditioning and relevant factors in addition to the western homestead experience. For one thing the Stevens Act as detailed by the Pennsylvania Radical set aside nine-tenths of the 394 million acres of confiscated rebel land for sale to the highest bidder—an open invitation to the speculator and monopolist. It is possible that these types might have behaved toward the black homesteaders of the South in much the same way they behaved toward the white homesteader in the West. If so the probability of success for the philanthropic part of the Stevens Act is appreciably diminished.

Prospects of success for the Stevens Act are also illuminated by the history of a Southern Homestead Act that actually *was* adopted by Congress. There were 47,700,000 acres of public land in five of the Confederate states in 1861, more than the amount of rebel estates set aside for freedmen by the hypothetical Stevens Act. In 1866 the Radicals pushed through a drastic bill applying exclusively to these lands, reserving them to homesteaders at 80 acres per holding, and favoring freedmen by excluding ex-Confederates from homesteading privileges. These lands were generally less accessible and less desirable than those of confiscated estates might have been, and as in the case of the Western act no provision was made for furnishing credit and transportation to homesteaders. These conditions probably explain why extremely few blacks seized upon this opportunity to double the elusive 40 acres. In that respect the act was a failure and, at any rate, Congress reversed the policy in 1876 and threw open this rich Southern empire to unrestricted speculation. There ensued a scramble of monopolists that matched any land rush of the Wild West, and the freedmen were thrust aside and forgotten. Admittedly this episode offers further discouragement for the chances of the revolutionary Stevens Act.

Determined revolutionists are not disheartened by reverses, however. They merely press forward with more heroic measures. Perhaps Thaddeus Stevens was not revolutionary enough. There is the problem of the rebel resistance to Radical Reconstruction and federal authority in the defeated states. My own researches have impressed me deeply with the seriousness of this resistance. It was often open, defiant, organized, and effective. White Southerners repeatedly insulted, persecuted, and sometimes murdered federal officials, army officers included. They scoffed at the law and ridiculed the courts. They did everything to black citizens the law forbade their doing and invented mistreatments that law never thought of. How any self-respecting government put up with such defiance unless, indeed, it was at least subliminally sympathetic with the resistance, it is difficult to understand. With overwhelming power in its hands, even an ordinary respectable non-revolutionary government could have done better than this.

Let me remind you, however, that this is a revolutionary program that we are pursuing. Here Thad Stevens lets us down. He raises the question whether any Republican, Senator Charles Sumner included, really deserved the name "Radical." It is true that his rhetoric against the "proud, bloated, and defiant rebels" was violent enough, that he promised to "startle feeble minds and shake weak nerves," that he ridiculed "the prim conservatives, the snobs, and the male waiting maids in Congress," that he asked, "How can republican institutions, free schools, free churches . . . exist in a mingled community of nabobs and serfs," and that he thundered the promise to "drive her nobility into exile," or worse. But when it came right down to it he confessed that he "never desired bloody punishments to any extent." This admission of bourgeois softness proves that Stevens has exhausted his usefulness as a guide to revolutionary solutions.

It is becoming a bit tiresome (and it is entirely unnecessary) to be flanked on the left in speculative audacity. Armchair bloodbaths can be conducted with impunity by anyone, even a professor emeritus. Let us then pursue the logic of the revolutionary process on past Stevens and Sumner, past the Old Left and the New Left, and out to the wild blue—or rather infra-red—yonder. Let us embrace in our revolutionary program, along with the Stevens Act, an act for the liquidation of the enemy class. There is ample precedent for this in the history of revolutions. Even the American Revolution drove the Tories into exile. Mass deportation, considering the merchant marine's state of total disrepair in 1865, is unfortunately not a practicable option. That leaves available only the messier alternatives. It is true that the Alaska purchase from Russia made providentially available an American Siberia in 1867, but that would take care of relatively few, and again there is the tedious problem of transportation. The numbers are formidable, for the counter-revolutionary resistance extended beyond the planter class through a very large percentage of Southern whites. A few hundred thousand Northern Copperheads can be handled in concentration camps, but in Dixie harsher measures are indicated. Let no true revolutionary blanch at the implications. Remember that we must be cruel in order to be kind, that we are the social engineers of the future, that we are forestalling future bloodbaths, race riots, and relieving our Northern metropolitan friends of problems that trouble their thoughts and for a time threatened to destroy their cities. If our work is bloody our conscience is clear, and we do all that we do—compassionately.

Having liquidated the white resistance down to the last unregenerate lord of the lash and the last bed-sheeted Ku Kluxer, let us proceed unencumbered to build the true Radical Reconstruction. We will find it expedient to import managerial talent in large numbers to replace the liquidated white resistance, and place them in charge of agriculture, industry, railroads, and mines. They will doubtless come from the same states the carpet-baggers hailed from, but they must be carefully screened to eliminate the more objectionable types and certified as non-racists and non-Copperheads. We will also establish a permanent Freedmen's Bureau, perhaps modeled on the Indian Bureau, and place in command of it the very finest talent. If not General O. O. Howard, perhaps we can get the nomination of Frederick Douglass through a miraculously radicalized U.S. Senate, after a radicalized U. S. Grant had executed a Pride's Purge of half the members.

After these Draconian, Cromwellian, Stalinist measures had removed all resistance and interference from Southern and Northern racists and Kluxers and nightriders, silenced all Confederate orators, and shut down the last obstructionist press, the revolutionists should have had a perfectly free hand. What then would have been the consequences for fulfillment of Reconstruction purposes? Would these additional measures have converted failure into success? One would surely hope so after paying such a bloody price.

But again, no one can say for sure. And again we turn to the comparative method for possible illumination. I hope that I am sufficiently alert to the dangers of these comparisons. I realize that no analogy is complete, that no two historical events are identical, and that the risks of drawing conclusions by such reasoning are most formidable. I have tried to guard against such risks and to be very tentative about drawing conclusions, but I suspect I have already outraged respected historians by mentioning Grant in the same breath with Cromwell or Stalin. Nevertheless I shall take heart and venture one last excursion into the treacherous field of comparative or counterfactual history.

Once again the comparison is close to home and contemporaneous with the Reconstruction period. Moreover, the same electorates, the same congressmen, the identical presidents and judiciary, the same editorial chorus and clerical censors are involved in the one as in the other—one cast for two dramas. The second drama also has as its plot the story of reformers using the federal government to bring justice and rights and decent lives to men of color. This time the theater is in the West instead of the South and the colored minority is red instead of black. Since we have "controlled the variable" (as the quantifiers say) of Confederate slave owners' resistance in the South—with a regrettable amount of bloodshed to be sure—the two theaters are more readily comparable. For while the reformers in the West had their own problems, they were not encumbered by die-hard Confederate reactionaries, former owners and masters of the red people, and not dogged at every step by determined and desperate nightriders. In these respects they had a relatively free hand.

The personnel and policies of the white guardians of the blacks and the white guardians of the reds were often interchangeable. General W. T. Sherman moved from command of the Southern District to command of the Western District in 1867, from the final arbiter of the black freedman's destiny to final arbiter of the redskin's fate. Many other military officers including General O. O. Howard moved back and forth from South to West. While General Howard, who had been head of the Freedmen's Bureau, was serving as president of an all-black Howard University in 1872 he was dispatched by Grant to conclude a treaty with the Apaches; in 1874 he was placed in command of the Department of Columbia, and in 1877 he led a punitive expedition against the Nez Perce Indians. Black regiments served in West and South under the same white officers. In the educational field Samuel Armstrong of Hampton Institute, Booker Washington's mentor and model, took Richard Henry Pratt, the great Indian educator, as disciple and assistant, and the two of them integrated and taught black and red students at Hampton. Later Pratt took the Armstrong-Booker Washington gospel to Indian schools. The same missionaries, preachers, editors, and reformers often concerned themselves with the problems and destinies of both colored minorities.

What can be said, in view of the relatively free hand they had in the West, of the performance of the American reformers toward the Indian, as compared with their performance toward the Negro, when they did not have the free hand I have imagined for them? Was it any better? As a matter of fact the two problems were solved in much the same way. The red man like the black man was given to understand that the white man's will was supreme, that he had few rights the white man was bound to respect. He was promised land and the land was taken away. He was promised integration and then segregated, even more completely than the black man. He was degraded, exploited, humiliated, and because he offered more resistance he was cut down ruthlessly by military force or vigilante action. Idealists like Richard Henry Pratt who operated in both South and West were as frustrated in their efforts for red man as they were with the black man. White supremacy forces were as triumphant over Eastern "Indian lovers" in Arizona and Colorado as they were over Northern "nigger lovers" in Mississippi and Alabama.

But this comparison is an outrage against established compartmentalizations of historical thought, a preposterous violation of respected conventions. Everyone knows what a "good Indian" was. And what but confusion of the undergraduate mind can possibly come from comparing Colorado and Alabama? I apologize for this travesty against sound canons of the profession. Nevertheless, I confess that these irresponsible speculations have raised such doubts in the mind of one dedicated revolutionary arm-chair ultra-radical as to palsy his hand and sickly over with the pale cast of thought the native hue of resolution. Almost am I persuaded to countermand belatedly the order for the Confederate liquidation.

I owe further apologies. Having invited you to consider the causes of the failure of Reconstruction, I have produced nothing but negative results. While applauding the revisionists for their excellent work, I have questioned the emphasis on the idealism and sincerity of the Radicals and their ephemeral triumphs as an adequate indication of their ultimate failure. In the second place, I have raised doubts about moralistic and uniquely American explanations for post-emancipation failure in the protection of freedmen on the ground that much the same pattern of forced labor occurred everywhere in the world as a sequel to abolition. Thirdly, having embraced the Stevens policy of rebel land confiscation and redistribution, I am forced to admit that contemporaneous experience with federal administration of public lands discourages optimism about the freedman's chances. And finally, after eliminating Confederate resistance with bloody measures I am overcome with doubts, caused by belated reflections on the fate of the poor red man, that even these drastic steps would ensure success. With the candor I have urged upon other historians I am obliged to confess a failure of my own, the failure to find a satisfactory explanation for the failure of Reconstruction.

The problem remains unsolved. The assignment still goes begging. It deserves high priority among the unfinished tasks of American historiography. Those who next undertake the task will not, I hope, rely too uncritically on the received ideas, the shared moral convictions and political values of their own time to sanction their premises. They should give scrupulous attention to uniquely American conditions, but remember that the post-emancipation problem they attack was not unique to America. They may well profit from consideration of allegedly idyllic race relations on happy islands in the Caribbean sun, but remember that their home problem was environed by Protestant Anglo-American institutions of a temperate zone unblessed by Pope or tropical sun. They should give due weight to constitutional issues without fruitlessly pining for an English-type constitution to deal with states' rights, a Russian-type Czar to distribute land among the emancipated, or a Soviet-type commissar of security to liquidate mass resistance.

I hope those who accept this challenge will not take these reflections as the counsel of despair, or as intimation that Reconstruction was doomed to failure, or that our ancestors might not have done better by their experiment than they actually did. Nor should other historians be discouraged from revolutionary speculations by the inconclusive results of my own. Let them be as far-out left as is currently fashionable. But in the transports of revolutionary imaginings, arm-chair edicts, and dreams of glory, they would do well to keep in mind the human materials and the historic context of their problem. If they do this, they will face up to the fact that nineteenth-century Americans (and some in the twentieth century as well) were fatefully stuck with a perverse mystique of squatter sovereignty. The tenets of this perversion of the democratic dogma, this squatter sovereignty, were that whatever the law or the Constitution or the Supreme Court or world opinion or moral codes said to the contrary notwithstanding, the will of the dominant white majority would prevail. And where whites were not in the majority it would prevail anyway. How it was, and how early, we got stuck with a commitment to this caricature of democracy is a long story, a very long story, and the story did not begin in 1865, and the commitment was not confined to the South.

IV

HISTORY
AND FICTION

For the last century or more American historians of the academic sort have tended to put distance between themselves and literary folk. The amount of distance has varied depending on the seriousness with which the historians happened to be stressing their aspirations as scientists. The more scientific, the more distance. Interludes of cordiality, largely sponsored by historians of journalistic background or sympathies, have occurred. Indeed an organization to foster the waning affinity still exists. Of late, however, the chill of scientific exclusiveness has increased and the dissociation has widened. Among the more exclusionist are some professionals who are uncomfortable with the very expression "historical literature," or the admission that they share with literary craftsmen the use of narrative, the employment of metaphor, or any serious concern with the quality of their prose.

The theme running through the pieces in this section of the book is a concern that historians may allow themselves to be deprived of benefits they could well derive from exploring the interests, subjects, problems, and techniques they share with creative writers as fellow craftsmen. On both sides of the line separating scholarly from creative writers are some who would resist any traffic whatever across the border. On one side are historians properly intent on preventing the blurring of distinctions between fact and fancy and illicit borrowing of the novelist's license, along with those who resist the thought that history might conceivably entertain as well as instruct. On the literary side of the dividing line are those with comparable scorn for Clio's earth-bound, fact-enslaved servants and with resistance to their literal-minded and lowly concepts of truth. On both sides, however, I would hope that a majority would admit that both history and fiction attempt to present and in some measure account for human conduct, use much the same vocabulary in their efforts to do so, and often write about people of the same class, nationality, or locality. With that much in common, it would seem sufficient to justify, if not require, an ongoing dialogue between the two crafts, the scholarly and the creative. In addition, I admit that the maintenance of such relations might serve another cause that I privately cherish—that of restoring the claims of history to membership-in-good-standing in the humanities.

11

Why the
Southern Renaissance?

Here the theme of fiction and history takes the form of using historical method and insight to test hypotheses that have been offered to account for a literary phenomenon. No historian who began his professional career in the South of the early 1930s could be unaware of the explosions of literary productivity going on around him. Reading books by then little known or unheard of writers who were later to become world famous was an exciting but confusing experience. Careful to curb expressions of regional pride and expose provinciality, the young Southerner took pains to consult the pronouncements of critical moguls on the Hudson. They were then dismissing works of some of the best Southern writers as dull, pretentious, commonplace, or meaningless. The youthful reader nevertheless read on while publicly conforming to New York fashions of the time. To my embarrassment I find myself as a very junior instructor parroting metropolitan wisdom back in 1938, shamelessly remarking that William Faulkner seemed to draw his subjects out of abandoned wells. I hope the following essay, published in 1975, profits from more mature perspective.

Why the Southern Renaissance ever occurred is still something of a mystery. All that is attempted here is an analysis of some explanations that have been offered by others and a few additional speculations. Before turning to the critical *why*, however, it is necessary to determine just what it is we are talking about. In the first place, we are stuck with a misnomer in the very word "renaissance." For neither in its literal sense nor in its classic historical usage is this French word really applicable to what happened in the South. As for the literal meaning when applied to that phenomenon, Allen Tate has observed that "it was more precisely a birth, not a rebirth." Certainly nothing comparable had happened before in the South that could conceivably be said to have been reborn in the twentieth century. The second and more common historical usage of "renaissance" is the one to describe the evocation of the ghost of a dead civilization, as the ghost of Hellenic culture was evoked in thirteenth- to fifteenth-century Italy. And surely nothing of that sort took place in the South. Nevertheless, we are stuck with this misnomer and will continue to use it. It has been applied with comparable looseness to New England in the early nineteenth century and by F. O. Matthiessen to Northern letters in the 1850's.

In continuing to apply the word "renaissance" to the twentieth-century Southern phenomenon it is well to remember that the movement was pretty strictly limited to the literary arts—poetry, fiction, and drama. It did not spill over to any significant degree to the visual or performing arts. There was no Southern Renaissance in music,* painting, sculpture, or architecture, so far as I am aware. To turn H. L. Mencken's famous quip in "The Sahara of the Bozart" upside down, one could say that an oboe player or a drypoint etcher was much rarer than a poet down there at a time when poets—to use another Menckenism—had become as common as evangelists or snake-oil salesmen.

Assuming agreement, therefore, that our subject is confined

---

* Michael O'Brien in *Rethinking the South* makes jazz a product of the Renaissance, but I think of it as a traditional form rediscovered.

to an explosion of literary productivity, the next question is *what* literary products we are taking about. There is no doubt whatever that Southern writers were remarkably active in this period, that the presses roared with their products, and that hucksters sold some of them by the millions. With their special regard for numbers, the sociologists have come forward with a sort of quantification of the Renaissance. Howard Odum estimated that in the first half of the twentieth century Southern writers turned out no fewer than five thousand titles of what he described as "full-sized-book literature." Classifying half of these as "literature in the traditional sense," he broke these down into 1,000 volumes of fiction, 500 of biography, 400 of poetry, 125 of drama, and threw in 800 volumes on history and 800 on Negro life for good measure. Not content with purely quantitative standards, he ventured into what he called "the qualitative measure" by pointing out that "Pulitzer awards have been made to Southern authors in more than half of the years since the first awards in 1917" and that "of the eleven best sellers that have exceeded or approximated a million copies, ten were by Southern authors."

We immediately run into difficulties with the quantitative standard, however, when we discover that "the most widely read American writer of the twentieth century" was Erskine Caldwell, that one of his works sold more than 6,500,000 copies and six others more than 2,000,000 copies each. And this at a time when all of William Faulkner's novels save *Sanctuary* had gone out of print. Clearly there is something misleading about market figures in this field. The case for them is not very much improved by a literary critic who has compiled a list of some 700 so-called "Renaissance authors" of "book-length volumes which have been issued by reputable publishers of more than local prestige." He even apologizes for inadvertent omissions. One trouble is that in scanning the columns of this list state by state compiled ten years ago one so rarely runs across a recognizable name. If we are not talking in terms of millions of books or hundreds of authors, then in just what terms are we talking? Briefly, the answer is, in much smaller terms.

When Allen Tate was pressed to "invoke certain names"

a decade ago he said that "if the Elizabethan Age would still be the glory of English literature without Shakespeare, the new literature of the Southern states would still be formidable without Faulkner." He then suggested in support of that view the names of twenty additional writers. How that list will stand up after another fifty or a hundred or three hundred and fifty years one cannot know. About some of the names there is already dispute among critics. But if as many as ten remained undisputed by the end of the century and as many as three after another century, that would still constitute a formidable record indeed—a phenomenon worthy of comparison with distinguished periods in Western literary history.

If this suggests the scope of the phenomenon, it remains to agree roughly on the time of its appearance and its duration. It is sometimes said to have taken place between the two world wars. There would probably be less difficulty agreeing about its beginnings than its endings. Some of the major figures are still alive and still productive, while some of the younger writers may not yet have reached their full stature. It is generally agreed that the Renaissance began in the 1920s, though there is some dispute about just how early in that decade.

I like to think of the year 1929 and those immediately following as specially significant. In 1929 appeared Faulkner's *Sartoris* and *The Sound and the Fury* and within three years *As I Lay Dying, Sanctuary,* and *Light in August*—all with blinding suddenness and little comprehension from critics or public. In 1929 came Thomas Wolfe's first novel, *Look Homeward, Angel* and first books by Robert Penn Warren and Merrill Moore. Katherine Anne Porter's first book *Flowering Judas* came in 1930 and on its heels followed the first books of Caroline Gordon, Andrew Nelson Lytle, and Lillian Hellman. Tate, Ransom, and Davidson had already published. A second generation of authors was already in the wings and a third one was to come. Together they dominated the literary scene in America for three, perhaps four, decades. Their influence fluctuated over that period, as did individual productivity, and full recognition of the stature of some was slow in coming. But the dramatic suddeness of the coming was unmatched by any previous burst of creative literature in American history.

A few critics caught a glimmering of the Southern movement's significance quite early, but only a glimmering. In 1927 Herschel Brickell believed that it was no "exaggeration to speak of a Renaissance of literature in the South," and in 1930 Howard Mumford Jones agreed, though he predicted that it would "remain merely charming and interesting." As late as 1942 Alfred Kazin, while acknowledging Faulkner's experimental boldness, could pronounce him "curiously dull, furiously commonplace, and often meaningless, suggesting some exasperated sullenness of mind, some distant atrophy or indifference." The French were quicker to acclaim the eminence of Southern achievement, and by 1954 the London *Times Literary Supplement* could say without challenge that "the literature [of the South] . . . has solidly established itself as the most important, the most talented, interesting, and valuable in the United States."

Turning to the question of *why* one should remember first how crude and inappropriate for the task at hand are the instruments of the historian. Typically history deals with groups rather than individuals—with nations, classes, political parties, governments, industries, interests. True, writers may be described as a group, but their significant acts, motives, purposes, values, habits, and achievements at the level we are talking about are highly individual. I have rarely met one who could give me a coherent account of what made him tick—much less a convincing account of his peers. His is a lonely trade. The only important thing he does in his whole life, so far as we are concerned, he does alone in a room by himself, quite unobserved. The task of explaining and understanding him is better suited to the skills of the biographer or the psychologist than to those of a historian.

Those historical forces the historian deals with in writing of wars, revolution, religious and ideological conflicts, and movements like industrialization and urbanization are ill adapted to fathoming the mysteries of human mind in its rare moments of high creativity. It is important to remember that we are dealing here not with thousands of people or hundreds, but with a mere handful—fewer than one in a million. And remember too that they are scattered over a vast area, in villages, towns, cities, or remote country places. Their formative years are behind them before they meet each other. They may congregate briefly in Nashville, Charleston, Richmond, or New Orleans in small numbers, but what they do in common is of less significance than what they do alone. And the important shaping influence on the writer's are may not be his daily drinking companion in Nashville or New Orleans but a man he has never met in Dublin or Rome or for that matter in sixteenth-century London or thirteenth-century Florence.

Some skepticism is advisable toward historians who are willing to tell you just why it was that Sophocles, Aeschylus, and Euripides appeared in fifth-century Athens, or a handful of poets suddenly got active in second-century Rome, or a Dante and a Petrarch turned up in Italy when they did. To take a more recent instance, one contemporary with, though greater than, the Southerners under scrutiny here, there is the mystery of the creative explosion of artistic, literary, scientific, and philosophical talent that occurred in Austria-Hungary at the time when that atrophied, ramshackle, and rather ludicrous Empire staggered to its dissolution in 1918 and before it swooned into the arms of Adolf Hitler in 1938. That was the heyday of Vienna, Prague, and Budapest, from which sprang major shaping forces of Western intellectual and artistic life in the twentieth century. In due time some historian will undertake to explain just why the whole thing happened. As a matter of fact, there is one already at work on the subject, a learned one at Princeton.* Learned or not, I still advise skepticism about learned explanations—reasons *why*.

From Vienna and Budapest to the Mississippi boondocks, the Tennessee hills, the Carolina lowlands is a far cry, but the problem is much the same—the reasons why, reasons in a field of endeavor where the non-rational so often holds sway.

First, to dispose of a few explanatory hypotheses that will not take much time. They are predominantly sociological in

---

* Reference is to Carl Schorske, *Fin-de-siècle Vienna: Politics and Culture* (New York, 1980).

character and seek to correlate the Renaissance with various social changes in the South. Among the social variables that have been suggested are increasing prosperity, the industrial revolution, the rise of cities, the "leaven of liberalism," changing attitudes toward the Negro, and a transfusion of "new blood" from the North. Were I an impatient man—and such hypotheses certainly provoke impatience—I would simply say "nonsense" and pass on. But I am an academician indoctrinated with the creed that sociologists (and historians who imbibe their theories) like other disciplines must be treated with due respect and their arguments patiently answered.

In the first place the Renaissance was a depression phenomenon and if correlated with any social condition it was certainly not prosperity. Secondly, both industries and cities had been growing at a desultory rate for several decades without producing any literary phenomenon of this sort, and when cities and industries really did start booming in the forties and fifties they produced no discernible effect on literary output. Thirdly, if the major literary figures can be tagged with any ideological identification (and I am reluctant to do so), it was not liberalism. If there were any appreciable change in attitudes toward the Negro in the twenties and thirties, the two major Negro figures in the Southern Renaissance, Richard Wright and Ralph Ellison, failed to note such change. And, incidentally, in the period since such changes in racial attitudes *have* occurred, no black author in the South has attained the stature of Wright or Ellison. And finally, whatever "new blood" came south, it is distinctly old blood that we are dealing with here.

Donald Davidson, among others, has taken particular delight in making paradoxes out of the sociological determinants. Pointing out that "By every cultural standard that the sociologist knows how to devise, Mississippi rates low in the national scale during William Faulkner's formative period," Davidson challenges the sociologists to explain why Faulkner "or some novelist of comparable stature, did not appear, during this period, somewhere north of the Ohio—say in Massachusetts or Wisconsin." He goes on to say that in view of the "extremely forbidding" and backward condition of Mississippi in that period he "can hardly see how Mr. Faulkner survived, much less wrote novels," and that in view of reliable sociological evidence "a William Faulkner in Mississippi would be a theoretical impossibility" and "would have to originate in, say, Massachusetts, where the cultural factors were favorable to literary interests." Allen Tate has taken the argument a step further by expressing his "paradoxical conviction . . . that the very backwardness of Mississippi, and of the South as a whole, might partially explain the rise of the new literature. . . ."

We shall return later to the half-serious, perhaps quarter-serious, part of Tate's explanatory paradox—for I think there is at least a grain of truth in it, enough to be refined and preserved. For the present, however, we shall be content to use it along with the other evidence to lay to rest forever the cruder sociological explanations of the Southern Renaissance. Needless to say, there are subtler and more sophisticated sociological variables and subtler sociologists that deserve consideration.

It is now time to turn to theories of more substance. One of these is the theory that the basic impulse behind the sudden release of Southern literary creativity, the "cause" if you prefer that tricky word, was profoundly defensive—an urge to defend the native region from unjust attack and repel the invasion of alien values. This theory had perhaps its most explicit formulation from W. J. Cash, who called it "the decisive factor." As he put it, "the outburst proceeded fundamentally from, and represented basically the patriotic response of men of talent to, the absorbing need of the South to defend itself, to shore up its pride at home, and to justify itself before the world." Since this theory, or some variation on it, has also received support from some of the major Southern men of letters, it cannot be dismissed out of hand and must be weighed with care.

Of the intensity of the attack and the incentives for patriotic defense there can be no doubt. The bleak and shabby cultural landscape of the Old Confederacy was the favorite butt of wits, caricaturists, and debunkers in the twenties. H. L. Mencken set the pace and led the pack with enormous gusto and glee. Dixie, he declared, was a land of "paralyzed cerebrums." It was "almost as sterile, artistically, intellectually, culturally, as the Sahara Desert. There are single acres in Europe that house more first-rate men than all the states south of the Potomac. . . ." As for "critics, musical composers, painters, sculptors, architects and the like . . . there is not even a bad one between the Potomac mud-flats and the Gulf. . . . In all these fields the South is an awe-inspiring blank—a brother to Portugal, Serbia and Albania." The intellectual vacuity begged comparison with interstellar space. It reminded him of "Asia Minor, resigned to Armenians, Greeks and wild swine, of Poland abandoned to the Poles." Granting the glories of the old régime, "One could no more imagine a Lee or a Washington in the Virginia of today than one could imagine a Huxley in Nicaragua." As for Georgia, which was "little re-moved from savagery," here was "a state with more than half the area of Italy and more population than either Denmark or Nor-way, and yet in thirty years it has not produced a single idea." The whole region was "a vast plain of mediocrity, stupidity, lethargy, almost of dead silence." Realizing that he had struck a funny bone of his public, Mencken continued his attack in the *Smart Set* and later in his *American Mercury* and was joined by scores of imitators.

Two things about this assault of South-baiters complicate the problem. One is simply the substantial amount of truth in it. That is precisely what constitutes the main mystery of the sud-den flowering of literature in such a desert. In the second place, one difficulty about explaining that phenomenon as a defen-sive reaction to the assault is the initial response of many of the alleged defenders. The fact is that many of them joined the assault. As Cash himself remarks, "baiting the South in [the *American Mercury*'s] pages was one of the favorite sports of young Southerners of literary and intellectual pretensions." It was the surest way of establishing one's credentials, of shaking off the abhorred stigma of provincialism. Sufficient stridency about the boobs and yokels below the Potomac might even overcome the handicap of a young Southerner's tell-tale accent during visits to New York.

The most curious manifestation of this foible was its out-cropping among those who later became the most militant de-fenders of the South. In fact, Mencken is said to have "long been an ideal of the literary young men at Vanderbilt" and that "even Tate went around with Mencken under his arm." In 1925 young Tate, a temporary exile in New York, published in the *Nation* an essay he called "Last Days of the Charming Lady," in which he declared that the Southerner "does not inherit . . . a native culture compounded of the strength and subtlety of his New England contemporary" and that an "essential" Southern litera-ture was made impossible by the inability of Southerners to repudiate "outmoded general notions which have lost their roots in an existing reality" and consequently had "no tradition of ideas, no consciousness of moral and spiritual values." About the same time his friend Donald Davidson despaired of finding "a single Southern writer of merit who in his thinking and manner of expression is as clearly of the South as Robert Frost is of New England." Southerners felt that "the gallantries of the Lost Cause, the legends of a gracious aristocracy, the stalwart tradi-tions of Southern history" had been "mouthed over and cheap-ened." They felt homeless between the abhorred slogans of "New South" and "the treacly lamentation of the old school." John Crowe Ransom declared that "If there is a significance in the title of the magazine [*The Fugitive*], it lies perhaps in the senti-ment of the editors (on this point I am sure we all agree) to flee from the extremes of conventionalism, whether old or new." And in the preface to the first number of that journal he wrote, "*The Fugitive* flees from nothing faster than the high-caste Brahmins of the Old South."

The turning point for these three and for others of the Nashville group came in 1925 with the trial of Scopes at Day-ton, Tennessee, for the violation of the state law against teaching evolution. This brought the whole tribe of South-baiters, boob-jeerers, and yokel-tormentors led by Mencken himself to Nash-ville's doorstep. From there they broadcast their mockery of the moronic idiocy of the Southern boobs. It was too much for the Nashvillians and then and there they "took their stand." Tate declared, "I've attacked the South for the last time" except in so far as it has produced the "New South." Davidson replied that he was "delighted at your own annunciation of the True Southern Spirit," and Ransom rallied to the colors. Dayton "broke in upon our literary concerns like a midnight alarm," wrote Davidson, To him it seemed that a " 'cold Civil War' began from about that moment . . . a long sustained bombardment. . . . We were religious bigots. We were Ku Kluxers. We were lynchers. We had hookworm, we had pellagra, we had sharecroppers, we had poll taxes, we had poor whites, we had fundamentalists. We did not have enough schools . . . paved roads . . . skyscrapers . . . modern plumbing. . . . Our women were too hoity-toity about ancestors. Our men all chewed tobacco or drank mint juleps and sometimes did both." It seemed to him incredible "that nobody in the South knew how to reply to a vulgar rhetorician like H. L. Mencken," and that "no real defense was being made," that "a kind of wholesale surrender was in progress," and that "the Trojan Horse of liberalism had disgorged a horde of social scientists" within the walls.

Avoiding the discredited strategy of the late Confederates, the Nashvillians decided promptly that the best defensive was an offensive and assumed the aggressive posture from the start. Taking their native South as "the best available existing model of the traditional society," they professed to set it in contrast "with the giant industrialism, anti-traditional in all its features, that had possessed the North" and was making inroads into their own region. "In championing this South," wrote Davidson, "we were abandoning the defensive attitude of the nineteenth-century South" of Henry Grady "and the servile collaborationism of the modern Southern liberals. For the first time since Lee's invasion of Pennsylvania in 1863 we were taking the South into an offensive movement. We were attacking not retreating. But this time it was an intellectual offensive, executed at the highest level and in the broadest terms we could command."

No Gettysburgs, no Bloody Angles ensued, and the invaded could scarcely have been less aware of the invasion. But the invaders vicariously derived the thrills of conquest and vengeance from their crusade. In the words of Davidson, the most ardent crusader, theirs was "the cause of civilized [i.e., traditional] society, as we have known it in the Western world, against the new barbarism of science and technology controlled and directed by the modern power state." It was, in fact, a kind of counter-culture movement, and partook inwardly—though with none of the outward trappings—of some of the élan and some of the perversity of its more recent counterpart.

There were really very few active participants, and of the Twelve Southerners who took part in their major manifesto, *I'll Take My Stand*, in 1930, only five, Ransom, Tate, Davidson, Warren, and Andrew Nelson Lytle could be said to have figured in an important way in the literary Renaissance. Other prominent Southern writers of no connection with the Nashville group were no doubt influenced and excited by some of their ideas. The very posture of cultural defiance and independence, coming as it did on the heels of the Panic of 1929 and accompanying the deflation of industrial pretensions, suffused among many Southerners a new mood of release and autonomy from dominant national values. As Davidson wrote Tate in late October, 1929, "The terrific industrial 'crises' now occurring almost daily . . . give present point to all the line of thinking and argument we propose to do. . . . It all means more ammunition to us." There is some truth in the observation of Edward Weeks in the *Atlantic* that "it is the Depression which really marks the fountainhead of Southern genius. . . . No area of North or West could match that quality of competition."

I personally recall a visit to Vanderbilt in the early 1930's in the company of a small delegation of Chapel Hillians who had the temerity to accept a challenge to debate the Agrarians on their own turf. The visitors were clearly suspected of having emerged from the Trojan Horse. The verve, confidence, and spirited conviction of the Agrarians gave them an enormous advantage and an overpowering sense of purpose. It is quite probable that the values they invoked often found their way into work of serious literary character.

It is one thing to grant the excitement of a defensive movement voiced by a few eloquent and passionate men, some of whom were then or later became distinguished writers. It is quite another thing to say, as W. J. Cash did, that the defensive purpose was "the decisive factor" behind the Southern Renaissance, or that its literary treasures "represented basically the patriotic response . . . of the South to defend itself." What sort of Southern defense is *The Sound and the Fury* or *The Violent Bear It Away* or *Flowering Judas* or *Brother to Dragons?* What mad propagandist would perpetrate such works to defend any cause, just or unjust? For the language of defense or attack is the language of propaganda, however high a cause it serves. It finds no place in literature of the level that commands worldwide acclaim.

It is true, of course, that numerous works of Southern writers, particularly those in the best-seller lists, are clearly recognizable as pro-Southern or anti-Southern and are in some degree tracts of celebration or exposure. The latter typically choose as their subject matter the more degraded elements in the population. *Tobacco Road* and *God's Little Acre* come to mind as examples. It is not the subject matter that is significant, however. The same class of people is the subject of Faulkner's *As I Lay Dying* and O'Connor's *A Good Man Is Hard to Find.* The fact that Cash could equate Faulkner with Erskine Caldwell is a clue to his qualification as critic. The "pro-Southern' or celebratory novel often takes as its subject the tragedy of the Civil War and the fall of the planter régime. But one has only to think of *Gone With the Wind* in connection with *Absalom, Absalom!* to evaluate the "defense" thesis. Those who bring forward Tate's "Ode to the Confederate Dead" in support of the thesis had best give that poem another reading—a more careful one this time. Racial injustice in the South is the theme of numerous novels, and here, with apologies, I invite a comparison between a forgotten but onetime best-seller, *Strange Fruit,* on the one hand and *Light in August* on the other. I shall leave the defenders of "defense" to make what they can for their causal hypothesis out of such works as *Night Rider* or *World Enough and Time,* out of *Losing Battles* or "The Petrified Man," out of "The Artificial Nigger" or "The Bear," out of *Pale Horse, Pale Rider* or "A Rose for Emily."

Here I quote from an essay I first published in 1956. "The best of the Southern novelists have never set out to defend the values or the prejudices or the errors of any particular age or section. It is true that their books are often filled with tales of horror and lust and betrayal and degradation. But they have not paused to reckon their popularity in attacking the values of their own age or any other. They have not set up as defenders of a cause, either one lost or one still sought. They have proved themselves able to confront the chaos and irony of history with the admission that they can fit them into no neat pattern and explain them by no pat theory." I have found no reason to change these views over the years. None of these writers was a purveyor of what Warren once labeled "The Great Alibi"—and incidentally Warren never implied that they were.

Abandoning the defense thesis as hopeless, I turn next to one of wider currency and more acclaim. This is Allen Tate's "backward-glance" theory. "With the war of 1914–1918," he writes, "the South re-entered the world—but gave a backward glance as it stepped over the border: that backward glance gave us the Southern renaissance, a literature conscious of the past in the present." In an earlier essay he had said: "The Southern novelist has left his mark upon the age; but it is of the age. From the peculiar historical consciousness of the Southern writer has come good work of a special order; but the force of this consciousness is quite temporary. It has made possible the curious burst of intelligence that we get at a crossing of the ways, not unlike, on an infinitesimal scale, the outburst of poetic genius at the end of the sixteenth century when commercial England had already begun to crush feudal England. The Histories and Tragedies of Shakespeare record the death of the old régime, and *Doctor Faustus* gives up feudal order for world power."

Robert Penn Warren offers a similar theory by suggesting "a parallel between New England before the Civil War and the South after World War I to the present. The old notion of shock, a cultural shock, to a more or less closed and static society—you know, what happened on a bigger scale in the Italian Renaissance or Elizabethan England. After 1918 the modern industrial world, with its good and bad, hit the South; all sorts of ferments began. . . . There isn't much vital imagination, it seems to me, that doesn't come from this sort of shock, imbalance, need to 're-live,' redefine life."

There is a generous amplitude and an imaginative insight about these theories that inspires credibility. Of "the peculiar historical consciousness of the Southern writer" there can be no question. It is the hallmark of the regional genre. And scores of instances spring to mind that substantiate the characterization of "the Southern renaissance [as] a literature conscious of the past in the present." It is in the present or the recent past rather than in the Old Regime that the major Southern fiction writers have most often sought their subject matter. No matter how contemporary or recent the period they treat, however, the past is always a part of the present, shaping, haunting, duplicating, or reflecting it. The past is indeed an essential dimension of the present. Examples from the work of William Faulkner, Robert Penn Warren, Katherine Anne Porter, Eudora Welty, Andrew Lytle, Allen Tate, Thomas Wolfe, and Tennessee Williams provide ample illustration.

It is, indeed, difficult to imagine this body of literature without resort in some measure to the "backward-glance" or "crossroads" hypothesis. It was almost a necessary condition of the phenomenon. Without it there is no satisfactory accounting for powerful inner conflicts of these writers, the unrelenting tensions between what Warren once called "the Southerner's loyalties and pieties—real values, mind you" and "his religious and moral sense, equally real values." The "pieties"—blood kin, regional pride, manners, history—clashed with moral values of the present. It was the conflict between a traditional society and a modern one. The conflict necessitated a coming to terms with the past. The "crossroads" and the "backward-glance" are necessary conditions to what happened.

But "necessary conditions" are not historical explanations. The logicians properly insist on a distinction here. The conditions can exist without the event to which they are necessary occurring. After all, feudalism was overwhelmed by commercialism in many other countries without producing the Elizabethan literary phenomenon. And when we rely on the "crossroads" theory to explain the Southern Renaissance we have to admit that our "crossroads" are not as fixed in time or place as firmly as would be convenient to accounting for the suddenness and apparent co-ordination of this cultural happening. Or for that matter its continuation. Southerners had been encountering historic crossroads for quite a while before the 1920's. It is true that the major figures of the first generation of Renaissance writers were all born within a few years around the turn of the century. But that leaves a second and perhaps a third generation of writers missing the crossroads or facing different ones. Yet they manifested many of the characteristics and inner conflicts of the first generation. I am thinking here particularly of the generation of Flannery O'Connor and William Styron.

Perhaps the historian had best concentrate on "necessary conditions" and leave causation and explanation to non-historians, who are less hobbled by logic. Cleanth Brooks presents a promising list of what he calls "the elements in the life of the South which have an important bearing on its literature." Without asking his permission, I shall call them "necessary conditions." They are as follows: "(1) the concreteness of human relationships, including the concreteness of moral problems; (2) the conflict and tension which everywhere confront one in the Southern scene and which, because they are conflict and tension, make for drama; (3) the pervading sense of community; (4) the sense of religious wholeness—I dare say that the South is the last part of the country which still believes instinctively in the supernatural; (5) the belief that human nature is mysterious and relatively intractable, and that it is not a kind of social putty which can be shaped as the politician or the social scientist may be tempted to shape it; and (6) a sense of the tragic dimension of life." He adds that "If the South still believes in the 'American dream,' it is at least chastened in its belief, not naïve and uncritical." In his opinion these "elements" brought the South "closer to the older European tradition" than were any other parts of America.

Brooks admits that his six "elements" are only a few of many that might have been named, only a few of what I choose to call "necessary conditions." He would be the first to concede that his elements had been there a long time—waiting for a Renaissance to happen. They can, therefore, hardly qualify as "causes"—only conditions. It is one of the most important contributions the critic and literary historian can make to define, explore, and understand such necessary conditions. The task is endless, for there is no end to the conceivable number of them. But assuming the impossible and imagining that we did succeed in putting together a complete and accurate compilation of them, what then? I am afraid our task of finding the cause of it all would still be a failure, and like some modern Sisyphus we would be condemned to start all over again.

I suppose I am forced in the end to agree with Donald Davidson when, in seeking the explanation for just one aspect of the Renaissance, he wrote: "I do not think the literary historian can ever explain, by piecing together bits of fact and theorizing from cause to effect, just how this particular group of young men happened to become a group of poets in Nashville, Tennessee." He then promptly and rashly and inconsistently proceeds to "venture an hypothesis"—another hypothesis, which takes the form of a question: "Suppose that Ransom had been a Californian, Tate a native of Iowa, Warren of Kansas, Davidson of Maine," etcetera, etcetera. Of course, the obvious answer to Davidson's question is that thousands of young men of equally authentic Southern heritage gathered in those same years at scores of other Southern colleges—and nothing much happened.

Besides, we are left with an endless number of other questions, many of them yet unasked, which might be equally important. For example, why was it that of the major writers all over the South, as Warren has observed, "almost all of them of that period had some important experience outside the South, then returned there—some strange mixture of continuity and discontinuity in their experience—a jagged quality." And if we venture beyond the South, as we most certainly should in any thorough search for the causes of things, the mysteries thicken and multiply. What about that strange young man of Dublin, Paris, and

Trieste and how his influence happened to penetrate to Oxford, Mississippi, at a particular moment? And there are similar questions about the influence of an American exile from St. Louis who settled in London and of another American exile from Idaho who wound up in Rapallo.

12

History in
Robert Penn Warren's
Fiction

The occasion for this heretofore unpublished paper was a conference on Warren's work at Yale University in August 1987, in which four specialists in American literature from the Soviet Union and five American scholars participated. Mine was the only contribution by a historian, all the other participants, Soviet as well as American, being students or critics of literature. This explains in part my emphasis on historical aspects and my neglect of aspects treated by my colleagues with skills I do not command.

O NE OF THE APPEALS Robert Penn Warren has for historians is that it is he who has repeatedly taken the initiative, come forward to exchange views, and in his own work often addressed historical themes, problems, and theories and done so with sympathy, understanding, and originality. He has never written fictional history or what is commonly called "historical fiction," but both his fiction and poetry are permeated with sensitivity, respect, and awareness for historical dimensions of human experience. These are only a few of the reasons why Warren's name is among the first to come to mind in any discussion of the relations between American literature and American history.

Another reason for his special appeal for historians is undoubtedly the fact that he has often made historians prominent characters and even protagonists in his fiction. They are in and out of Warren's novels as graduate students, apprentices, amateurs, and as narrators employed to tell the story. Novels about novelists, poets, soldiers, heroes, and outlaws are common enough, but fictional historians are rather hard to come by. Yet in one of Warren's novels we read the dissertation of one and see him through his researches for two other historical investigations that prove to be turning points in his life and in the novel about him. I am thinking here, of course, of Jack Burden in *All the King's Men*. Is it any wonder that historians take special interest in a novelist who is capable of taking them and what they do so seriously? I suspect that pride of calling and something like vanity are involved here.

But for Warren, history is more than grist for the mill of his fiction. He insists that "I wouldn't think of sitting down and writing a piece of history. . . . I'm terribly interested in history, but writing it is not for me." He nevertheless speaks of himself as "ferociously restudying American history" and having "read a lot of history—for a nonprofessional I read a lot, anyway." He is keen on defining the differences between history and fiction, not merely the essential and obvious ones, but also the attitudinal and subtle ones. Both historian and novelist write of the past, the former a past that is provable, the latter one not provable, but both about a past that must be imagined before it can be written about at all. He continues:

> Now the big difference here between history and fiction is that the historian does not know his imagined world; he knows *about* it, and he must know all he can about it, because he wants to find the facts behind that world. But the fiction writer must claim to *know* the *inside* of his world for better or for worse. . . . Historians are concerned with the truth *about*,

with knowledge *about;* the fiction writer, with the knowledge *of.* . . . This is a fundamental difference, it seems to me.

Both are seeking the truth. "The rules are different, though, in this sense: the historian must prove points, document points, that the novelist doesn't have to document." Yet the novelist is conditioned by the "historically possible," and "tied to the facts of life."

I constantly encounter two types of historians: one type that makes outlines and one that does not. It has always seemed to me that the first type is engaging in an enterprise that is essentially unhistorical. For one thing he is writing about the future instead of the past and engaging in a species of prophecy, idle prophecy as I perversely see it. For another he is writing his conclusions, however speculative, before the evidence is in, blazing a path before he gets to the woods. The other type of historian, the one who proceeds without an outline, waits to read what he writes in order to find out what he thinks. I do not know whether novelists fall into those two categories or not, but I am interested to find Warren saying that "A writer doesn't know what his intentions are until he's done writing." He goes on to explain:

> If you look on a work as the writer's exploration of possibilities, then the question takes on a different complexion. A work represents a growth of meaning. You, the writer, are chiefly involved in finding, in growing toward a meaning, but you haven't got a fully organized intended meaning when you start off . . . not a specific intention. Intention is closer to result than to cause.

There are discriminating tastes of readers in the varieties of history as there are in kinds of literature. Taste governs preferences in subject as well as author and extends to choices in style, theme, mood, and purpose. Those historians will find Warren's fiction most congenial who share his tastes in history, and these tastes lean toward subjects and themes of complexity, ambivalence, paradox, and irony. Deterministic history, whether determined by divine will or dialectic forces, is not for him. We have his word for it that he early overcame a boyhood appetite for he-

roic simplicities and grand overall theories that explained everything. The boyhood addiction was for H. T. Buckle's *History of
Civilization*, but having become disenchanted with it by the age
of thirteen he retained an abiding skepticism of any theorist offering one key to history.

Warren's prototypical protagonist in fiction is John Brown,
a historical figure and the subject of his first book, which he
wrote while a graduate student at Yale. And it was this youthful
work in history, he tells us, that "led to fiction," that proved in
an unpremeditated and "instinctive way" to be in his writing career "a step toward fiction." In the vast corpus of that fiction are
to be found again and again characters of prominence who are
reminiscent in some degree of old John Brown. They are usually
idealists who intervene recklessly and self-destructively in events
of great complexity with results that are unanticipated and often
tragic or ironic or both.

Unlike much fashionable history and fiction that deal with
controversial figures, periods, or issues, however, Warren's work
never promotes a cause, illustrates a theory, vindicates a neglected
minority, or sets out to foster civic virtue. Nor does it champion
any cause that was lost or picture any past that was golden. It
teaches no burning lessons for the present contrived by imposing
modern values on the past. If the past he summons up sometimes
serves as a rebuke to the present, it is not a relevance achieved by
sly anachronism. The numerous periods he reconstructs are scrupulously faithful to historical evidence. Whatever is to be made
of Warren's dismissal of the importance of research for his fiction, it is clear that such exacting fidelity to archaic patterns of
manners, morals, idiom, dress, firearms, and theology is not based
on intuition or guesswork. A historian can recognize skilled craftsmanship when he sees it, whether in history or fiction.

A writer of national and international prominence, Robert
Penn Warren is nevertheless narrowly confined in subject matter and geographical range to provincial limits. These limits are
not so finite as William Faulkner's "postage stamp" of a Mississippi county (and Faulkner left that county far behind more
than once), but they are narrow enough, almost entirely South-

ern, and for the most part within the western section of Kentucky and Tennessee. It never entered his head, he told Ralph Ellison, that he "could write about anything except life in the South." To a remarkable extent the historic episode or event inspiring his works took place within a short distance of his birthplace, "around my home section" as he said of *World Enough and Time,* or "around my home, that part of Kentucky," as he said about events suggesting *The Cave,* and as he might have said about events in *Night Rider* and *Brother to Dragons.* Typically such events inspired a wealth of folklore and word-of-mouth legend that were part of the world of his youth. "I had no romantic notions about it," he told a British enquirer. "I was just naturally steeped in it and I knew that world. I also read a good deal of Southern history and was partly raised by a grandfather who was a great reader of history and talked it all the time." It was also that grandfather who kept alive for him memories of the Confederacy, the Civil War, and the years afterward.

The events that suggested (or shall we say are suggested by) Warren's work, in so far as they have such connections, stretch from the early nineteenth century to the mid-twentieth century. They all involve violence of some sort. In order of chronological occurrence they are events of 1811 associated with *Brother to Dragons,* the 1820s with *World Enough and Time,* the Civil War with *Wilderness,* Reconstruction with *Band of Angels,* the Indian war of 1877 in *Chief Joseph,* the early twentieth century with *Night Rider,* the 1920s and 30s with *At Heaven's Gate,* and *All the King's Men.* The other novels and some other poems can be placed in time, of course, but not associated with particular historic occurrences or figures.

We must sympathize with Warren's frustrating and continuous battle to keep readers from identifying fictional characters and events with historic characters and events. He has taken elaborate precaution in the writing of his books to prevent this, and the failure of these efforts partly explains his irritation with the label "historical novel." He willingly permits that description to be applied to *World Enough and Time* alone. The novel that has caused him greatest annoyance of the kind is *All the King's*

Men. Of that he has declared with some exaggeration that he had "no idea what [Huey] Long was really like" and would not have known how to put him in a novel if he had.

The parallels and similarities between historical prototype and fictional creation are nevertheless undeniable. The life and death, the career and tragedy of Huey Long unavoidably suggest the life, death, career, and tragedy of Willie Stark. That, however, by no means converts Warren's novel into fictional history with the names changed. The resemblances are external. New dimensions and meanings are given the facts by the introduction of Jack Burden, as Warren says, "to serve as a kind of commentator and *raisonneur* and chorus." More than that, Burden extracts from the story or speaks for the author in extracting, the meaning for Burden as well as for the reader. Using the spiderweb metaphor, Burden relates the past to the future and the present to the past and shows how past, present, and future are interrelated. He derives these truths from his three jobs of historical research, the history of Cass Mastern, the history of the Upright Judge, and the history of himself and Willie Stark.

We are familiar with Allen Tate's description of the Southern Renaissance as "a literature conscious of the past in the present," and his reference to "the peculiar historical consciousness of the Southern writer." Warren put this idea in personal terms. Speaking of the "relevance of history to my way of thinking or feeling," he told Richard B. Sale, "I don't think there's been much change. You know the habits, how things were in the South. If you lived, say, in my generation, you still live in two kinds of time. The elements of the past, the tale told. . . . The sense of the past and the sense of present are somehow intertwined constantly. This was a cultural factor in the South; the telling of tales was part of it." More than any other writer of his distinguished generation, it seems to me, Warren manifested in his work "the peculiar historical consciousness" that is said to be the hallmark of the Southern Renaissance.

The fact that, as Warren puts it, the past and the present "somehow intertwined constantly" for his generation may explain the trouble he had with the use of the term "historical" to characterize his novels. That plus the occurrence of some of the events during his own lifetime. "The first one was *Night Rider,* about the tobacco wars when I was a child," he told John Baker, "and I saw it, so I guess that's not historic. . . . It wasn't then you see. And also the novel about Nashville in the thirties, *At Heaven's Gate*—it wasn't history then. I was living there when I was twenty-five years old, and I was seeing these things happen. Then *All the King's Men* was not history. I never did a day's research in my life on those novels. They were coming out of the world I lived in, but not a historical one."

He is comfortable with the use of the adjective "historical," then, only when it applies to events before his own time and cannot be recorded without appreciable research. That definition will, of course, accommodate much of his work, notably *Brother to Dragons, World Enough and Time, Band of Angels,* and *Wilderness,* though the fact that the events of the first three took place in Kentucky and that the story that inspired one of them was "a very well known one in middle Kentucky, or was at one time" seems to temper the historical identification for him to some extent. There can be no denying evidence of serious and diligent historical research in support of all these latter works. Scrupulous attention to detail eliminates anachronism from his pages.

There remains to consider the deliberate anachronism, what James H. Justus (with the Coleridge poem in mind) calls the "Mariner theme." This is the interpolated narrative of a contemporary who in the three early novels is impelled to tell the story of his own crime and punishment of an earlier time or, in one instance, by the device of a memoir from an earlier generation. The interpolated confession serves as a subliminal or direct commentary on the experience of the protagonist. In *Night Rider* Willie Proudfit plays Mariner to protagonist Perce Munn; in *At Heaven's Gate* Ashby Wyndham is the guilt-ridden Mariner and, like Proudfit, an unlettered countryman. *In All the King's Men* Jack Burden, narrator and protagonist, becomes his own confessional

Mariner, a highly literate and sophisticated one, but Burden also interpolates the instructive confessions of an ancestor, the diary of Cass Mastern.

In these and subsequent novels Warren is experimenting with the narrative voice, and in so doing demonstrates the great variety of effects that different narrators have on the history being narrated, on substance as well as manner. Whether it is intended or not, the experiments amount to satirical comment on the historian's pose of objectivity and detachment. Jack Burden as narrator is a takeoff on the modern historian's posture of cynical skepticism. The narrator of *World Enough and Time* is presented as another history student, a modern one with different style and temperament, writing not as an autobiographer but as editor of the journal of the protagonist, Jeremiah Beaumont, and related materials. He puzzles in bafflement over the self-deceptions of Beaumont. Finally, in *Band of Angels,* the compulsive Mariner is again the protagonist. Amantha Starr reveals more to the reader than she understands herself, while from the interpolated narrator Hamish Bond, with whom she is paired, she appears to learn nothing at all, even though the reader does.

Creator of narrator and narrated alike, the author will not tip his hand, tell us whom we can trust, who shares our values, who speaks for the reader or the author. Like the true historian, he will share what evidence there is, assess its reliability, and on that basis tell what was said and done. But not who or what to believe or trust. In *World Enough and Time* he gives the anonymous historian-narrator the opening lines, addressed directly to the reader:

> I can show you what is left. After the pride, passion, agony, and bemused aspiration, what is left is in our hands. Here are the scraps of newspaper, more than a century old, splotched and yellowed and huddled together in a library. . . . Here are the diaries, the documents, and the letters yellow too, bound in neat bundles with tape so stiffened and tired that it parts almost at your touch. Here are the records of what happened in that courtroom, all the words taken down. Here is the manu-

script he himself wrote, day after day, as he waited in his cell, telling his story.

Our historian-narrator does not bow out after this intriguing prologue, but takes us by the hand and leads us all the way to the end as guide, interpreter, and indispensable intermediary between us and the baffling, self-contradictory protagonist Jeremiah Beaumont and his remote frontier Kentucky. Since he knows we must rely upon his judgment, skill, fairness, and integrity, the historian-narrator is at pains early on to establish his credentials, his *bona fides,* and win the confidence of the reader. Immediately after the opening paragraph describing the faded archival sources, the "what is left" of his story, he pronounces them "the lies and half-lies and the truths and half-truths," but not, he adds, "the Truth." He follows that flourish of reassuring skepticism with a statement about the protagonist that, "It was a drama he had prepared, an ambiguous drama," perhaps one that he "had to prepare in order to live at all, or in order, living, to be human." He goes on to say that, "The drama which Jeremiah Beaumont prepared was to be grand, with noble gestures and swelling periods, serious as blood," but that, "At times it was only a farce, though a bloody farce, which, with its comic parody of greatness, struck a desperate doubt into his soul." And toward the end, after a frustrated attempt at suicide by Beaumont and his beloved we have this:

> So after the fine speeches and the tragic stance, the grand exit was muffed. The actors trip on their ceremonial robes, even at the threshhold of greatness, and come tumbling down in a smashing prat-fall, amid hoots and howls from the house, and the house gets its money's worth.

So much for the pretensions of the protagonist's autobiographical account, and of his romantic baring of bosom. And so much for "the lies and half-lies, the truths and half-truths" of the faded archival documents. What then of the trustworthiness of the historian-narrator? Is he any more reliable? We are beguiled by his likening himself to "the scientist fumbling with a tooth and a thigh bone to reconstruct for a museum some great, stupid beast extinct with the ice age." We are reassured by the distance he maintains between himself and this "land of the fiddle and whisky, sweat and prayer, pride and depravity." We are tempted by his implicit invitation to join him on the peaks of twentieth-century rationality to survey the sad wreckage of nineteenth-century delusions and pretensions.

For all that, we gradually build up our own skepticism of the anonymous narrator's pretensions as well. And that, I believe, is the author's intention. Otherwise, why does the narrator protest so much? Do we not catch him patronizing his distraught subjects, often condescendingly? And what of the ambiguities of his detachment and sympathy? In numerous interpolations between quoted documents he seems eager to help out, to clarify the protagonist's meanings and justify his motives and claims. In the alternative passages of nineteenth-century romanticism and twentieth-century rationalism distinctions of style become blurred by the narrator. Is he not caught in the plight in which the guild historian, particularly the biographer, is often ensnared? Immersed so completely in the writings of his subject, every word of which is put down in vindication or defense, the author unwittingly becomes a participant in an adversarial brief. Occasional asides of impatience or outbursts of derision by the anonymous narrator do not entirely absolve him from suspicion.

Warren has said, in regard to the relationship between the modern historian and the historic figure who is his subject, that in *World Enough and Time* the relationship between historian-narrator and Jeremiah Beaumont is the same as that in *All the King's Men* between Jack Burden and Cass Mastern. The importance he attaches to the narrator in his fiction is indicated by his statement that this is the first and most crucial decision he makes about any novel he proposes to write: who is going to tell the story. Jack Burden, of course, has another story to tell—really three: not only that of Cass Mastern but that of Willie Stark and thirdly that of his relationship with Stark. And all three stories are about his own moral dilemmas and identity. In any case the novelist is once and sometimes twice removed from the story told.

The historian, unlike the novelist, is always the narrator. Historians have a great deal to learn from a craftsman so keenly conscious of the narrator's role and of the difference in the story a difference in narrators can make.

All this about the teller and the tale and about the interlocutor between the reader and what is read. What then about the setting, the place and time of the subject matter? Some would dismiss the question as of no real importance. Everything has to happen somewhere: Caesar's Rome, Hamlet's Elsinore, what does it matter? Who cares about the Rubicon and where it was crossed? Is the poet a gardener who cultivates a vegetable that grows only in one latitude? Certainly the author of *Hamlet* was all over the place—from ancient Athens, imperial Rome, and medieval Europe to Elizabethan London. Geography did not seem to matter much to him. It did, however, to the poet under discussion, though not as a limitation or handicap.

One of the most misguided suggestions ever ventured by a critic of Warren was that he is one of those Southerners "who wear the South about their necks like the albatross." And there is more about guilt-ridden poets who brood and worry about the sins and faults and failings of their unfortunate region and its heritage of wickedness. Such writers, we are told, are mired in an unchanging state of mind and must be made mindful that "fast transportation, mass production, and other such blessings" have rendered their morbid preoccupations outmoded. It is difficult to see how a faithful reader of Warren can find in his work any obsession with regional sins, any need for communal confession or expiation, or apology or penance. Individuals in the region commit sins, work evil, and are covered with guilt, and their offenses are committed in the South and not in Salem, Massachusetts. But that is another matter. A Southerner, Warren surely is, but not one governed or obsessed by that identity.

Although he has lived outside his native region for much the greater part of his life, Warren has repeatedly said that he has remained a Southern writer, that he could not well be anything else, and that the setting of all his novels is in the South. That does not pretend to say, however, that he has written about all parts or aspects of the vast region. No serious writer has attempted to do that. All write about the part they know best, usually their native part from which, as Warren put it, "your early images survive."

Warren's South is not Faulkner's black-belt, cotton culture, half-Negro, Mississippi deep South, and the demography of his fiction reflects that. His is not plantation country. There are no planter patriarchs in Warren's novels, no Compsons, Sartorises, or deSpains. The nearest he comes to an aristocratic ambiance is Judge Irwin of *All the King's Men* and he had to dip far down into Louisiana for him. Colonel Fort of *World Enough* is certainly of the gentry, but hardly to the manner born. Plain folk of the middling sort abound and rural intellectuals turn up regularly. Blacks are relatively more rare, and none so memorable as Faulkner's Dilsey, Clytie, Lucas Beauchamp, or Joe Christmas. The plainer of the plain white folk, including poor whites, command more attention and often more respect. He will not suffer slurs on their piety, their customs, or their accents. They can produce individual specimens as beastly as those produced by their social betters, but not beastliness as a mark of class.

Attachment to place, to region, to locality is not withdrawal or confinement for Warren, but rather the mining of an extraordinary concentration of riches in subject matter. It is with Warren as it was with Thomas Hardy, the prodigality of opportunity and variety at his doorstep rather than provinciality of interests that defined his subject matter. I like to compare the attractions the region has for the historian with those that appealed to the novelist and the poet. For historians the lure of the Dragon Country is definitely off-limits, along with the appeal of other legendary monsters and the furtive wisps that flit in and out of folklore. Apart from the forbidden territory of magic and myth, however, wide stretches of common ground exist.

Dark and bloody ground of Kentucky border country itself, for example, divided the state in an incestuous war between brothers. And more than that, the South of the founding fathers, the South of the frontier, the South of slavery and secession and civil war and defeat and military rule and reconstruction and poverty and racial oppression, the black South, the white South, the South of humiliation and submission, the South of siege mentality and defiance. For neither poet nor historian does any richer material exist, at least in the New World. And beyond that is the South's exemption from the claims of American exceptionalism. Its record of defeat, misfortune, and humiliation endows its past with a universality denied its more fortunate fellow countrymen. This is what opens the door of the South's history to comparability. Just recently, for example, appeared a book comparing Russian serfdom with American slavery. The similarities prove as fascinating as the differences.

I believe I know full well the risks of opprobrium I may incur from members of my own guild for posing this analogy, this invidious comparison, of history and literature. It revives the ancient rivalry of the two crafts over control of the past. It was Aristotle, I believe, who first weighed their rival claims and concluded that those of the poets, particularly the tragic poets, were superior and that the past was safer in their hands than in those of historians. Since then it has been the defensive strategy of historians to put distance between themselves and literary folk, particularly so since the novel was invented and later presumed outright to contest with history the control and interpretation of the past. Historians have never taken well to these presumptions, and in general I understand and share their resistance and insist on maintaining important differences and distinctions between history and fiction.

Some of Clio's servants go too far though, I believe, in holding that historical sense and poetic sense are contradictory if not antithetical. On this question I find welcome support for my position in a passage from the Foreword of *Brother to Dragons* that Warren retained in all essentials in his extensively revised edition of the poem twenty-six years later in 1979. "I am trying to write a poem, not a history," he says, but adds that "a poem dealing with history is no more at liberty to violate what the writer takes to be the spirit of history than it is at liberty to violate what he takes to be the nature of the human heart." And so, he continues, "I have tried in my poem to make, in a thematic way, historic sense along with whatever kind of sense it may otherwise be happy enough to make." And then the famous confirmatory sentence: "Historical sense and poetic sense should not, in the end, be contradictory, for if poetry is the little myth we make, history is the big myth we live, and in our living, constantly remake."

13

Fictional History
and Historical Fiction

*The following discussion of two genres of fiction and their ob-
ligations to history takes the form of an essay review of William Safire's novel about Lincoln and the Civil War entitled
Freedom.*

M UCH AS THEY MAY DEPLORE THE FACT, historians have no
monopoly on the past and no franchise as its privileged interpreters to the public. It may have been different once, but there
can no longer be any doubt about the relegation of the historian
to a back seat. Far surpassing works of history, as measured by
the size of their public and the influence they exert, are the
novel, works for the stage, the screen, and television. It is mainly
from these sources that millions who never open a history book
derive such conceptions, interpretations, convictions, or fantasies
as they have about the past. Whatever gives shape to popular
conceptions of the past is of concern to historians, and this surely
includes fiction.

Broadly speaking, two types of fiction deal with the past—

historical fiction and fictional history. The more common of the two is historical fiction, which places fictional characters and events in a more or less authentic historical background. Examples range from *War and Peace* to *Gone With the Wind*. Since all but a few novelists must place their fictional characters in some period, nearly all fiction can be thought of as in some degree historical. But the term is applied as a rule only to novels in which historical events figure prominently. Fictional history, on the other hand, portrays and focuses attention upon real historical figures and events, but with the license of the novelist to imagine and invent. It has yet to produce anything approaching Tolstoy's masterpiece. Some fictional history makes use of invented characters and events, and historical fiction at times mixes up fictional and nonfictional characters. As a result the two genres overlap sometimes, but not often enough to make the distinction unimportant.

Of the two, it is fictional history that is the greater source of mischief, for it is here that fabrication and fact, fiction and nonfiction, are most likely to be mixed and confused. Of course historians themselves sometimes mix fact with fancy, but it is a rare one who does it consciously or deliberately, and he knows very well that if discovered he stands convicted of betraying his calling. The writer of fictional history, on the other hand, does this as a matter of course, and with no compunction whatever. The production and consumption of fictional history appear to be growing of late. Part of the explanation for this is probably the fragmentation of history by professionals, their retreat into specializations, their abandonment of the narrative style, and with it the traditional patronage of lay readers. Fictional history has expanded to fill the gap thus created but has at the same time gone further to create a much larger readership than history books ever had.

Emboldened by their success, some writers of fictional history do not stop at justifying their license to mix fact with fiction but go on to blur or confuse important distinctions between the two. They can end by denying any significant difference at all between history and fiction. As the novelist E. L. Doctorow puts

it, "There is no fiction or non-fiction as we commonly understand
the distinction: there is only narrative." With that assumption he
asks, "Why should fiction writers be denied the composition of
history?" After all, the novelist does historical research too, even
though he must take care "not to know too much." Any danger
of that would seem precluded by his research method: "My idea
of research is idiosyncratic and accidental, to find something to
confirm your hunch, and not to look for it until you need it."
Such a method would comport well with a somewhat frenzied
manner of composition: "I just started to type," he relates about
writing *The Book of Daniel*, "very angry, full of despair, and
with an intense feeling of self-mockery. I started typing—whatever
it was, I didn't know."[1]

   To turn from Doctorow's work to Alex Haley's *Roots* is to
turn from history by "hunch" to history (or genealogy) by "feel."
His book, he says, is "a novelized amalgam of what I *know* took
place together with what my researching led me to plausibly *feel*
took place." Far from minimizing research, however, Haley emphasizes it—twelve years and half a million miles of it "in fifty-
odd libraries, archives, and other repositories on three continents."
A stunning commercial success, *Roots* sold more than a million
and a half copies the first year; a six-part TV adaptation attracted
a hundred million viewers and won an award as the season's best
show. A special Pulitzer prize was created to honor this combination of fact and fiction, for which its author suggested the ill-
conceived name "faction." Examined by historians and genealo-
gists later on, the factual pretensions of the "faction" collapsed
disastrously, the genealogical foundations totally.[2]

   One of the most prolific writers of fictional history now

---

[1] Doctorow is quoted in Bruce Weber's article "The Myth Maker," *The
New York Times Magazine* (October 20, 1985). On the blurring of fact and
fiction in contemporary letters more broadly see Cushing Strout, "Traveling
in Border Country: American History, Fiction, and Biography," *The Southern Review*, Vol. XXIII (April 1987), pp. 295–308.

[2] Alex Haley, *Roots* (Doubleday, 1976), pp. 565–584 for the quotations.
Also Richard N. Current, "Fiction As History: A Review Essay," *Journal of
Southern History*, Vol. LII (February 1986), pp. 82–85; and Elizabeth
Shown Mills and Gary B. Mills, "The Genealogist's Assessment of Alex
Haley's *Roots*," *National Genealogical Society Quarterly*, Vol. LXXVI
(March 1984), pp. 35–47.

practicing the art is Gore Vidal, who has so far published, in addition to fifteen other novels, five of an ongoing cycle about various periods of American history between the time of Thomas Jefferson and that of Harry Truman, all of them starting high in the best-seller lists. One, for instance, entitled *1876*, simplifies a complex contested presidential election. But whether representative or not, his *Lincoln: A Novel* (1984) will be considered here as an example of Vidal's brand of fictional history. The novel treats Lincoln during his presidency, with a few references to earlier years. The book profits from some acquaintance of the author with scholarly literature on the period as well as from his wit, imagination, and gift for story-telling. In an afterword Vidal says that he has invented some characters and events, but that "the principal characters really existed and they said and did pretty much what I have them saying and doing." Like Doctorow, he is persuaded that he surpasses historians (hagiographers, he calls them) in accurate portrayal of real figures, in this instance Abraham Lincoln. His book was extravagantly praised by both novelists and historians—a few of the latter at least.

Some of the foremost Lincoln scholars do not share these views. After listing numerous historical blunders and errors of the novel, Richard N. Current, a leading Lincoln biographer, declares that "Vidal is wrong on big as well as little matters. He grossly distorts Lincoln's character and role in history." Roy P. Basler, editor of *The Collected Works of Abraham Lincoln*, estimates that "more than half of the book could never have happened as told," and that another 25 percent consists of "episodes that might have happened, but never as told by Vidal." He concludes with something Lincoln once said about Stephen A. Douglas: "He has no right to mislead others, who have less access to history."[3]

---

[3] Richard N. Current, "Fiction as History," pp. 78–82; Roy P. Basler, "Lincoln and American Writers," *Papers of the Abraham Lincoln Association* (1985), Vol. VII, pp. 7–17; see also Gabor S. Boritt, "The Sandburg for Our Time? Gore Vidal's Lincoln," a paper read at the American Historical Association convention in December 1986. Vidal's extended rejoinder and my brief reply may be found in *The New York Review of Books*, April 23, 1988, under the title "Gore Vidal's Lincoln? an Exchange."

With these examples of recent fictional history in mind, it is only natural to approach the latest and most ambitious venture in this field with some misgivings. William Safire's *Freedom* bears on the jacket, though not the title page, the subtitle, *A Novel of Abraham Lincoln and the Civil War*. Its publisher announces a "National Six-figure Advertising, Promotion, and Publicity Campaign." The product is of dimensions proportional to the scale of promotion. Mr. Safire's novel is nearly twice the size of Mr. Vidal's bulky *Lincoln* and since it covers less than half the time span Vidal encompassed, it more nearly quadruples than doubles the proportions of the earlier novel. *Freedom,* in military chronology, runs from First Manassas (Bull Run) in July 1861 through Antietam in September 1862 and on through Murfreesboro at the end of the year. It ends with Lincoln signing the Emancipation Proclamation on January 1, 1863. The war is by that time not half over, and neither is Lincoln's presidency. A sequel to this volume is not announced, but one of equal or greater length would seem a natural expectation.

The issue of fact versus fiction is addressed by both the publisher and the author. Jacket copy, for which the author cannot be held responsible, calls it "a profoundly moving novel" as well as "a significant work of history" by "a historian with the singular insight of a novelist" who "uses fiction to reveal the truth." The author more modestly writes, "In general, the credibility quotient is this: if the scene deals with war or politics, it is fact; if it has to do with romance, it is fiction; if it is outrageously and obviously fictional, it is fact." Safire goes further and adds an "Underbook," 147 pages on "Sources and Commentary" and bibliography in which, he writes, "the author cites his sources, points out controversies that have aged and ripened for a century among historians, justifies his own judgments, and makes clear where reporting ends and imagination begins. The primary purpose here is to separate fact from fiction."

What with all this scholarly paraphernalia lying around, one occasionally forgets where one is and starts looking for an index that isn't there, or wishing the footnotes were at the bottom of the page "where they belong." Until, that is, one bumps into a bit of stage scenery and is forced to face up to the facts of fiction. At any rate, evidence exists that this time we are not in the hands of another unbridled poststructuralist bent on denying any difference between fact and fiction and demonstrating that the probing imagination never meets any resisting reality in exploring the past. Safire undoubtedly mixes up fiction with fact, but he acknowledges that there is some difference between them and that fictional history is not a tennis game without a net on a court without lines.

The Lincoln that takes shape in these pages grows with the demands history makes on him. He is not the hero Carl Sandburg drew for his credulous times, nor the crafty manipulator Vidal draws for his cynical times. Safire's Lincoln at least suggests the one scholars debate and often differ about. The novelist is aware of some of their controversies and how his own position relates to them. For example, in the notes at the back he acknowledges that he "tilts away from the historians' traditional tolerance for Lincoln's excesses," meaning the dictatorial power the President paradoxically used to deny freedom in the name of freedom. And yet he can quote Professor Don E. Fehrenbacher with approval as saying, "The transcendent humaneness of the man lent the Civil War much of its luster, but it was his inveterate toughness that helped determine the outcome." All that appears in the "Underbook," while up front in the novel a familiar figure lumbers through the "Mansion" (as it was then usually called) under near day-by-day scrutiny. He is a Lincoln racked by debilitating depression (which he called melancholia), agonizing over the daily choice of evils, and seeking relief in one of his that-reminds-me stories. He is by turns Saint Sebastian, Machiavelli, Pericles, and an oversize, countrified Puck.

While Lincoln is viewed primarily as a political animal—as is virtually every soul in the long cast of characters—he is endowed with other dimensions and more personal qualities than any other contemporary we meet in the book. Not merely chief executive, head of state, and commander in chief, he is writer, reader, political theorist, and round-the-clock philosopher. He is also (more dimly) husband, father, and bosom friend, who kept his counsel and set limits to intimacy. Mary Todd Lincoln is not given a leading role in the novel and is granted rather less sympathy than usual. She is seen most often through the disdainful eyes of her husband's young secretary, John Hay, who refers to her habitually as "the Hellcat." The death of her small son Willie paralyzes her with grief, puts her in mourning, drives her into the mercies of spiritualists, and keeps her out of sight most of the time.

The President's habitual companions and the novelist's leading characters are politicians, generals, and journalists—important ones. Almost everybody who was anybody in wartime Washington (and nobody who wasn't) is in the picture. Whatever fictions he invents about them, Safire's characters are real, not fictional. At least I never identified an invented one. The distinction quoted above that the author draws between "fact" if it's war or politics and "fiction" if it's romance is not very helpful. Reunited lovers go to bed talking presidental war powers, wake up thinking miiltary strategy, and report political dreams. The "romance" in these pages is of the kind that prompts the following reflection from old Francis Preston Blair, one of Lincoln's advisers:

> It never ceased to amaze him how the human element, especially in its sexual dimension, could stir politicians and affect the makeup of cabinets, the presidential succession—perhaps the fate of armies and the control of the conduct of wars.

Blair might have taken the words right out of Safire's mouth, so to speak. It is Safire who reports in detail the curious services rendered a prominent Union senator by "the most exciting woman in Washington," Rose Greenhow, the Confederate spy. Union detective Allan Pinkerton spied on the spy during the exercise from a bedside boudoir window and reported that he could not tell from the look on her face "how much was sexual and how much political." Here fact and fiction seem as confused as sex and politics.

Senators, cabinet members, generals, political dynasts, and pundits reflect in their conduct the course of military and political developments. Secretary of State William H. Seward changes from aggressive rival to valued ally of the President. Secretary of the Treasury Salmon P. Chase pursues his devious ambition to take Lincoln's place, and his glamorous daughter Kate cooperates by marrying the needed money. Senator Bluff Ben Wade earns his nickname and his radical credentials once again. The old sage Blair coaches his sons Montgomery and Frank, Jr., on the mysteries of power seeking and advises the President to pursue policies to those sons' advantage. And Edwin M. Stanton will capture the War Office "no matter what duplicity, . . . what hypocrisy, . . . what demeaning flattery or false promises were required."

Not all readers will agree with his rendering of these familiar stories, but Safire's versions are engagingly told. None more so or with closer attention to detail and complexity than the controversy between Lincoln and General George B. McClellan—and Stanton's part in it. The events that led to McClellan's being relieved of command of the Union armies are the very core of military politics in this part of the war. While wearing his other hat as historian, Safire (in his notes at the back) is dead right, I think, in saying that the important difference between the President and the general he fired was political rather than military: that the general's "real insubordination was in presuming to set national goals," which is a president's job, and that the President was wrong to "interfere in detail" with the fighting, which is a general's job.

The present-mindedness in the pundit-historian peeps out from behind the scenes when a blundering and jealous Congress is pictured trying to take over the President's job of running the war and foreign policy. When nobody is looking the novelist will borrow the pedagogue's hat and teach some history lessons. For example, he instructs us that the central idea of majority rule" was "the unshakable political religion of the land" in Lincoln's mind. That was a curious religion for a president elected by a minority of those voting in 1860, one who approved the secession of a minority of Virginians to form the new state of West Virginia while he was fighting a war to *prevent* a majority in eleven old states from achieving secession from the Union.

An experienced pedagogue could have warned him about awkward questions from unidentified students at the back of the room.

Mr. Safire is more cautious about the centrality of the idea of emancipation suggested by the title chosen for his book. No cynic about freedom as a war aim, he is no idealist either, and is better described as a realist. It would, in fact, be difficult to find a more astute political analysis of the purposes behind the Emancipation Proclamation than those he puts in the President's mind. It was among other things "using the issue of black freedom to subjugate white rebels." By one stroke the Great Emancipator saw himself creating a new source of Union manpower, reducing rebel manpower, planting terror behind enemy lines, reinvigorating war sentiment in the North, blocking foreign threats of intervention in the war, justifying "seizing more property than any despot in history," and, whether as afterthought or not, providing moral justification for the greatest blood-bath of the century. And incidentally freeing millions of human beings from bondage—eventually, piecemeal, and whether constitutionally or not.

Watching the novelist hover over Lincoln's shoulder calling shots of syntax, word choice, and sentence structure is like watching a skilled pro admire an intuitive artist at work. One is reminded that Safire once served as a president's speech writer himself. Here is the President revising a famous passage in a message to Congress in his head: "He added 'quiet' to the past and 'stormy' to the present" and substituted "dogmas" for "beliefs" to add negative connotations. Other aspects of Safire's career are suggested by features of the novel. One is the prominence, influence, and insight attributed to the press, including editors, owners, and reporters. For example, the New Yorkers, including Greeley of the *Tribune,* Bennett of the *World,* Raymond of the *Times.* Journalists are in and out of the President's office all the time and sometimes seem omniscient. They are also up on all the gossip. The most interesting and brilliant woman in the novel is Anna Ella Carroll of Maryland, a journalist, a military strategist, and a charmer. Safire wants to present a Washington insider's view of the Civil War and a view from the top down. The cast consists largely, in Anna Carroll's words, of those who know "whom to see and what could be done and how to ask for it." Most of the actions viewed take place within residences or streets on the four sides of Lafayette Square—including the Mansion across Pennsylvania Avenue.

We do get out on the battlefields occasionally, though usually with the reporters or Mathew Brady's photographers or in some general's tent. Two spectacular battlepieces, one on Shiloh and one on Antietam, each in all its appalling slaughter and horror, are persuasive evidence that the old reporter has more than desk-bound talents and interests. Of course the reporter's instinct that the big news comes out of headquarters' tent may account for it, but one does get the impression that this war was fought by generals rather than enlisted men and officers of junior rank. Johnny Reb and Billy Yank provide the casualties by hundreds of thousands, but they don't have much to say for themselves.

Another conspicuous omission is the other side. Occasionally we glimpse southern rebels, principally women spies and generals in the field. But only one Confederate, General John Breckinridge of Kentucky, is given the attention and space that dozens of Union figures receive. His is a very moving and appealing portrait indeed (and he is rewarded by being endowed by fiction with Anna Carroll as mistress), but as the novelist himself points out, "The Breckinridge family was on both sides, and so, in a sense," was the general. Other figures in gray are largely tagged with stereotypes. As if in caricature of his own prose the author refers in one passage to "the dashing Johnston, the fainthearted Beauregard, the bull-headed Bragg, the acquiescent Buckner, the reckless Morgan, the doubting Breckinridge." Jefferson Davis comes on briefly with some incredibly wooden lines. Lee, Longstreet, Jackson, and Forrest get short shrift, though Lee is still the marble man. It only remains to add that the novelist has a perfect right to treat only one side. This a book about Washington, not Richmond.

More doubtful is Safire's neglect of the large black presence and part in the Civil War. Elizabeth Keckley, Mrs. Lincoln's seamstress and White House companion, was a former slave, and some plausible scenes between her and the President are invented. We are also given a shocking glimpse of the whip-mangled back of a fugitive slave. One book of the nine into which the novel is divided is indeed entitled "The Negro," but it is largely concerned with other matters, with only four or five pages on blacks, and most of that is what whites said or did about them, not what they said and did themselves. As a whole they are granted fewer than twenty-five lines of their own to speak. None of their prominent leaders are introduced, and Frederick Douglass is not mentioned. Lincoln speaks his sad lines to a silent black delegation: "It is better for us both, therefore, to be separated." And that's about it. Nowhere does this huge book face up squarely to the impact of slavery and the complexities of race.

For a story stopped in midcourse, January 1, 1863, the author contrives a strong ending—or better, curtain, for it is more of a stage device. The scene is the annual New Year's Day reception at the Executive Mansion. The Lincoln family in the receiving line stands in the Blue Room and the callers file by, diplomatic corps and military in dress uniform and the rest in their Sunday best. All the cast present in the city at the time take a final bow, with appropriate words from the President for those who have played leading roles. Then the Great Emancipator goes upstairs with a numb right hand to massage and many reflections to ponder before squaring away to sign the proclamation.

Then what is there to quarrel with about this stupendous performance? Specialists can pick flaws in the history, as they regularly do in work of historians. There are some to be picked all right, but this is a novel, after all, and by a novelist who has taken the unprecedented pains (as far as I know) to back up his fiction with 147 pages of notes on sources. And that includes a long and well-chosen bibliography with which he demonstrates familiarity. Aren't the scholars playing hard to please? Putting aside minor slips, and assuming as many as a dozen bloopers in all, that would average out in a book this size to only one blooper

per hundred pages. Many historians do worse, and less is expected of novelists.

Is the book readable? Decidedly. But is it worth reading? That is a more difficult question. Much depends. Of the thousands who are expected to read it, many will find it entertaining enough to answer the question. It is a lot of book and entertainment for the price. Since it includes more than seventy-five photographs, most of them full page and many from Mathew Brady's camera, it could also answer for a Civil War picture book, a good one, too. The pictures form important parts of the documentation. As for historical reliability, many will pass that off with the reflection that one does not read fiction for historical facts but for how people felt and thought and experienced them.

That will not do for the more finicky and fastidious. With regard to his own study of the Civil War period, Edmund Wilson observed, "I don't know of any other historical crisis in which everybody was so articulate. . . . Their speeches and articles and diaries and letters and memoirs make most fiction about it seem pale; and a study of the literature of the period becomes more or less a history of what happened."[4] He is saying that with materials this rich, why invent new and imaginary ones, pale fictions? Why gild the lily? Safire himself can with authority cite Lincoln quoting Shakespeare's *Richard II*, Act III:

> *For God's sake, let us sit upon the ground*
> *And tell sad stories of the death of kings.*

And he can vary that by quoting (among many available) Abe's story about Frémont's grab for power: "Makes me think of the man whose horse kicked up and stuck his hoof through the stirrup. Man said to the horse, 'If you are going to get on, I will get off.'" With a protagonist and a cast ad-libbing lines like that, with everybody being so articulate, and with history providing a script that outdoes fiction for improbability, one can see why

[4] Edmund Wilson to Mamaine Koestler, December 5, 1953, in Elena Wilson, ed., *Edmund Wilson: Letters on Literature and Politics, 1912–1972* (Farrar, Straus and Giroux, 1977), p. 610.

Safire warns his reader that "if it is outrageously and obviously fictional, it is fact." If so, one might ask, why resort to fiction?

A large and thorough study entitled *The Unwritten War* by Daniel Aaron is devoted to the thesis that creative writers have never successfully risen to the challenge presented by the Civil War. He is able to cite impressive corroborative opinion going all the way back to Whitman's belief that "the real war will never get into the books" and William Dean Howells's view that the war "laid upon our literature a charge under which it has hitherto staggered very lamely." And on down to Robert Penn Warren, who writes of "the great single event of our history" that it was probably too "massively symbolic in its inexhaustible and sibylline significance" to be encompassed by fiction. At any rate, writes Aaron, "no Scott or Tolstoy appeared," and "the long anticipated 'epic' remained unwritten." He goes on to venture the opinion that, with the exception of a few "illuminating flashes" from poets and novelists, "in recent years, historians and biographers have more often come closer to 'the real sense' of the War than fiction writers, poets, and literary critics."[5]

In the face of this record of failure and skepticism and, I am sure, quite aware of it, Mr. Safire has nevertheless persisted with his enormous undertaking, spending, according to his publisher, "eight years in the research and writing." I cannot but admire such hardihood, even while sharing the skepticism I have expressed above and doubting the value of some of the devices of fictional history the author employs. For example, he invents many pages of diary for John Hay in order to provide inside views of Lincoln's actions and conversations and White House events. But then he will mix segments of Hay's real diary with the fictional diary and use the latter as evidence on controversial questions. Omniscience and mind reading are part of the novelist's license and are regularly used in writing of fictional characters

[5] Daniel Aaron, *The Unwritten War: American Writers and the Civil War* (Knopf, 1973), pp. xiv, xv, xvi, 129, 328–329; Robert Penn Warren, *The Legacy of the Civil War: Meditations on the Centennial* (Random House, 1961), pp. 80–81.

without special cause for wonder. But when the same license is used about real people, historical figures we know a great deal about, and whose impregnable secrets we have felt bound to respect, that is another matter. And here on the page facing their authentic full-page Brady photographs, they stand, stripped naked, their imagined secrets revealed. This constant juxtaposition and confusion of the real and the imagined gives the historian chills and fever, whether or not he shares the entertainment enjoyed by the laity.

I began by citing three unfortunate examples of fictional history that preceded Mr. Safire's experiment. I hope that by this time it has become clear that I am not placing him in their company except as a writer of fictional history. By way of compensation I offer a more attractive predecessor, though one whose example is not without an admonition of its own. This is Max Beerbohm, a novelist who also sought to become a servant of Clio, muse of history. In a chapter aside in the middle of his memorable novel *Zuleika Dobson,* first published in 1911, he pauses to tell how his petition to Clio was granted.

It seems that Clio had grown unhappy with her faithful servants, who thought of "nothing but politics and military operations" and produced "a mass of dry details which might as well be forgotten." For centuries she had "kept up a pretense of thinking history the greatest of all the arts" and "held her head high among her Sisters." But when novels came along she became addicted and spent all her spare time reading them. About this time Zeus took a shine to Clio and gave pursuit. Taking advantage of his infatuation, she begged a favor: "Zeus, father of gods and men, cloud-compeller," she began, and went on to ask him "to extend to the writers of history such privileges as are granted to novelists"—invisible presence at all events they describe and "power to see into the breasts of all persons" of whom they write. The slopes of Parnassus trembled with the wrath of Zeus over this absurd demand. But Clio smiled and Zeus was "induced to let her have her way *just once.*" Clio then picked Beerbohm to use this god-given once-for-all power to chronicle dire events she saw were about to take place in Oxford. It is thus that we have a novel by a writer whom G. B. Shaw aptly called "incomparable." But when Beerbohm sought to impose on her patience—and here's the admonition—Clio, he reports, "abused me in language less befitting a Muse than a fishwife."[6]

[6] Max Beerbohm, *The Illustrated Zuleika Dobson: Or an Oxford Love Story* (Yale University Press, 1985), pp. 178–186. The italics for the two words so printed are added.

14

Mary Chesnut in Search
of Her Genre

After the publication of my edition of her work, to which I gave the title Mary Chesnut's Civil War, *in 1981, and before the appearance in 1984 of* The Private Mary Chesnut: The Unpublished War Diaries, *I encountered a good deal of misapprehension about what the author was trying to do. Again, a central concern was the relation between fiction and history. In the following essay I tried to help the reader with this question as Mary Chesnut confronted and answered it.*

THE MOST ELEMENTARY and, I suppose, the most fundamental task of an editor is to discover, date, and authenticate the most reliable text of what he is editing and to bring that version to print as nearly as possible in the words and form the author intended. The task does not always turn out to be as simple as that sounds, as many editors have discovered. They may, in fact, in some cases find multiple versions of the text, each different from the other, yet all in the author's hand, and be confronted with complex and difficult choices and decisions.

That is the situation in which I found myself when I undertook to edit what was then known as the "diary" of Mary Chesnut. As any reader of Civil War history knows, this South Carolina woman was the author of the most often quoted personal record of the war experience from the Southern side. My purpose was to rescue a valuable work from what I knew to be the incompetence, unacknowledged abridgements, silent alterations, and misrepresentations it had suffered at the hands of previous editors. What gradually came to light in exploring the confusion of thousands and thousands of pages of manuscript, many of them unbound, was not one but four versions, two incomplete and the other two virtually complete, the third a rough draft of the fourth. Among them were the surviving parts of an original wartime diary, about a thousand pages of varying size. Sharing the instincts and biases of my guild, I first decided that this was my copy-text and that it was my duty to edit it and my obligation to inform Mary Chesnut's many readers that the text in which they had so long delighted was a garbled version of an afterthought of the 1880s.

I soon abandoned that plan for the time being for reasons I will explain. But I wish to add here parenthetically that, as a historian, I believe that a full and scholarly edition of the surviving parts of the original diary is needed and quite worth doing—and, in fact, I have one well along on the way toward publication.* Back to my reasons for abandoning or postponing that idea in the first place. For one thing, on comparing the first and last versions, I realized that by limiting my edition to the original diary I would be leaving the readers entirely dependent on the corrupt editions I wished to replace for the very part of Mary Chesnut's writings they cherished and rightfully demanded. For whatever values the hitherto-unpublished original diary possessed for the scholar—and I am prepared to defend them—it was not that but the expanded version of the 1880s written in the *form* of a diary that had established and justified her account as a pre-eminent classic of Civil War literature and won her thou-

* This was done in collaboration with Elisabeth Muhlenfeld and published as *The Private Mary Chesnut: The Unpublished Civil War Diaries* (New York, 1984).

sands of readers. If I used that version, however, I would be obliged to inform the readers they they had been misled by previous editors and that the book they had represented as a diary was actually written some twenty years after the war. As I remarked in the introduction to my edition, "It would be a regrettable and most ironic outcome of this effort to reveal the true nature of her work and provide an accurate text of what she wrote if it all resulted in lowering the esteem in which her work is held."

Light on these questions broke slowly during my years of growing acquaintance with a remarkable woman and a deepening understanding of her problems as a writer and of what she was trying to do. Mary Chesnut clearly realized that the four tragic years of the Civil War were the most profound experience of her life and the most poignant historical experience of her people— the death throes of a society. Alert from the start to the personal and historical significance the war might have, she felt the realization grow upon her that her own perception, experience, and understanding of the catastrophe were endowed with special, very unusual advantages. The possibility of giving some literary expression to the great experience of her life and that of her people seized her imagination. It would not let go, and she struggled with it for sixteen years before finding a solution. The question was into what form, what genre, should her work best fit: memoir, autobiography, fiction, chronicle, history? All these were possible for the purpose. If none of them would do, what other form might be used?

Her wartime diaries lay before her—many more of them available than now survive—as rich source material. And richer still a restless, tormenting memory teeming with more such material than there had been time or reason to record, or no more than briefly to mention. The idea of publishing the original diaries never occurred to her for reasons that seem fairly obvious. She kept them under lock and key. They were full of indiscretions, embarrassing confessions, self-exposures, and candid opinions of relatives, husband, friends, enemies, and allies. Then, too, they relied on hints and clues that had to be elaborated to be fully understood and they omitted so much that should be included. Themes had been left dangling, characterizations omitted or incomplete, potential metaphors unexploited. No, the diaries obviously would not do.

Yet one of her numerous experiments was an abortive attempt to *make* them answer her purposes, an extended effort she carried out in the mid-seventies, ten years after her last entry in the diaries. This venture took the form of a more or less simple revision of the original diaries, smoothing out, eliminating trivial, indiscreet, or irrelevant parts, rounding out incomplete or fragmentary notes, and filling in gaps. A comparison of surviving parts of this 1870s version, some 400 pages out of many lost, with her ultimate 1880s version indicates that the former fell far short of the latter. The words were faithful enough to the preceptions of her original diary, but they lay inert on the page and refused to bring to life her real experience. She gave it up.

She then returned to her experiments with fiction that she had put aside to try the journal revision. The first of these was a war novel she called "The Captain and the Colonel." Her first effort to exploit the material in her wartime journals, it contains recognizable characters and episodes from them. Unmistakably fiction, it is a serious, ambitious, and quite unsuccessful novel. Its drafts and revisions, however, are interesting evidence of a writer seeking to establish a narrative voice, shape her style, master dialogue, and come to terms with her subject matter. As Elisabeth Muhlenfeld, the closest student of the fiction, suggests, Chesnut must have realized that "the novel was simply not nearly so interesting as the material on which it was based—the Civil War journals themselves." It was probably that realization that inspired her abortive and unsuccessful revision of the journals just described.

After abandoning the latter effort in 1876 she went back to revise another novel in progress that she called "Two Years—or The Way We Lived Then," a title inspired by Trollope's *The Way We Live Now*. It is clearly autobiographical fiction, written in the first person with fictional names and incidents paralleling events in the author's early adventures on the Mississippi frontier. Like its predecessor, it was a failure, but it was also filled with instructive writing experience that proved to be of value later. If this novel is a fair test, Chesnut lacked the genuine autobiographical impulse and was more interested in re-creating the life of the past and portraying her part in it. She wisely abandoned the fictional solution after another try at a war novel she called "Manassas."

In none of these experiments did Mary Chesnut find what she was looking for. The answer seemed to be hidden in the old wartime journals, but literal transcription or smoothing them up did not give her the range and freedom she needed. Autobiography, whether fictional or otherwise, led her away from her vital interest, which was not her inner self but herself as witness, and narrator, of historical and social drama and tragedy. She proved impatient with the fictional conventions of her time—contrived incidents, elaborate plot, the story line—and never mastered them. Instead she rebelled against them. Besides, the drama of real life, the historical and social drama in which she had been both actor and witness, was so much more gripping. As she later wrote about her reactions at the time of the battle for Richmond:

> Now, for the first time in my life, no book can interest me. But life is so real, so utterly earnest—fiction is so flat, comparatively. Nothing, but what is going on in this distracted world of ours, can arrest my attention for ten minutes at a time.

Mary Chesnut combined among her literary impulses and needs those of both the creative writer and the historian, with components characteristic of the novelist, the journalist, the memorialist, and to some extent the autobiographer, the social satirist, and the literary critic—especially at the juncture where literary tradition intersects with real life and shapes the memory and conception of experience. Her controlling impulse, however, was to write about real flesh-and-blood people caught in the turmoil and anguish of a great historical crisis and about herself as participant. She never forgot that she had seen "a world kicked to pieces." She required a form none of the above genres could adequately supply. Such a form would have to permit her to be both witness and narrator, to speak in her own colloquial, witty, and ironic style, and yet to convey the authority of first-hand experience. It would have to enable her to be analytical and opinionated in a way fiction would not. It would have to allow much flexibility to accommodate the sporadic character of personal and random experience and yet permit subtle characterization, full play to her genius for metaphor, and ample opportunity to embody the tide of historic drama as it mounted from the giddy mood of Fort Sumter to the anguish of Appomattox and overwhelmed her society in tragedy.

She eventually discovered her long-sought genre where she had started, in the old wartime diaries. She may have been influenced to a limited extent by the example of the English author, William Howard Russell, whose books, *My Diary in India in the Year 1858–1859* (1860) and *My Diary North and South* (1863), had employed the diary form to report his experience of two wars. Chesnut read Russell and quoted him in her book. But her own use of the same genre was far more ingenious, evocative, metaphorical, and sophisticated in realizing what Edmund Wilson has called "the literary possibilities" of her material. So innovative was her employment of the genre that she could more accurately be said to have invented than to have imitated it.

Critics do not normally attack writers for the genre they choose—whether it be autobiography as fiction, fiction as memoir, memoir as satire, social criticism as autobiography, or what not. (Henry Adams tried nearly all of them.) Rather the critic asks how effectively and successfully the writer uses the genre chosen for the purpose at hand. So it has been with the reception of Mary Chesnut's work, and among the more reputable, informed, and able critics whose opinions command respect the verdict has been virtually unanimous. They have pronounced it "a masterpiece," "a work of art," "a classic," and have suggested that it more fully realized the literary possibilities of the subject than most Civil War fiction. It is true that this opinion was uninformed about the origins and character of her work, though that was suspected by some. But the verdict has not been appreciably altered among our best qualified critics by full revelation of those circumstances. Henry Nash Smith, fully informed by the recent edition, pronounced it a "magnificent book" and went on to call it the making of "a kind of Southern *Charterhouse of Parma*," and to say that "Mary Chesnut might almost have been conceived by the same imagination that created the Duchess of Sanseverina: she had some of the Duchess's insight and spirit."

Of course the verdict has not been entirely unanimous. A few critics, fortunately very few, have reacted with a curious tone of outrage, betrayal, and indignation. Swept away by these emotions, they have gone so far as to apply to the book such terms as "hoax," "fake," "fraud," "disgraceful," "dishonest," "duplicitous," and pronounce it "one of the most audacious frauds in the history of American literature." When the book was awarded the Pulitzer Prize for history in 1982, one commentator went so far as to suggest a comparison with the prize for journalism awarded the year before to the Washington reporter who was later exposed as having made up the prize-winning story out of whole cloth. These charges, it would seem, are leveled not at scholarship or literary merit, but at morals. The perpetuation of fraud and deception are moral offenses. The criticisms are not only highly moralistic but *ad hominem,* and not only *ad hominem* but *ad feminam,* for they impute moral turpitude not only to the editor but to the author as well.

I might add in passing that these imputations have not caused the editor a moment's doubt about the editorial decisions under attack or about his estimate of the work he edited. He is supported in these opinions by better authority than that of the moralists. And I am pleased to report that the moral attack seems to have had no significant effect on the reception of the book save possibly to attract attention to this publication. (The cry of hoax not only gains the desired attention for the reviewer, but, incidentally, for the reviewed.) As for the suggestions that the editor conspired with the author to cover up discrepancies or contradictions between what she wrote in the sixties and what she wrote in the eighties, the evidence can be explored fully at their leisure by the censorious or the curious as soon as our edition of the 1860s journals is published. I shall happily abide with the results. And as for several unfortunate misrepresentations by the censorious, I prefer to assume that they are the consequences of fervor and not of malice.

The moral indictment of Mary Chesnut, however, is quite overt. She stands accused of deliberately deceiving the public about the true character of her book, of misrepresenting as a diary what she wrote much later in diary form. It is perfectly true, of course, that having adopted a form, she adhered faithfully to its conventions and demands. But so did her numerous contemporaries who wrote fiction in the form of memoirs, or memoirs or satire or jeremiads in the form of letters or diaries. Those were the rules of the game. Chesnut did depart from the rules once in her treatment of a period of some fifteen months in 1862–1863, during which she tells us she destroyed her wartime journals and would "fill up the gap from memory." After this interlude in memoir form, which takes up fifty-nine pages in my recent edition, she returns to the diary genre. By way of comparison, it took her 233 pages to cover one period half that long for which we have her original journals.

How she might have presented her book to the reader in a preface we will never know, for she did not write one. She had been dead nearly twenty years when the first appalling edition was published and she certainly had no hand in writing its preface or in chosing the trivializing and deceptive title, *Diary From Dixie*. Deceit of the kind imputed is not consistent with what we know of her. She lived and wrote in a goldfish bowl, told her friends what she was writing, and preserved ample evidence of its origins. Whatever her intentions, any responsible editor would have set the reader straight right off about the true nature of her book. My guess is that the outrage and indignation of the critics stems more from the irresponsible conduct of the earlier editors than from the alleged perfidy of Mary Chesnut or her latest editor. The outraged critics felt they had been taken in, betrayed. And in a measure they had—though not by the author.

The indignation of the moralists need detain us no longer and would not have detained us at all had they not, quite unintentionally, served to introduce questions of more significance.

These are questions regarding the nautre of diaries, the historians' expectations of them, the distinctions we draw between diaries and memoirs, the classification of the one as primary and the other as secondary sources, the reliance upon memory as a source of history, and the ambiguities of memory itself. These are more and larger questions than can be handled here, and we can only consider them in part.

The special significance the historian attaches to the diary lies in its contemporaneity with events recorded. It is assumed to deny the diarist knowledge of the future, to preclude hindsight, and to minimize the clouding of memory by the passage of time. These characteristics set the diary apart from other types of personal records, including memoirs. It is an important distinction, and I have no intention of abandoning it. It is only natural, however, to wonder how many diaries actually measure up to the abstract concept. Diarists' own diaries are often their favorite reading, and as they pore over them later, sometimes years later, they may often be tempted to delete, correct, supplement, smooth out, bring up to date, revise. In editing Chesnut's wartime diary, for example, we have been at pains to recover many erasures, delete afterthoughts, and weed out the work of helping hands of later date. It often happens that the nightly session with the diary has to be postponed, sometimes for weeks—in the instance of Boswell, for months—and reconstructed later when there is time. In such experiences, which I believe are not uncommon, opportunities for the introduction of hindsight are not lacking. And if the diary is published, industrious editors and publishers get involved, not all of them as scrupulous about hindsight and revision as they might be.

Fresh and instant memory is another standard virtue of diaries that is weakened and diminished in such circumstances. But even the most dedicated diarist, who never misses the nightly vigil, no matter how small the hour and how weak the flesh, is still dependent on memory. And everything that is filtered through the human memory is transformed in some degree. Thomas Hobbes may have put it too strongly in *Leviathan* when he wrote that *"Imagination* and *Memory,* are but one thing, which for divers considerations hath divers names." But he had a point. And the point calls in question the sharp distinction historians have conventionally drawn between primary and secondary sources when classifying diaries and other writings on personal experience. For all that, I believe historians are right in their special sensitivity about the integrity of diaries, their authors, and their editors. That sensitivity may help account for strong feelings upon the disclosure that what they had always assumed to be one thing was in reality another.

Does the revelation of the true nature of the Chesnut book, then, undermine its integrity or relegate it to some inconsequential category of entertainment literature? It can certainly no longer be regarded as a diary. But would that be to assume that the authentic diary is the only legitimate and worthwhile way in which personal perception of historic events can find expression? Of course the worth and utility of memoirs are acknowledged by the copious use historians have made of them, hundreds of them—hindsight and time lapse notwithstanding. Chesnut's book has been classified as memoir, but I do not think it fits that category much better than that of diary. It has also been called an autobiography—"one of the best in American letters," according to one historian—but that classification seems misleading too. And in spite of the history award it won, I confess doubts about the appropriateness of the category assigned by the citation. The book has some characteristics of all these genres, but does not fit convincingly into any one of them. It is both less and more than any of them and different from them all.

While the genre she chose as a solution to her problem may be unique, the problems she faced in her search are certainly not. In *The Great War and Modern Memory* (1975), Paul Fussell has addressed such problems as they were faced by "writers who have most effectively memorialized the Great War as a historical experience." In it he has also attempted "understanding something of the simultaneous and reciprocal process by which life feeds materials to literature while literature returns the favor by conferring forms upon life." In seeking to express the deeper meaning of their experience of the First World War, British writers found the daily diaries they kept inadequate and turned to memoir. "The significancies belonging to fiction," writes Fussell, "are attainable only as 'diary' or annals move toward memoir, for it is only the ex post facto view of an action that generates coherence and makes irony possible." Mary Chesnut did not turn to memoir, but neither did she abandon the diary *form* or its conventions. Instead she sought by her adaptation of the form to combine historical with figurative and fictional truth and thus to generate the coherence and irony she sought. She does not claim, or make, a distinction between a world of historical fact and one of figurative or fictional truth. Chesnut sought rather to make the two coincide and illuminate the great experience she tried to express.

Mary Chesnut's Civil War must be understood as a creative work that uses personal experiences, real people, and actual events instead of invented or fictional material. If anything, the author is more careful about historical accuracy than she was in her diary. But history is not what she is about, nor is historical fact what we seek from her. She uses historical events, memory, her old diary, and other documents to re-create and breathe life and reality into past experience, to evoke the crisis and chaos and agony of people at war. She recaptures memory by the use of sensory vignettes, disparate images, snatches of conversation, chance encounters, whispered confessions, secret military intelligence, telegrams, and letters—a palimpsest, a montage of disparate scraps of realities and mentalities.

Conscious art enters into the apparent confusion, and deliberate metaphor emerges subtly but powerfully between the lines. These devices that were developed in her experiments in fiction reflect the narrative persona she had established, with its colloquial and ironic pitch. But the new genre permits freedoms that are precluded by fiction—for example, the free expression of her personal anger, dismay, delight, excitement, grief, disgust, revulsion. The diary form required her to speak in the temper and mood of an earlier era, the time of the war itself, and thus exempted her from the post-Confederate pieties, nostalgias, and sentimentalities that cloyed much Southern writing about the war published in the eighties. Her writing stands in marked contrast to that of her contemporaries since it remains remarkably faithful to her wartime perceptions. Through them ran powerful themes of skepticism, irony, scorn, exasperation, pessimism, and doom. They were moods of a time before the Confederate myths were constructed and before the "Old South" was invented. Had she adopted history as her genre, the conventions of the craft in her day would not have encouraged the amount of attention she gave to slaves, free blacks, poor whites, overseers, and yeomen, or for that matter to the cruelties, insensitivities, and hypocrisies of slave masters, and the wretched plight of Southern white and black women under the patriarchal order.

It is difficult to see, after all the alternatives are considered, what other genre might have answered her purpose so well as the one she eventually chose. None of the others could have given her the latitude she required—the range of subjects, the episodic license, the witness's authority, the occasion to use an anachronistic voice, tone, mood of a bygone era, the freedom to employ to the fullest her ample endowments of intelligence, wit, learning, keen perception, and detachment, all combined with privileged position—to give literary expression to the great experience of her life. What writer would under these circumstances deny her the choice of genre she made? Could such denial possibly be justified on the ground that there is no precise precedent for this use of the diary form? That would be to set rather arbitrary limits to literary innovation. And what would Joyce or Conrad or Chaucer have said to that? And what do historians have to say about a denial on the ground of some alleged sacredness of the diary form, once it is plain that it is a chosen genre and not a bungled deception?

Paul Fussell's *The Great War and Modern Memory* focuses on the point "where literary tradition and real life notably transect." Commenting on Robert Graves's *Goodbye to All That* (1929), Fussell writes: "Its brilliance and compelling energy reside in its structural invention and in its perpetual resourcefulness in imposing patterns of farce and comedy onto the blank horrors or meaningless vacancies of experiences. If it really were a documentary transcription of the actual, it would be worth very little, and would surely not be, as it is, infinitely readable." I think Robert Graves would have understood what Mary Chesnut was doing about an earlier war.

V

BEHIND
THE MYTHS

While a major concern of historians is to keep myth
from replacing history and to purge the past of myth, they would
have to admit that myths are an inevitable component of their
regular subject matter. Myths are right there along with facts,
working to determine and explain human behavior and the
course of events. It would be stupid to ignore or underestimate
them. Not all myths are associated with defeated or discredited
causes and their defense. In fact the most hardy, secure, and
numerous myths are the product of victories and vindicated
causes and embody live and cherished values. Myths of the latter
type have sometimes taken the place of history, as pointed out in
the first of the following essays. The second is admittedly a ten-
dentious exercise done to demonstrate obliquely that virtue and
public morals have not been entirely a regional monopoly. And
the third deals with historians themselves as creators and critics
of mythic historical understanding.

15

The Antislavery Myth

SLAVERY AND THE CIVIL WAR were prolific breeders of myth, and their fertility would seem to wax rather than wane with the passage of time. Neither the proslavery myths of the South nor the antislavery myths of the North ceased to grow after the abolition of the Peculiar Institution. In fact they took on new life, struck new roots and flourished more luxuriantly than ever. Both myths continually found new sources of nourishment in the changing psychological needs and regional policies of North and South. The South used the proslavery myth to salve its wounds, lighten its burden of guilt and, most of all, to rationalize and defend the system of caste and segregation that was developed in place of the old order. The North, as we shall see, had deeply felt needs of its own to be served by an antislavery myth, needs that were sufficient at all times to keep the legend vital and growing to meet altered demands.

In late years the proslavery myth and the plantation legend have been subjected to heavy critical erosion from historians, sociologists, and psychologists. So damaging has this attack been that little more is heard of the famous school for civilizing savages, peopled with happy slaves and benevolent masters. Shreds and pieces of the myth are still invoked as props to the crumbling defenses of segregation, but conviction has drained out of it, and it has been all but relegated to the limbo of dead or obsolescent myths.

Nothing like this can be said of the antislavery myth. Its potency is attested by a steady flow of historical works by journalists and reputable scholars. It is obvious that the myth can still dim the eye and quicken the pulse as well as warp the critical judgment. Apart from the fact that it is a creation of the victor rather than the vanquished, there are other reasons for the undiminished vitality of the antislavery myth. One is that it has not been subjected to as much critical study as has the proslavery myth.

Before turning to evidence of the exuberant vitality of the antislavery myth, however, it is interesting to note two penetrating critical studies of some of its components. Larry Gara, in *The Liberty Line: The Legend of the Underground Railroad*,[1] addresses himself to a limited but substantial element of the myth. No aspect of the myth has so deeply engaged the American imagination and entrenched itself in the national heritage as the underground railroad, and no aspect so well reflects what we fondly believe to be the more generous impulses of national character. It is a relief to report that Mr. Gara is a temperate scholar and has avoided handling his subject with unnecessary rudeness. By the time he finishes patiently peeling away the layers of fantasy and romance, however, the factual substance is painfully reduced and the legend is revealed as melodrama. Following the assumptions that the better critics of the proslavery legend make about the slave, he assumes that "abolitionists, after all, were human," and that the "actual men and women of the abolition movement, like the slaves themselves, are far too complex to fit into a melodrama."

One very human thing the authors of the melodrama did was to seize the spotlight. They elected themselves the heroes. It was not that the abolitionists attempted to stage *Othello* without the princely Moor, but they did relegate the Moor to a subordinate role. The role assigned him was largely passive—that of the

[1] Lexington, Ky., 1961.

trembling, helpless fugitive completely dependent on his noble benefactors. The abolitionist was clearly the hero, and as Gerrit Smith, one of them, put it, the thing was brought off by the "Abolitionists and the Abolitionists only." As Mr. Gara points out, however, it took a brave, resourceful and rebellious slave to make good an escape, not one temperamentally adapted to subordinate roles—no Uncle Tom, as abolitionists often discovered. Moreover, by the time he reached the helping hands of the underground railroad conductors—if he ever did in fact—he had already completed the most perilous part of his journey, the southern part.

Another important actor in the drama of rescue who was crowded offstage by the abolitionists was the free Negro. According to the antislavery leader James G. Birney, the assistance of the fugitives was "almost uniformly managed by the colored people. I know nothing of them generally till they are past." The fugitive slaves had good reason to mistrust any white man, and in the opinion of Mr. Gara the majority of those who completed their flight to freedom did so without a ride on the legendary U.G.R.R.

Still another human failing of the legend-makers was exaggeration, and in this the abolitionists were ably assisted by their adversaries, the slaveholders, who no more understated their pecuniary losses than the abolitionists underestimated their heroic exploits. Under analysis the "flood" of fugitives diminishes to a trickle. As few as were the manumissions, they were double the number of fugitives in 1860 according to Mr. Gara, and by far the greater number of fugitives never got out of the slave states. Another and even more fascinating distortion is the legend of conspiracy and secrecy associated with the U.G.R.R. The obvious fact was that the rescue of fugitive slaves was the best possible propaganda for the antislavery cause. We are mildly admonished that the U.G.R.R. was "not the well-organized and mysterious institution of the legend." "Far from being secret," we are told, "it was copiously and persistently publicized, and there is little valid evidence for the existence of a widespread underground conspiracy."

But there remains the haunting appeal and enchantment of the secret stations, the disguised "conductors," and the whole "underground" and conspiratorial aspect of the legend that is so hard to give up. "Stories are still repeated," patiently explains Mr. Gara, "about underground tunnels, mysterious signal lights in colored windows, peculiarly placed rows of colored bricks in houses or chimneys to identify the station, and secret rooms for hiding fugitives." These stories he finds to be without basis in fact. While we must continue to bear with our Midwestern friends and their family traditions, we are advised that, "Hearsay, rumor, and persistent stories handed down orally from generation to generation are not proof of anything."

The most valuable contribution this study makes is the revelation of how the legend grew. It was largely a postwar creation, and it sprang from a laudable impulse to be identified with noble deeds. Family pride, local pride and regional pride were fed by abolitionist reminiscences and floods of memoirs and stories. "Every barn that ever housed a fugitive, and some that hadn't," remarks Mr. Gara, "were listed as underground railroad depots." There were thousands of contributors to the legend, but the greatest was Professor Wilbur H. Siebert, whose first book, *The Underground Railroad from Slavery to Freedom,* appeared in 1898. In the nineties he painstakingly questioned hundreds of surviving antislavery workers, whose letters and responses to questionnaires Mr. Gara has reexamined. Mr. Siebert accepted their statements at face value "on the ground that the memories of the aged were more accurate than those of young people." The picture that emerged in his big book was that of "a vast network of secret routes," connecting hundreds of underground stations, operated by 3,200 "conductors"—the very minimum figure, he insisted. The work fathered many subsequent ones, which borrowed generously from it. There has been no lag in legend-building since. "The greater the distance," observes Mr. Gara, "the more enchantment seems to adhere to all aspects of the underground railroad, the legend that grew up around it, and its role in America's heritage."

A second and more elaborate aspect of the antislavery myth

is the legend that the Mason and Dixon Line not only divided slavery from freedom in antebellum America, but that it also set apart racial inhumanity in the South from benevolence, liberality and tolerance in the North. Like the Underground Railroad Legend, the North Star Legend (for lack of another name) was a postwar creation. Looking back through a haze of passing years that obscured historical realities, the myth-makers credited the North with the realization in its own society of all the war aims for which it fought (or eventually proclaimed): not only Union and Freedom, but Equality as well. True, the North did not win the third war aim (or if it did, quickly forfeited it), but it nevertheless practiced what it preached, even if it failed to get the South to practice it, and had been practicing it in exemplary fashion for some time.

For a searching examination of the North Star Legend we are indebted to Leon F. Litwack, *North of Slavery: The Negro in the Free States, 1790–1860*.[2] He starts with the assumption that, "The inherent cruelty and violence of southern slavery requires no further demonstration, but this does not prove northern humanity." On racial attitudes of the two regions he quotes with approval the observation of Tocqueville in 1831: "The prejudice of race appears to be stronger in the states that have abolished slavery than in those where it still exists." White supremacy was a national, not a regional credo, and politicians of the Democratic, the Whig and the Republican parties openly and repeatedly expressed their allegiance to the doctrine. To do otherwise was to risk political suicide. "We, the Republican party, are the white man's party," declared Senator Lyman Trumbull of Illinois. And, as Mr. Litwack observes, "Abraham Lincoln, in his vigorous support of both white supremacy and denial of equal rights for Negroes, simply gave expression to almost universal American convictions." These convictions were to be found among Free Soil adherents and were not unknown among antislavery and abolitionist people themselves.

One reason for the unrestrained expression of racial preju-

[2] Chicago, 1961.

dice from politicians was that the Negro was almost entirely disfranchised in the North and was therefore politically helpless. Far from sharing the expansion of political democracy, the Negro often suffered disfranchisement as a consequence of white manhood suffrage. By 1840 about 93 percent of the free Negroes in the North were living in states that excluded them from the polls. By 1860 only 6 percent of the Northern Negro population lived in the five states that provided legally for their suffrage. In only three states were they allowed complete parity with whites in voting. Even in those New England states doubts lingered concerning the practical exercise of equal political rights. As late as 1869, the year before the ratification of the 15th Amendment, New York State voted against equal suffrage rights for Negroes. Four Western states legally excluded free Negroes from entry.

In Northern courtrooms as at Northern polls racial discrimination prevailed. Five states prohibited Negro testimony when a white man was a party to a case, and Oregon prohibited Negroes from holding real estate, making contracts or maintaining lawsuits. Only in Massachusetts were Negroes admitted as jurors, and that not until the eve of the Civil War. The absence of Negro judges, jurors, witnesses and lawyers helps to explain the heavily disproportionate number of Negroes in Northern prisons.

Custom, extralegal codes and sometimes mob law served to relegate the Negro to a position of social inferiority and impose a harsh rule of segregation in Northern states. According to Mr. Litwack:

> In virtually every phase of existence, Negroes found themselves systematically separated from whites. They were either excluded from railway cars, omnibuses, stagecoaches, and steamboats or assigned to special "Jim Crow" sections; they sat, when permitted, in secluded and remote corners of theaters and lecture halls; they could not enter most hotels, restaurants, and resorts, except as servants; they prayed in "Negro pews" in white churches, and if partaking of the sacrament of the Lord's Supper, they waited until the whites had been served the bread and wine. Moreover, they were often educated in segregated

schools, punished in segregated prisons, nursed in segregated hospitals, and buried in segregated cemeteries.

Housing and job opportunities were severely limited. A Boston Negro wrote in 1860 that "it is five times as hard to get a house in a good location in Boston as it is in Philadelphia; and it is ten times as difficult for a colored mechanic to get work here as it is in Charleston." The earlier verdict of Tocqueville continued to ring true. "Thus the Negro is free," he wrote, "but he can share neither the rights, nor the pleasures, nor the labor, nor the afflictions, nor the tomb of him whose equal he has been declared to be; and he cannot meet him upon fair terms in life or in death."

In Northern cities with large Negro populations, violent mob action occurred with appalling frequency. Between 1832 and 1849 mobs touched off five major anti-Negro riots in Philadelphia. Mobs destroyed homes, churches and meeting halls, and forced hundreds to flee the city. An English Quaker visiting Philadelphia in 1849 remarked that there was probably no city "where dislike, amounting to hatred of the coloured population, prevails more than in the city of brotherly love!"

The Southern historian will be struck with the remarkable degree to which the South recapitulated a generation later the tragic history of race relations in the North. Once slavery was destroyed as a means of social control and subordination of the Negro, and Reconstruction was overthrown, the South resorted to many of the devices originally developed in the North to keep the Negro in his "place." There was more delay in the resort to segregation than generally supposed, but once it came toward the end of the century it was harsh and thorough. One important difference was that in the antebellum North the Negro was sometimes free to organize, protest and join white sympathizers to advance his cause and improve his position. His success in these efforts was unimpressive, however, for by 1860, as Mr. Litwack says, "despite some notable advances, the Northern Negro remained largely disfranchised, segregated, and economically oppressed." The haven to which the North Star of the legend guided the fugitive from slavery was a Jim Crow haven.

While these two studies of the antislavery myth are valuable and significant, they are slight in scope and modest in aim when compared with the far more ambitious—and traditional—book of Dwight Lowell Dumond, *Antislavery: The Crusade for Freedom in America*.[3] Elaborately documented, profusely illustrated and ornately bound, this massive volume is easily twice the bulk of an average-sized book. It covers the entire scope of the organized antislavery movement in this country, as well as pre-organizational beginnings. Represented as the result of "more than thirty years" of research by the Michigan historian, it is the outcome of a lifetime absorption in antislavery literature. It is doubtful that any other scholar has lavished such devoted study upon this vast corpus of writings.

The author's total absorption with his source materials is, indeed, the key to the theory of historiography upon which this remarkable work would appear to be based. That theory is that the purest history is to be derived from strict and undivided attention to source materials—in this case chiefly the writings, tracts and propaganda, running to millions upon millions of words, of the antislavery people themselves. If the author is aware of any of the scholarly studies of slavery and antislavery that have appeared in the last generation or more, he does not betray awareness by reference to the questions they have raised, by use of methods they have developed, or by incorporation of findings they have published. Neither the problems of slavery and antislavery that have been pressed upon the historian by new learning in psychology, anthropology, sociology and economics, nor the questions that have been raised by fresh encounters with Africa and Afro-Americans and by new experience with reformers and revolutionists and their motivation, receive any attention from the author. It is difficult to comment intelligently upon a work that so persistently and successfully avoids engagement with the contemporary mind, its assumptions, its preoccupations, its urgent questions, its whole frame of reference.

Mr. Dumond's treatment of slavery and the abolitionists ad-

[3] Ann Arbor, 1961.

mits of no complexities or ambiguities beyond the fixed categories of right and wrong. All of his abolitionists are engaged in a single-minded crusade wholly motivated by a humanitarian impulse to destroy an evil institution and succor its victims. They are moral giants among the pygmies who cross their will or fail to share their views. The single exception is William Lloyd Garrison, for whom he shares the strong distaste of his onetime collaborator Gilbert H. Barnes, the Midwestern historian. "In fact," writes Dumond (the italics are his), *"he was a man of distinctly narrow limitations among the giants of the antislavery movement."* Why Garrison falls so far short of the stature of the giants is not quite clear, but we are assured that he was "insufferably arrogant," given to "cheap cynicism" and withal "a timid soul except when safely behind the editorial desk."

Apart from Garrison, the antislavery leaders command Mr. Dumond's unqualified admiration, and his praise of them is unbounded. "What a combination of intellect, courage, and Christian faith!" he exclaims in describing the founders of the American Anti-slavery Society. The abolitionists are indeed due a redress of grievances at the hands of the historians, for they have had something less than justice from the craft. They are remembered more as pictured by caricatures such as Henry James drew in *The Bostonians* than for their good works and genuine merits. The wild eccentricities, the fierce come-outerism, the doctrinaire extravagancies and the armchair bloodlusts of some of the abolitionists have been stressed and repeated to the neglect of the dedicated and fearless work they did in the face of ridicule, mob violence and all the pressures that wealth and established order can bring to bear upon dissenters. Their cause was just, and among their numbers were men and women of courage, intelligence and moral force. They deserve their due and need a sympathetic defender.

The trouble with Mr. Dumond as historian of the antislavery movement is his total involvement. This involvement extends beyond hatred of slavery and approval of abolition. It commits him as well to the style and tone and temper, the immediacy of indignation, the very idiom and rhetoric of a movement of thought that took its shape from intellectual influences and social conditions existing nearly a century and a half ago. The effect is startling. The rhythm and color of his prose is in perfect keeping with the style and tone of the scores of lithographs and prints from old abolitionist tracts that serve appropriately to illustrate the book. The author paints just what he sees, but he sees everything through the eyes of the 1830s. The result is more than an anachronism. It gives the effect of a modern primitive, a Henri Rousseau of historiography.

Any treatment of the antislavery movement necessarily involves some treatment of the institution it opposed. Mr. Dumond's conception of slavery would seem to have taken shape in considerable degree from the antislavery literature he has so thoroughly mastered. At any rate, he quotes liberally from this literature in characterizing slavery. Among other things, he quotes a poem by Timothy Dwight, published in 1794, the year before he became president of Yale. The last stanza of it reads as follows:

> Why shrinks yon slave, with horror, from his meats?/ Heavens! 'tis his flesh, the wretch is whipped to eat. / Why streams the life-blood from that female's throat? / She sprinkled gravy on a guest's new coat!

"Poetic license?" asks the historian. "Exaggeration? Fantasy? *Only half the truth, if a thousand witnesses are to be believed.*" And they, he assures us, are to be believed.

Mr. Dumond selects Theodore Dwight Weld's *American Slavery As It Is,* published in 1839, as "the greatest of the antislavery pamphlets," and still the best historical authority on slavery. "It is an encyclopedia of knowledge. It is a book of horrors," he writes. Weld himself correctly described it as "a work of incalculable value" to the abolitionist cause. "Facts and testimonies are troops, weapons and victory, all in one," he wrote. The principles governing its composition are suggested by a letter to Weld from two editorial advisers, Sereno and Mary Streeter: "Under the head of personal cruelty [you] will be obliged to reject much testimony; and this is not because the facts are not well authenticated but because those which are merely *horrid* must give place to those which are absolutely diabolical." Absolutely diabolical or not, in the opinion of Professor Dumond, "It is as close as history can come to the facts." According to his theory of historical evidence, "Diaries and plantation records are largely worthless because slaveholders never kept a record of their own evil ways."

The strong sexual theme that pervades antislavery literature often took a prurient turn, but in Mr. Dumond's hands the pruriency is transmuted by bold treatment. The presence of miscegenation is attested by the Census of 1860 and the proportion of the colored population of the South that was of mixed blood. But to Mr. Dumond, sexual exploitation becomes very nearly the basis of the institution of slavery. "Its prevalence leads to the inescapable conclusion," he writes, "that it was the basis—unspoken to be sure—of much of the defense of the institution." Ulrich B. Phillips, the Southern historian of slavery, doubtless betrayed a certain blindness when he reported that in all the records he studied he could find only one instance of deliberate "breeding" of slaves, and that an unsuccessful one in colonial Massachusetts.[4] To Mr. Dumond, however, it is plain as day that the "breeding" was practiced by *all* slaveholders: "That is exactly what slave owners did with the slaves, and there were no exceptions." To the Georgia historian there were no instances, to the Michigan historian no exceptions! What is one to tell the children?

Mr. Dumond's main subject, of course, is not slavery but antislavery. In his treatment of this great theme the myth is slightly muted, but it nevertheless pulses powerfully through the whole narrative. The Underground Railroad is described as "a highly romantic enterprise" that became "well organized." In these pages it operates with all the enchanting conspiracy and secrecy of the legend, with fugitive slaves "secreted in livery stables, in attics, in storerooms, under featherbeds, in secret passages, in all sorts of out of the way places." There was one hayloft in Detroit that "was always full of Negroes."

---

[4] John Jossylyn of the commonwealth recorded in 1636 that Mr. Maverick owned a slave woman with whom he commanded his male slave, "will'd she nill'd she to go to bed to her—which no sooner done than she kickt him out again."

In Professor Dumond's history the North Star Legend is given very nearly full credence. In striking contrast with the account rendered in detail by Mr. Litwack, we are informed that Negroes "continued to vote without interruption in New Hampshire, Vermont, Rhode Island, and in the two slave states of New York and New Jersey," and that there were never "any distinctions whatever in criminal law, judicial procedure, and punishments" in any New England states. "Negroes were citizens in all of these [free?] states," he writes (leaving it unclear how many). "They were citizens by enjoyment of full political equality, by lack of any statements to the contrary in any constitution or law, by complete absence of legal distinctions based on color, and by specific legal and constitutional declaration, and any statements to the contrary by courts, federal or state, were contrary to historical fact and are worthless as historical evidence." There is no hint of the thoroughgoing system of Northern segregation described by Mr. Litwack. It is admitted that one might "find a less liberal attitude toward free Negroes" in the Midwestern states, but that is easily accounted for: "There was a preponderance of Southern immigrants in the populations." In spite of this, we learn that in Jackson's time, "the Northern people, freeing themselves of the last vestiges of slavery, moved forward in a vast liberal reform movement."

The theory Mr. Dumond applies to the antislavery movement colors and coerces his reading of the whole of American history from the Revolution through the Civil War. This reading amounts to a revival of the long discredited theory of the Slave Power Conspiracy, a dominant hypothesis two or three generations ago. Slavery, we are told, "gave clay feet to Patrick Henry . . . and I suspect to Washington and Jefferson as well." Of the Revolutionary leaders he writes: "Those men were perfectly willing to spread carnage over the face of the earth to establish their own claim to freedom, but lacked the courage to live by their assertion of the natural rights of men." Of the presidential contest of 1800 we are told: "This election enabled Jefferson to lay solidly the foundations of the party of agrarianism, slavery, and decentralization." Any mention of Jefferson is accompanied by a reminder that he owned slaves. The achievement of a group is discredited with the phrase, "slaveholders all." The Virginia Dynasty, its heirs and successors of the next three decades, and most of their acts and works including the Constitution, fare pretty harshly under this rather restricted historical criterion.

The whole sectional conflict that eventually erupted in the Civil War is construed, of course, in terms of right versus wrong, North against South. Civil War historians will be interested to learn that "there was complete co-ordination by the Congress, the President, and the field commanders of the Army" in their mutual determination to abolish slavery at the earliest possible moment. This revelation will require a good deal of revision in accepted views, which take into account a great lack of coordination among those distracted branches of the wartime government.

It is possible that Professor Dumond's interpretations of American history might be traced directly to an unfortunate theory of historical method. Neither this nor the extended criticism of his work already undertaken would be worth the effort, however, were it not for what the book reveals about the present vitality and amazing persistence of the antislavery myth. His book is the latest and fullest embodiment of the myth. Yet it comes with endorsements of unqualified praise from leading authorities in the field. The wide flaps of the dust jacket bear such recommendations from the three foremost present-day historians of the American Civil War, followed by the equally enthusiastic praise of prominent historians from four of our most respected universities. These are not men who share Mr. Dumond's restrictive concepts of historiography, nor are they given to bestowing praise lightly. They undoubtedly mean what they say. What two of them say is that this book is "definitive," and all agree that from their point of view it is wholly satisfying.[5]

One would like to know more about their reasoning. Several of them refer directly or obliquely to present-day social problems that are a heritage of slavery, meaning segregation and the move-

[5] Among the more unqualified endorsements are those by Paul Angle, Ray A. Billington, Bruce Catton, Oscar Handlin, Richard B. Morris, Allan Nevins, and Carl Sandburg.

ment for Negro rights. But surely one can establish his position upon such clear-cut contemporary moral problems as these without compromising the standards of historical criticism. And by this time, one hopes, it is possible to register a stand on the slavery issue without feigning the apocalyptic rages of a John Brown. No, these are not adequate or convincing explanations, at least for the reactions of these particular historians.

In all probability the real reason why this ponderous, fierce and humorless book is handled with such piety and solemnity is the very fact that it does embody one of the great American myths. We have never faced up to the relationship between myth and history. Without tackling the semantic difficulties involved, we know that *myth* has more than pejorative usages and that it can be used to denote more than what one deems false about the other man's beliefs. In the nonpejorative sense myths are images, or collections of them, charged with values, aspirations, ideals and meanings. In the words of Mark Schorer, they are "the instruments by which we continually struggle to make our experience intelligible to ourselves." Myths *can* be, in short, "a good thing." No man in his right mind, and surely not a responsible historian, will knowingly and wantonly destroy a precious thing. And no doubt some would hesitate to lay hands on a book that, improperly though it may be, got itself identified as a repository of cherished values.

Serious history is the critique of myths, however, not the embodiment of them. Neither is it the destruction of myths. One of the great national myths is the equality of man, embodied in the Declaration of Independence. Tocqueville's study of equality in America is a valid critique of the myth, with neither the intention nor the effect of destroying it or doing it injury. Henry Nash Smith's *Virgin Land* provides a valid critique of the West's Myth of the Garden and symbols of the frontier without succumbing to impulses of iconoclasm. There is no comparable critique of the more elaborate myth—one might say mythology—of the South. What has been done in this respect has been mainly the work of imaginative writers rather than historians of the South. Historians have made a beginning, however, and a recent contribution by William R. Taylor, *Cavalier and Yankee*,[6] which illuminates the legend of aristocratic grandeur, is an excellent illustration of what is needed.

As a result of such studies, intelligent, contemporary Americans can speak of the myth of equality without self-consciousness or cynicism, and embrace it without striking the pose of a defiant Jacksonian of the 1830's. Contemporary Westerners are able to cherish and preserve frontier values without assuming the role of a Davy Crockett. And Southerners can even salvage some of the aristocratic heritage without wallowing in the Plantation Legend.

As yet, however, the Yankee remains to be fully emancipated from his own legends of emancipation. Confront him with a given set of symbols and he will set his sense of humor aside, snap to attention and come to a full salute. In the ensuing rigidities of that situation, conversation tends to lag. The pertinent interjections by Mr. Gara on the U.G.R.R. and by Mr. Litwack on the North Star Legend, already noticed, may help to break the ice, but the thawing will probably be slow. The orthodox text is obviously still the gospel according to Mr. Dumond.

The big assignment on the Antislavery Myth still awaits a taker. The eventual taker, like any historian who would make myth the proper subject of his study, should be involved without running the risks of total involvement. It would help a great deal if he could contrive to bring detachment as well as sympathy to his task. It is also to be hoped that he might make legitimate use of irony as well as compassion. And, finally, no aspirant with inappropriate regional identifications need apply.

[6] New York, 1961.

16

Southerners Versus
the Southern Establishment

THE BOOKS AND COLLEGE COURSES and memories that come to
mind when southern history is mentioned are not filled with subversives and radicals and revolutionaries. This is hardly surprising when it is remembered that the great bulk of what passes as
the history of the South is the 150 years Walker Percy has called
"the long Southern obsession," the century and a half that began
when the South succumbed to the combined temptations of slavery and cotton gin, an era that has only recently come to an end.[1]
Throughout most of that period southern whites were on the defensive. For half of it they had an increasingly discredited institution on their hands, and for the other half they closed ranks to
protect a precarious compromise on racial policies under attack.
Under the circumstances it is no wonder that the South had little or no patience for opposition from subversives and radicals in
their own ranks and that the pages of history covering the years
of the Great Obsession are dominated by conservatives or reactionaries.

The wonder is the South of that long era produced or toler-

[1] Walker Percy, "Random Thoughts on Southern Literature, Southern
Politics, and the American Future," *Georgia Review* 32 (1979), 499–511.

ated any white subversives or radicals at all. The fact that it did produce a surprising number, even if they were not often tolerated for long, seems to me to deserve more attention than it has had. I have been criticized for overemphasizing them in some of my books. In *Thinking Back* I undertook to reply to my critics.[2] But there were too many critics and criticisms—most of them quite justified, incidentally—and I could not reply to them all. One criticism that I did not get around to was that I overplayed the role of the radicals. I would say that my critics are probably right, but that I have a number of excuses to offer. One is that it got a bit lonely and tiresome making a career of living exclusively with conservatives; another is that making a living telling stories without the spice of contrast can be dull.

Southern liberals, until the civil rights movement, did not provide the needed spice of contrast. Most of them followed the so-called liberal tradition as laid down a century ago by Henry Grady, Henry Watterson, and Walter Hines Page. Theirs was a cheerful gospel of progress, prosperity, industry, and nationalism with a sugary icing of reconciliation of all classes, sections, and races—all of course under proper white supremacy. In other words southern liberalism, old school, was conservatism under another name. With liberals like that, you don't need any conservatives. No spicy contrast there. Of course there was a small handful of genuinely liberal white Southerners a century ago, people like George W. Cable, whom I will get around to later. But they horrified the so-called liberals of the Henry Grady type who pronounced them dangerous and drummed them out of the South. Cable wound up teaching in New England, a latitude virtually uninhabitable for native-born Southerners.

I must make apologies in advance for neglecting one large and authentic category of subversives from the South, black Southerners. They provided the spiciest and most numerous subversives of all. I offer several reasons for omitting them here. One is the large number and relatively greater neglect of white subversives. Black subversives come as no surprise. After all, they

[2] C. Vann Woodward, *Thinking Back: The Perils of Writing History* (Baton Rouge, 1986).

had so much to be subversive about. It is surprising that blacks produced any conservatives at all, or tolerated the ones they had, like Booker T. Washington. Black subversives from Nat Turner to Martin King, with scores in between, are already famed in song and story. Not that history has done them justice or that they do not deserve more attention and investigation than they have had. But here I have enough on my hands with whites. I must be content with acknowledging the debts that southern whites owe southern blacks for liberating them from the Great Obsession, first by their indispensable contribution to abolishing slavery and second by initiating, fighting, and winning the civil rights movement and thereby sparing us and themselves more of the Obsession.

Turning then to southern white subversives, I begin with the most famous and most successful and therefore the least typical of all—Thomas Jefferson. He was untypical because he was successful—a revolutionist whose cause prevailed. Having challenged and overthrown by force of arms the old establishment, Jefferson came to preside temporarily and uneasily over a new establishment of his own that replaced the old. I say "uneasily" because Jefferson remained suspicious and distrustful of all establishments. When Shays's Rebellion, an uprising of Massachusetts farmers in 1786, frightened conservatives out of their wits, Jefferson wrote home from Paris: "what country can preserve its liberties if their rulers are not warned from time to time that their people preserve the spirit of resistance? Let them take arms. . . . The tree of liberty must be refreshed from time to time with the blood of patriots & tyrants. It is its natural manure."[3]

This comes as no surprise from the author of The Declaration of Independence, in which he was even more sweeping in justifying revolution. He repeated these sentiments more than once in those years, writing to Abigail Adams in 1787, "I like a little rebellion now and then," and suggesting one every twenty years or so. Jefferson in these years, however, was thinking less

[3] Dumas Malone, *Jefferson and His Times*, Vol. 2 (Boston, 1951), pp. 164–65.

about the scene in America than about the governments of Europe, which he described as merely "the general prey of the rich on the poor,"[4] and rotten to the core. American minister to France at the time, he was in close personal touch with the revolutionists of 1789 in Paris, and they regarded him as Mr. Revolution himself, leading world authority on the subject. They earnestly sought and he gladly gave advice on the subject. "Our proceedings," he wrote James Madison, referring to those of the American Revolution, "have been viewed as the model for them on every occasion; and though in the heat of debate men are generally disposed to contradict every authority urged by their opponents, ours has been treated like that of the Bible, open to explanation but not to opposition." Jefferson went to witness the demolition of the Bastille himself and contributed to the widows of those who fell in its taking.[5] He left for home in September 1789 with strong sympathy and high hopes for the revolution, but before it took the bloody course he could not approve.

Early southern opponents of the establishment sometimes extended their subversive attacks to national institutions that had southern supporters but were increasingly thought of as northern. Pre-industrial capitalism, its Federalist supporters, and the legislative favors, privileges, patronage, and exemptions they lavished upon commercial enterprise met a formidable critic in John Taylor of Caroline, Virginia, planter and friend of Jefferson. In one fiery book and pamphlet after another, such as *Tyranny Unmasked* (1822) and *Construction Construed* (1820), Taylor tore into this "aristocracy of paper and patronage," as he called it. Denouncing it as "luxuriously rich and arrogantly proud," he accused the bankers, merchants, and capitalists of extorting 40 percent of the earnings of farmer and laborer and leaving them impoverished. Writing before the day of industrialism and wage labor, Taylor anticipated Karl Marx's theory of surplus value and the source of profit. There is something wildly improbable about this master of scores of slaves raising the banner of rebellion and

[4] Ibid., pp. 158–63.
[5] Ibid., pp. 226–31.

declaring that "we farmers and mechanics" must unite in common cause.[6]

An even more ferocious and improbable attack on capitalism came a generation later from George Fitzhugh, also from Caroline County, Virginia. Fitzhugh was an outspoken defender of slavery, but presumably on the theory that the best defense is an offense, he devoted most of the pages in his *Sociology for the South* (1854) and his *Cannibals All!* (1857) to the failings and horrors of free society and wage slavery. He contended that wage slavery was "far more cruel than the Black Slave Trade, because it exacts more of its slaves." Proof of this was the greater profitability of wage slavery, since all profit is derived from withholding from labor values it creates. Wage slavery was also "more cruel in leaving the laborer to take care of himself and family out of the pittance which skill or capital has allowed him to retain."[7]

Using the same evidence and many of the theories that Karl Marx used to attack capitalism, and lifting arguments freely from the *Communist Manifesto* of 1848, Fitzhugh assaulted the capitalist establishment with a ferocity rivaling that of his communist contemporary. But even if that establishment did have southern friends, it was essentially the northern, not the southern, establishment he was attacking. Moreover, he was attacking wage slavery as a means of defending chattel slavery, which was, by his time, an exclusively southern establishment. Fascinating as Fitzhugh is as a menace to the establishment, it was not the southern one he menaced, and he deserves only passing mention in this connection.

Genuine and sometimes heroic opposition to the southern order of things is best illustrated by southern antislavery leaders in the thirty years preceding the Civil War, after sectional feeling became bitter, tolerance vanished, and the going got rough. Before that happened, and while the influence of the revolution-

[6] John Taylor, *An Inquiry into the Principles and Policy of the Government of the United States* (Fredericksburg, 1814), pp. 22, 31, 262–64; Robert E. Shalhope, *John Taylor of Caroline, Pastoral Republican* (Columbia, S.C., 1980).

[7] C. Vann Woodward (ed.), George Fitzhugh, *Cannibals All! Or Slaves Without Masters* (Cambridge, 1960), pp. 25–27, 107–9, 167–76.

ary generation lingered, antislavery feeling was still tolerated. Scarcely one of the great Virginians of that generation, including Washington, Jefferson, Madison, Patrick Henry, and George Mason, failed to go on record as favoring emancipation. They came forth with no effective plan for achieving it, but several emancipated their own slaves, and that was the generation that outlawed the foreign slave trade and prohibited slavery in the Northwest Territory. Up to 1830 the large majority of antislavery societies was in the southern states. Shortly after the Nat Turner Rebellion of 1831, the Virginia legislature debated the last serious attempt of a southern state to abolish slavery. In that debate Thomas Jefferson's grandson, Patrick Henry's grandson, and John Marshall's son were leading proponents of abolition.[8] But the effort failed, and repression of dissent closed in over the South.

In the early years of the nineteenth century, up to the time repression set in, antislavery sentiment in the South was found in the upper class. While an occasional aristocrat joined up later, the main source of recruits in the South for the abolitionist crusade was the middle class, and they were likely to be Quakers, Methodists, or other evangelicals. They were also likely to pack up eventually and move north of the Ohio River, either to gain freedom of speech or to escape association with an institution they hated. One example was John Rankin, a native of Tennessee who moved to Ohio and became known as the "Martin Luther of Abolitionism" and a tower of strength for the cause in the decades before the Civil War. Another was James Gilliland, born and raised in South Carolina, who moved to Ohio and was elected vice-president of the American Anti-slavery Society when it was organized in 1833. A third was Levi Coffin of North Carolina origins and later of Indiana, who has been called "the most important figure" in the Underground Railroad and "president" of that rather shadowy organization. Edward Coles, of aristocratic Virginia birth, secretary to President Monroe and friend of Jefferson, took his slaves to Illinois and liberated them, was elected

8 Joseph C. Robert, *The Road from Monticello: A Study of the Virginia Slavery Debate of 1832* (Durham, 1941), pp. 20ff.

governor, and led a successful movement to prevent slavery being legalized in that state. Among other abolitionist leaders of southern origins in the Middle West were Jesse Lockhart of Tennessee, Alexander Campbell of Virginia, and William Williamson of South Carolina.[9]

It was Southerners who launched the antislavery press in America. Charles Osborne of North Carolina wound up in Ohio, where he founded the *Philanthropist,* which holds disputed title of being the first paper in the United States to advocate immediate and unconditional emancipation. Elihu Embree, a slaveholding Quaker of Jonesborough, Tennessee, had the distinction of publishing in his own state what Clement Eaton calls "the first periodical in the United States devoted exclusively to the abolition of slavery," first under the title *Manumission Intelligencer,* later changed to the *Emancipator.* Benjamin Lundy, another Quaker, published his *Genius of Universal Emancipation,* wherever he happened to be living, first in Ohio, then four years in Tennessee, then in Baltimore. Lundy hired an assistant named William Lloyd Garrison, who thus began his famous publishing career in the South before launching his *Liberator* in Boston. (I hasten to add that I am *not* claiming Garrison as a southern hero.) Another disciple of Benjamin Lundy, however, was a North Carolinian named William Swain who founded his *Patriot* in Greensboro, fiercely defended free speech, and opened his columns to antislavery writers. When the state passed laws suppressing such publications, he swore in 1834 that he would take his own life rather than surrender his freedom to "a motley crew of office-hunters, despots, demagogues, tyrants, fools and hypocrites." Swain continued his publication unmolested, true to his faith in defiance of law and storms of abuse. Another North Carolinian, Daniel Reeves Goodloe, edited the most influential abolitionist paper of its time, the *National Era,* from Washington in the 1850s.

---

[9] For this and the following two paragraphs on southern antislavery, see Dwight L. Dumond, *Antislavery: The Crusade for Freedom in America* (Ann Arbor, 1961), pp. 83–108, 185–203; Clements Eaton, *Freedom of Thought in the Old South* (Durham, N.C., 1940), pp. 139–41, 252–74.

Other antislavery editors were not so fortunate. James G. Birney had moved from his native Kentucky to Alabama, established himself as a lawyer, mayor of Huntsville, and a slaveholding planter when he turned against slavery. Despairing of speaking out against it in Alabama, he returned to Kentucky, freed his slaves, and prepared to publish an antislavery paper. Confronted with a mob that threatened to destroy the press that was to print his paper and having no other means of publishing it in the South, he moved to Cincinnati. By no means intimidated, Birney went on to become national leader of the political wing of abolitionists and was twice, in 1840 and 1844, their candidate for president on the Liberty party ticket. Birney's father warned him never to return to his native state, even for a visit. Another errant antislavery son to receive the same orders from an indignant southern father was Moncure Daniel Conway of Falmouth, Virginia. The elder Conway wrote his son that because of his "horrible views" he deserved the intolerance of old neighbors, and that however willing he was "to expose your own person recklessly, I am not willing to subject myself and family to the hazards of such a visit." Stay away, stay away was again the word of father to son: you can't go home again.

It is impossible to include here more than a sample of southern opponents of slavery, and I must pass up even such notable ones as Hinton Rowan Helper and Cassius M. Clay with only a mention. But it would be unthinkable to omit the famous Charleston aristocrats Angelina Grimké and her sister Sarah. With a father educated at Oxford and two brothers with national reputations as reformers or writers, the sisters Grimké chafed under paternal conservatism and Episcopalian orthodoxy and turned their backs on Charleston. After joining the Quakers in Philadelphia and finding them too straitlaced for their radical antislavery and feminist views, the sisters, with Angelina always in the lead, went all out as Garrisonian abolitionists and radical feminists. Angelina, the blue-eyed daughter of a slaveholder, set the Yankee radicals back on their heels by a series of eloquent lectures and pamphlets, one of which attacked Catharine Beecher, Harriet's sister, for her conservative views. She proceeded to marry Theodore Weld, one of the most famous northern abolitionists, and to collaborate with him in producing what was then the most powerful of all indictments of the institution, *American Slavery As It Is* (1839).[10]

A full and fair account of southern opposition to slavery would include a sample of those who kept their views to themselves but believed them passionately. I can afford only one illustration, that of Mary Boykin Chesnut of South Carolina, who less than one month before she witnessed the bombardment of Fort Sumter, wrote in her private diary that she held "slavery a curse to any land," and that Sen. Charles Sumner, whom her husband had recently denounced in the Senate for his slavery views, "said not one word of this hated institution which is not true."[11]

With that we must take leave of slavery and turn to the issues raised in Reconstruction. To represent southern subversives in this period, I choose a figure from Georgia, a state neglected so far. This is Amos T. Akerman of Cartersville, who was the only Confederate to serve in a Reconstruction cabinet. He was attorney general for a year in President Grant's first administration, and according to Prof. William S. McFeely of the University of Georgia, "no attorney general since his tenure . . . has been more vigorous in the prosecution of cases designed to protect the lives and rights of black Americans." Lest I be accused of fudging a point, I must admit that the man was born and received a good education in New England at Exeter and Dartmouth. But Akerman came to the South when he was only twenty-one and had lived there nearly thirty years before he joined Grant's cabinet. He fell in love with the region, read law, established a practice in Cartersville, acquired land that he cultivated with slaves, raised no question about the institution, went along with secession, saw service in the Confederate Army, and the last year of the war married a southern woman who was to

[10] Gerdar Lerner, *The Grimké Sisters* (New York, 1967); Dumond, *Antislavery*, pp. 190–96.

[11] C. Vann Woodward (ed.), *Mary Chesnut's Civil War* (New Haven, 1981), p. 29.

bear him eight sons. He returned to Cartersville in 1865 impoverished and shattered in health to raise his family.

What engaged Akerman in the issues of Reconstruction was his dedication to the law. All about him he saw the law violated and trampled on by many, including the state legislature and the Ku Klux Klan, mainly with the intent of depriving black freedmen of their rights or their lives. He joined the Republican party and was appointed United States district attorney for Georgia, where one of his chief concerns was violations of the Civil Rights Act of 1866. With the object of protecting the lives and rights of southern Republicans, a party faction maneuvered the appointment of Akerman as attorney general, much to the surprise of all. Also to the surprise and dismay of some powerful Republicans, he took his duties with utmost seriousness and enforced the laws protecting black civil rights from the Ku Klux Klan with unprecedented effectiveness. This was not quite what was expected of an ex-Confederate. The Republican party was withdrawing from the protection of the rights and privileges it had won for Southern blacks. His cabinet colleagues grew bored with his grisly stories of Ku Klux atrocities, and the railroad barons complained he did not understand their needs. He was removed from office in 1871 and returned quietly to Cartersville to live out his years, which ended in 1880.[12]

George W. Cable of New Orleans could claim the right to speak as "a native of Louisiana, an ex-Confederate soldier, and a lover of my home, my city, and my state." He watched "the great Reconstruction agony," as he called it, "with his sympathies ranged upon the pro-Southern side of the issue, and his convictions drifting irresistibly to the other." Convictions won out, and in 1885 he published *The Silent South*, one of the most radical indictments of southern racial policy written by a Southerner in the eighties. He left the South the year his book appeared and never again lived in his native region, though he continued his

12 William S. McFeely, "Amos T. Akerman: The Lawyer and Racial Justice" in J. Morgan Kousser and James M. McPherson (eds.), *Region, Race, and Reconstruction: Essays in Honor of C. Vann Woodward* (New York, 1982), pp. 395–415.

critical attack on its policies. With their one-party system and exclusion of the blacks, Conservatives after overthrowing corrupt Reconstruction regimes had promised "pure government first, free government afterward." It had proved a "twin fallacy" and a "delusion," Cable wrote, that such a policy "could produce either free or pure government."[13] It had, he contended, produced neither.

Lewis H. Blair of Richmond was a striking example of aristocrat as subversive, an aristocrat with a family tree burdened with distinguished names from colonial times on down. Private Blair, however, returned from war service penniless, with name and fortune still to make. He made both as a successful merchant and manufacturer. Both self-made business man and old-family aristocrat, Blair was an uncommon source of subversive ideas. A kinsman who did not share his ideas at all could describe him as "a man of distinguished appearance and of a courtesy in manner that seemed to belong to an even older time." Yet this was the man who in 1889 at the age of fifty-five published in Richmond a book he called *The Prosperity of the South Dependent Upon the Elevation of the Negro*. It was a blistering and iconoclastic attack on the dogmas of white supremacy and black inferiority, on the paternalistic tradition of race relations, the plantation legend of slavery, the black-domination legend of Reconstruction, and the "brag and strut and bluster" of the complacent New South boosters. His book was also an eloquent plea for full equality for blacks, an uncompromising attack on racial segregation, discrimination, and injustice of all kinds, and a demand for full civil and political rights for the Negro, especially voting rights, which were "as absolutely essential for freedom as is the atmosphere for life."

The following statement, I would remind you, comes from the 1880s, not the 1980s, and from Richmond, not Boston. Wrote Blair in 1889:

[13] George W. Cable, *The Silent South* (New York, 1885), pp. 25, 47; and *The Southern Struggle for Pure Government, An Address* (Boston, 1890), pp. 10, 15–19.

The Negro must be allowed free access to all hotels and other places of public entertainment . . . to all theatres . . . to all churches, and in all public and official receptions of presidents, governor, mayor, etc., he must not be excluded by a hostile caste sentiment.

And this on school segregation:

Separate schools are a public proclamation to all of African or mixed blood that they are inferior and totally unfit to mingle on terms of equality with the superior caste. . . . Separate schools poison at its very source the stream whence spring the best and noblest fruits of education. . . . The doctrine of caste . . . seizes with its rigid, icy grasp the impressionable minds of the children and taints them; and the blind superiority thereby inculcated fosters [in white children] sentiments of false pride, disregard of the rights of others, and unfeeling haughtiness to all . . . whom they deem inferiors.

All this in 1889, the very eve of the white South's plunge into the depths of full Jim Crow segregation, disfranchisement, discrimination, and lynching, the worst period of racism in its history. That may explain why Lewis Blair's courageous book quickly sank from sight and was completely forgotten. But that is not the full measure of irony that seems fated to overtake southern heroes of resistance. Blair lived on until 1916, through the worst of the long period of racial extremism. Whether it was the influence of that period or that of the young wife he married at an advanced age who did not share his racial views, Blair sometime after his marriage in 1898 wrote a complete recantation of his views of 1889 and called for "absolute subordination to the whites" as "the only logical position for the Negro." The manuscript was found long after his death, unsigned, undated, untitled, unpublished. But there it was, another southern biographical enigma and the tragedy of another promise unfulfilled.[14]

[14] C. Vann Woodward (ed.), Lewis H. Blair, *A Southern Prophecy: The Prosperity of the South Dependent Upon the Elevation of the Negro* (Boston, 1964), pp. xii–xlvi, 136–51.

So far I have presented the historic challengers of the status quo as individuals and the main issue as racial. But the next challenge to the establishment from inside the South came from a political party. Southern Populists, the most radical wing of the national party, did not confine their attack to racial policy, but left few shibboleths, dogmas, or fictions of New South orthodoxy unchallenged. These included the gospel of progress, prosperity, and industrialization, the fictions of consensus, white solidarity, black contentment, and sectional reconciliation, and the themes of unity, continuity, and nationalism—all garnished with leftover myths of the Old South. Not only that, but the Populists put forth the most thorough American critique of corporate capitalism up to the 1890s, demanding government control of its excesses and nationalization of the railroads, telephone, and telegraph industries and others if they did not behave themselves.

Southern Populists were addicted to rhetoric that frightened conservatives out of their minds. The leading Populist journal of Texas proclaimed "a bitter and irrepressible conflict between capitalist and laborer" and called on workers to "overthrow the capitalistic class." Tom Watson entitled his 1892 campaign book *Not a Revolt; It Is a Revolution,* and the party candidate for president that year announced it to be "the eve of the greatest revolution the country has ever known." This sounds like nonsense today, but it did not then. Quite as scary, if not more so to some, was the Populist alliance between black and white voters, coming on the heels of Reconstruction and coinciding with a new effort in Congress for a second reconstruction to protect black voting and civil rights. Populists took up the black cause that met defeat in Congress and placed in their platforms denunciations of lynch law and convict lease and demands for full civil rights for blacks, including ballot protection, jury service, and equal justice. When all that is said, it must be admitted that the gains for blacks were limited and are easily exaggerated. The fact that this Populist alliance of races occurred at all in the South during this period of extreme reaction is the remarkable thing.

Had I used an individual to present the Populists, I would

have chosen Tom Watson of Georgia, their most prominent national leader. Had I done so I should have been obliged to include him as the prime example of the ironic fate, illustrated in the case of Lewis Blair, that so often overtook southern dissidents. Watson stands foremost among them because of the extremes to which he went at both ends of his personal political spectrum: from the courageous crusader of his early years to the matchless racist, demagogue, and master of mob rule in his late years.[15]

One does not think of Texas, Oklahoma, Louisiana, and Arkansas as seedbeds of radicalism nor the Southwest as a center of socialism. Yet in the years preceding World War I the American Socialist party won its strongest grass-roots support in precisely these states. To quote James Green, the leading authority on them, "Oklahomans built the strongest socialist state organization in the nation; their party claimed more dues-paying members than New York state and in 1914 the Sooner Socialists received 15,000 more votes than the Socialist party of the country's largest state," New York. In the same year they elected more than a hundred of their comrades to county and township offices. Mobilized against city slickers and modeled upon Oklahoma, the other states of the Southwest advanced the party cause with fifty-five weekly newspapers, recruiting debt-ridden farmers, timber workers, miners, and renegade preachers as members. Father Marx would have had moments of puzzlement had he witnessed their week-long "encampments" modeled on the old fundamentalist camp-meeting evangelistic revivals. Destroyed by vigilantes and government repression during World War I, the movement has been forgotten.[16]

Not forgotten yet, I hope, are worthy dissidents and their crusades of more recent times who have continued the great tradition of southern opposition to evils condoned, accepted, or ignored. There are too many to be mentioned or even fairly sam-

[15] C. Vann Woodward, *Tom Watson: Agrarian Rebel* (New York, 1938 and 1987); *Origins of the New South, 1877–1913* (Baton Rouge, 1951), pp. 239–58.

[16] James R. Green, *Grass-Roots Socialism: Radical Movements in the Southwest, 1895–1943* (Baton Rouge, 1978), pp. xi–xxi.

pled here. I must, however, mention Jessie Daniel Ames who headed and Mary McLeod Bethune who inspired the Association of Southern Women for the Prevention of Lynching which by 1939 had enrolled nearly 40,000 members. And while always remembering that it was the black people who began, fought, and won the Civil Rights Movement, I must at least mention some whites who helped. Such a list at a minimum would have to include the names of Lillian Smith of Georgia, Virginia Durr of Alabama, Will D. Campbell of Mississippi, James McDabb of South Carolina—but that is only a token, a beginning of those who deserve remembering.

I am assuming that the tradition of resistance and outspoken criticism to the powers that be is not ended merely because the Great Obsession of the South has tapered off. With that behind us, or nearly so, I would hope that oncoming dissidents could spare some of their critical talents for national problems. Rumor has it there are at least a few. Should it ever happen—and perish the thought that it might—that our country should become an embarrassment to its allies, a disgrace to its own traditions and principles, and a laughing stock among its enemies because of its leadership and their policies, I would hope that southern critics in their spare time might find targets worthy of their talents beyond the Potomac, starting just beyond perhaps.

17

Strange Career Critics: Long May They Persevere

This was written in 1988 at the request of the editor of The Journal of American History, *who published it in the same issue with a critical assessment of* The Strange Career of Jim Crow *in its various editions.*

Without the persistent attention of critics over the thirty-four years since its publication, *The Strange Career of Jim Crow* would have long since been forgotten. Lacking the demands for correction made by the flaws they discovered and the new findings they brought forth, I should have been hard put to justify the numerous revisions and new editions that have periodically helped revive interest in the subject. All along, of course, it has been the subject, rather than the book on the subject, that has explained the protracted attention and interest. I am nevertheless profoundly indebted to the critics for keeping the book alive along with the subject. I very much hope they will persevere.

I promise to return to questions raised by some of the more

recent critics.[1] First, however, I should like to enter the fray myself. If the best defense is offense, perhaps the analogous strategy for criticism is self-criticism. At any rate, I have a good bit of self-criticism bottled up that might be offered here on that theory. Some of it may answer or duplicate, and some may forestall, the criticisms of others, but I hope none of it will discourage or slow the continued flow of criticism.

Briefly stated, my main point is that work on this subject got started off on the wrong foot and that I bear heavy responsibility for the mischief. I am referring particularly to the question of racial segregation and its origins. What I did was to put the question *when* before the questions *where* and *how*, giving to time priority over circumstance and placing the chronology before the sociology and demography of the subject. I understand *why* I placed the issue of chronology foremost when I did. I believed then, and still do, that this ordering of priorities served a necessary and essential purpose. The fact remains that the approach did the historiography of the subject a disservice by giving it a wrong direction at the start.

I should have been persuaded to make these admissions earlier by the nature of evidence presented in other contributions to the controversy, notably those of Leon F. Litwack, Richard C. Wade, Ira Berlin, and Howard N. Rabinowitz. Each of them pointed to the existence of substantial racial segregation prior to the period of growth and legislation I had emphasized. I have accepted their findings in previous revisions or essays.[2] But since

---

[1] I am seeking to avoid repetition of response to earlier critics in two previous publications, C. Vann Woodward, *American Counterpoint: Slavery and Racism in the North-South Dialogue* (Boston, 1971), 234–64; and C. Vann Woodward, *Thinking Back: The Perils of Writing History* (Baton Rouge, 1986), 81–99.

[2] Leon F. Litwack, *North of Slavery: The Negro in the Free States, 1790–1860* (Chicago, 1961); Richard C. Wade, *Slavery in the Cities: The South, 1820–1860* (New York, 1964); Ira Berlin, *Slaves without Masters: The Free Negro in the Antebellum South* (New York, 1974); Howard N. Rabinowitz, *Race, Relations in the Urban South, 1865–1890* (New York, 1978). I should like to acknowledge belatedly the value of the contributions and sensible suggestions in Berlin, *Slaves without Masters*, which appeared too late for notice in the 1974 edition of *Strange Career*. C. Vann Woodward, *The Strange Career of Jim Crow* (New York, 1974).

it was on the timing of segregation's appearance that they addressed my thesis, I responded in kind by pointing out that, granting they were right, all were speaking primarily of race relations in cities or urban societies, of which there were extremely few in the nineteenth-century South. Even in 1900 scarcely one southerner in ten and an even smaller fraction of black southerners were classified as urban by the census.

While their qualifications and my rejoinder were true and lent support to the thesis of a delayed appearance of segregation in the South, that formulation eluded the more important point. The significant thing was not *when* it appeared but *where,* not the time but the circumstances. It appeared first in towns and cities and grew as they grew. It was essentially an urban, not a rural, phenomenon. That had been a legitimate, if unspecified, implication of Litwack's study of the free states (1961) and of Wade's study of the slave states (1964). It was a point in Rabinowitz's 1978 book on five cities of the South and was spelled out analytically by John W. Cell's comparison of the South and South Africa in 1982.[3]

In the 1974 edition of *Strange Career* I had pointed out the incompatibility of racial segregation with plantation slavery, given the necessities of policing, supervising, and exacting involuntary labor, receiving slave services, and attending to slave needs. Interracial contact, unwelcome as it might be on both sides, was unavoidable. Segregation was incompatible not only with slavery, but with much rural life after emancipation as well. Back on the farm, for example, many of the typical objects of segregation never existed. Streetcars, hotels, bars, restaurants, theaters, hospitals, public parks, and numerous other public facilities and services were not there to be segregated. If the purpose was to draw caste lines between superior and subordinate, those lines were made clear enough by slavery and then by its aftermath of paternalism and caste. If it was to maintain racial dominance and discipline, that was handled in the country by direct, personal, or "vertical" control—whether by the "boss man" or any white

[3] John W. Cell, *The Highest Stage of White Supremacy: The Origins of Segregation in South Africa and the American South* (New York, 1982).

who chose to keep blacks in their place. They were personally identifiable and rarely beyond white surveillance.

In the city things were different. There blacks enjoyed more autonomy and anonymity and rubbed shoulders with whites nearer their own class frequently and in new and unfamiliar circumstances. Although urban police did bring traditionally rural methods of intimidation into the city, the countryside reliance on direct or "vertical" control did not work well enough in urban conditions. To supplement the old methods, white urbanites added the "horizontal" system of segregation, an impersonal complex of interlocking economic, political, legal, social, and ideological components designed not only to separate the races but also to maintain white dominance and keep blacks in their place. As Cell puts it, Jim Crow was no rural redneck: "First and foremost he was a city slicker."[4]

While segregation was mainly (though not wholly) of urban origin, cities of the South differed in the haste and completeness with which they adopted and legalized the system. In that respect cities in which large numbers of whites and blacks were newcomers and where long experience of racial cohabitation was lacking took the lead. But scattered along the eastern seaboard were cities with roots deep in the colonial era. In that older urban South lived white and black families that had known each other for generations, whose lives after slavery continued to intertwine, as did the residential patterns of their streets.[5] They lagged behind the interior cities of the newer South in advancing segregation and were usually the last to support or adopt Jim Crow laws. I find that, as Rabinowitz says, it is mainly from such Old South cities—cities such as Charleston, Savannah, and New Orleans—that I draw evidence to support the thesis of delayed segregation, temporary fluidity, and diversity in race relations, the "forgotten alternatives." I would not deny, however, that

---

[4] Cell, *Highest Stage of White Supremacy*, 134. I owe the idea of rural methods of city police to J. Mills Thornton III, who expressed it in a personal letter.

[5] Berlin, *Slaves without Masters*, 254–57.

urban development, not chronology, contains the significant clue to the new order of race relations.

Given those concessions, how can I possibly maintain that putting chronology foremost nevertheless "served an important and essential purpose"? I have admitted that doing so was a disservice to progress in the historiography of race relations. But before a subject can have a historiography, it must be acknowledged to have a history. My first concern was to overcome the prevailing impression—and in southern ideology the firm conviction—that the subject had no history, that race relations in the South remained basically unchanged, that changes in law, whether associated with slavery, emancipation, Reconstruction, or segregation, had been superficial and resulted in no real change in relations between races. No changes, no history. The view was shared by those who wished to keep things the way they were and by many who wished to change things but despaired of ever being able to do so. It had adherents from the right, left, and center. Deeply rooted and expressed in various theories of continuity, the view still has followers, even in scholarly circles.

Since the essential component of history is change over time, it seemed necessary to prove that race relations had changed over time, in order to show that they had a history. That postulate placed time and chronology foremost on the agenda: Once upon a time things were different. If so, if the present order had not always existed, when did it start? What preceded it? Was that any better? And when did it come to an end? Time and origins thus took precedence over place and circumstances. The question of where and why things changed, if and when they had changed at all, had to await an answer. Such were the priorities and urgencies that presented themselves to me when I addressed the problem in 1954. They seemed clear and simple enough at the time.

I should have been forewarned by Marc Bloch's remarks on the ambiguities of the term *origins*: "a cross-contamination of the two meanings," beginnings and causes, he called it. Excessive preoccupation with origins reminded him of "that other satanic enemy of true history: the mania for making judgments."[6] The perils of establishing beginning in time were formidable enough, what with harbingers, portents, and precursors to contend with. In addition there was the debate about the comparative significance of custom and practice versus law and legally enforced segregation. The very contention, in a discussion of an existing evil, that things had been different before provokes the charge of romanticizing the past and suggests the existence of a golden age of race relations. Likewise, making a point of the relative recency of an evil and the role of the law in establishing and advancing it invites the hope that the evil is superficially rooted and can be easily uprooted by changes in the law.

Much time and energy that might have been profitably turned to important questions about race relations were thus diverted, often futilely, to the denial of false implications and misconceived hopes. Some of the contributors and many of the critics in the field paid a similar toll in diversion of time and effort. Granting all the costly diversions, false starts, and misleading implications, I still believe that starting with questions of chronological order served an important purpose. In the first place, it helped to force acknowledgment that race relations *had* a history. Second, it challenged the faith that race relations had "always been that way" and were as impervious to change as the characters of the two races involved. That faith was the foundation of the status quo of race relations in the South.

To defend the faith, now that it was challenged, was perforce to resort to historical argument and to admit that race relations had a history. To do so was to open a Pandora's box of troubles: the possibility, for example, that the status quo was neither invariable, inevitable, nor unalterable. While those possibilities were not strictly legitimate concerns of historians, they had practical consequences that served to stimulate, not to say enliven, legitimate historical investigation and controversy. To get off on the wrong foot is perhaps better than not to get off at

[6] Marc Léopold Benjamin Bloch, *The Historian's Craft*, trans. Peter Putnam (New York, 1964), 30–31.

all. In the meantime historians have differed over the time, cause, degree, character, and importance of change in race relations, but no one, so far as I know, any longer denies the existence of change. Having overcome the ideological denial of the phenomenon's existence, we could at last get on with the investigation of its origins and historical significance.

Among recent critics of *Strange Career,* very few have contributed more constructively than Howard Rabinowitz. By establishing exclusion as an antecedent of segregation, the latter as an improvement over the former, and cities of the inland South as the place of origin for both, he advanced the argument substantially. I had already urged in 1971 that we "conceive of the historical problem of segregation not as one of dating origins at a point in linear time but of accounting for the phenomenon in whatever degree it appears." It was not when any form of segregation first appeared, but rather, as I repeatedly stated, when and how it appeared "in the rigid and universal form it had taken by 1954" and enforced by law. What with all the "guarded qualifications" and fine distinctions between urban and rural, de facto and de jure, antebellum and postbellum circumstances, I do not wonder that Rabinowitz has found that the debate "has often been frustrating for Woodward's critics." The implication that they have been compelled to cope with a rather elusive fellow is not entirely unjustified, nor is the complaint that the argument "often seemed to come down to whether the bourbon glass was half full or half empty."[7] I have sympathy to spare for their frustration and nothing but praise for their patience.

I nevertheless agree with Rabinowitz that the debate has been "fruitful" and hope to gain his admission that it has appreciably narrowed differences by concessions on both sides. At least I have come to agree that more segregation, both de facto and de jure, existed earlier in the nineteenth century than I had originally allowed. And, on the other hand, I fondly believe that most

[7] Woodward, *American Counterpoint,* 242, 237; Woodward, *Thinking Back,* 82–83; Howard N. Rabinowitz, "More Than the Woodward Thesis: Assessing *The Strange Career of Jim Crow*," *Journal of American History,* 75 (Dec. 1988), 842–56.

of my critics now concede that toward the end of the century an escalation in white fanaticism resulted in a rigidity and universality of the enforcement of discriminatory law that was a sufficient change to mark a new era in race relations. Joel Williamson, one of the first critics to question the limited extent of segregation I saw in Reconstruction, has later agreed that "race relations in the South and in America had been diverse and evolutionary" and "had not frozen with the end of either slavery or Reconstruction."[8] On the other hand, I would agree with Rabinowitz and others that I somewhat overstated the rigidity of segregation in the early twentieth century. And it will expand the area of agreement to concede that such innovations as elevators and phone booths were segregated without resort to law, and that further research is needed on the Jim Crow statutes themselves. I would repeat once more that "laws are not an adequate index" to segregation.

I agree that "the First and Second Reconstructions not only differed in their chances for success; they were about very different things." But what I had in mind was an analogy, and as dictionaries have it, analogy means "correspondence in some respects . . . between things otherwise dissimilar." Few would claim more than that between events of the 1860s and those of the 1960s. It is no argument against the use of analogy to say it is dangerous. So is the historian's use of evidence, comparison, imagination, or, for that matter, metaphor. Analogy itself is an abridged metaphor. History is a perilous craft. History without analogies, however, would be a meaner thing, no more than a social science, perhaps one that speaks of analogies as "models" and misconceives their uses. Of course analogies never prove anything. They only provoke things. They can even provoke thought. Considering the amount provoked by the instance at hand, I have no hesitation in continued defense of the use of analogy in history.

With characteristic generosity Rabinowitz has compared and assessed the various editions of *Strange Career,* pointing

---

8 Joel Williamson, *The Crucible of Race: Black-White Relations in the American South since Emancipation* (New York, 1984), 491–92.

out changes, inconsistencies, and additions. I never consciously sought to turn the original lectures into a textbook, as he assumes. Rather, the changes and additions in successive editions were inspired by efforts to keep abreast of criticism, ongoing research, and changing events during the turbulent decades following the original edition. As the issue of segregation diminished in comparative importance (and similarly the issue of its origins), new issues and developments demanded attention, and the book underwent changes in successive editions beyond those normally described as "revision." I might have done well to start over with a new title—*The Second Reconstruction*, say. Instead, I stuck with the old one and added chapters. It is ungracious of the beneficiary to complain of critical approval, but it must be admitted that if a fifth edition is undertaken, the final chapter of the previous edition, the "contribution" most generously praised, will undergo the greatest changes. I shall return to those changes presently.

Before that, however, I wish to respond, as I have not been able to do earlier, to the engaging assessment of my efforts by John W. Cell. I must pass over his comparisons of race relations in South Africa and the American South, as "remarkably tidy" as he proves them to be. Nor have I space to address anything but his discussion of my treatment of segregation and race relations. In observations on other subjects of common concern, Cell finds valid reasons for disagreement with certain positions I have taken. For example, he holds that I exaggerate the fall of the planter class and the transition of planters from labor lords to landlords, and he believes that the New South was "less bourgeois than Woodward supposed." On the other hand, he pronounces the "Prussian Road" critique of my emphasis on bourgeois over planter leadership of industrial development "fundamentally misleading" and has generous things to say about my attempts to synthesize the major themes of the period.[9]

In his discussions of the controversy over the origins of segregation and the shaping of race relations in the South, Cell also

[9] Cell, *Highest Stage of White Supremacy*, 144–54, 165–68.

maintains an independent position, finding place for criticism as well as agreement. In general, however, I believe that we are more in agreement than otherwise on such matters. Only rarely is he misled, as for example in his understanding me to say "the South before the 1890s was in practice a comparatively open society, in which white and black competed on surprisingly equal terms." That statement attributes to my outlook a degree of optimism to which I plead innocent. I must also disavow the illusion that the South ever enjoyed "a democratic, tolerant, [racially] integrated society." Apart from that slip and one overlooking my acknowledgment that segregation by custom and practice preceded segregation by law, Cell succeeds in representing my position and those of its critics with exemplary fairness and understanding.[10]

Weighing the pros and cons, criticism and response, revision and modification in the long controversy, Cell finds persuasive arguments on both sides. "The outside observer finds it hard to choose," he confesses, and he speculates that "this may be one of those relatively few cases when both sides are right." At the root of it, however, he believes there lies a "failure in communications," that "the debaters have talked past one another"; that "Woodward and his critics do seem to be discussing different problems." He goes on to observe that "the revisionists are talking mostly about practice and attitudes, Woodward about political rhetoric and law; they about social and economic structure, he about political and ideological superstructure." Those distinctions should prove clarifying for all participants save those who read dismissive connotations into the terms law, ideology, and superstructure and assume them to be of little effect on practice and attitudes. I do not believe that Cell is of that persuasion.[11]

It is his opinion that "the revisionists have failed or refused to meet Woorward on his own ground," that "Woodward's interpretation centers on the 1890s," and that "at both ends his critics have largely avoided him." Cell agrees about the importance and centrality of the 1890s, a turning point in economic and politi-

[10] *Ibid.*, 92, 83.
[11] *Ibid.*, 91, 94, 103.

cal, as well as racial, history. Yet he professes puzzlement that although a "most controversial" theme of my earlier work had been stress on economic determinants, I disengage politics from economics in explaining race relations and insist that the new order was "shaped and defined by political means and measures, not to meet the needs of commerce and industry but the needs of politicians." The brunt of the accusation of inconsistency is borne by a previous work, *Origins of the New South,* and follows from the charge that it overdoes the rise of the bourgeoisie. He may have a point, but that is another book and another debate, and here I must focus on book and debate at hand.[12]

On the forces behind change in race relations, Cell agrees with J. Morgan Kousser (as I have come to) that privileged, rather than underprivileged, whites were mainly responsible and that their ends were primarily political. In explaining the new racial order in the agrarian South, Cell concludes that "economic determinism will not work. On that, as with so many of his conclusions, Woodward is absolutely right." He does believe that segregation was "linked in significant ways to the early, formative industrial growth of the region" (as it was in South Africa), that it helped to divide and weaken the work force and to forge bonds between its white members and their oppressors. However, he concludes that in the long run, the new order of race relations was "not economically determined," was "not based on economic but on political grounds," and that "it grew directly out of political responses to circumstances that were mainly political." It was "an organic part of a massive systemic change by which the Old South was giving way to the New. . . . It was in the New South that the highest stage of white supremacy evolved." Cell's formulation leaves some issues unresolved but substantially narrows the differences between us and brings gratifying support on the reality, the chronology, and the basic reasons for significant change in race relations.[13]

---

[12] *Ibid.,* 91–92, 95–97.
[13] *Ibid.,* 119–21, 142–43, 153–54, 169–70; J. Morgan Kousser, *The Shaping of Southern Politics: Suffrage Restrictions and the Establishment of the One-Party South, 1880–1910* (New Haven, 1974), 238.

To return to the revision of the final chapter of the 1974 edition ("The Career Becomes Stranger") for a possible fifth edition of *Strange Career* is to face still another of the ironic turns both the history and the historiography of this subject have taken. Paradox and ironies, most of them revealed by new investigation, have prompted revisions from the start. Litwack confirmed Alexis de Tocqueville's view that the strongest racial prejudice was to be found in the states that had least encounter with slavery, and he discovered the origins of segregation "north of slavery." Ira Berlin disclosed that early laws of segregation in slave state cities not only kept blacks from whites but also separated free blacks from slave blacks. He also found residential segregation in the antebellum South to be less than in the North. Rabinowitz discovered that during Reconstruction segregation was regarded as an improvement over exclusion of blacks and was supported by freedmen and Republicans.

The movement to overthrow segregation was afflicted by even more ironies and paradoxes than the development of segregation. No sooner had the Civil Rights Act of 1964 and the Voting Rights Act of 1965 marked the triumph of the key objectives of the movement than violent rebellion broke out in urban ghettos of the West and North and for four summers spread flame and ruin in more than 150 major riots, most of them in the North. It was a rebellion allegedly fired more by hope than by despair, but not the hope for integration through nonviolence, the watchwords of the southern-born movement led by Martin Luther King, Jr. The new leaders rejected integration and assimilation by nonviolence for black separatism and racial polarization by "the basic tool of liberation: the gun," in Huey P. Newton's words. For the black nationalists, integration was "a dirty word." They converted few of their people during their short-lived crusade, but they left undeniable evidence that a successful movement against black segregation could spawn a violent black crusade for racial separatism. Most of those ironies have been acknowledged, but a more poignant one needs to be explored to bring revision up-to-date.

The inspiration, the energy, the power, the recruits, and the leaders of the mighty movement against segregation came out of the tightly segregated black communities and institutions of the South. The whole thing is inconceivable without those all-black churches, colleges, and schools. When the demonstrations started and met with violence, they had the support of united communities that included all classes, ages, and conditions. Class differences there were among blacks, but their residential commingling and racial unity were imposed to a large degree by the system they were fighting to overthrow. And the very success of their fight threatened and depleted the unity that made it possible.

The success of the civil rights movement had limits, but the movement did enjoy considerable fulfillment with regard to its professed aims of individual liberty, equal rights, equal opportunity, and equal justice. Thanks to a thriving economy as well as to gains won by the movement—the new opportunities and the lowering or removal of old barriers—hundreds of thousands of black people were able to improve their economic and social position substantially. The black population registered striking gains in political office and representation, educational achievement, and white-collar positions. The percentage of blacks achieving middle-class status increased sharply. As they moved up the economic ladder they moved out of the old ghetto confines, and those who departed were the able, the strong, and the resourceful.

In stark contrast with the condition of those who escaped was the plight of those who remained behind in the ghetto. The latter accounted for most of the 30 percent of black families who suffered a plunge into deeper poverty than ever following the civil rights movement. Among them unemployment increased faster than ever. To look at particular cities with large populations of poor blacks, New York welfare rolls doubled in the ten years after 1965, those of Chicago doubled in half that time. Throughout the country households headed by females of all races increased 72 percent in the 1970s. The great increase in child mothers and fatherless families meant further proliferation of impoverished, unschooled, unskilled, and unemployable city youth and the Hobbesian war of all against all that is now under way.[14]

It may be well at this point to distinguish what I am saying from what I am not saying. I am not saying that the civil rights movement or the struggle against segregation was a mistake or that their shortcomings explain the mounting desperation in the slums. Nor am I attributing the social and moral deterioration of the ghettos to the withdrawal of the black middle class. And I certainly do not wish to appear to be yielding to impulses of nostalgia for the return of a segregated past. But I do admit wondering how teenage mothers with fatherless families in crime-infested and drug-plagued ghettos will fare bereft of such communal support and protection as the old black segregated communities were able to give their young, their unfortunate, and their helpless, and such unified backing as they furnished the crusade that emancipated the more fortunate and resourceful. All these grim and paradoxical sequels to a noble cause will have to be incorporated before our revision of its history is completed and its story brought up-to-date.[15]

Thirty-five years of involvement in the ongoing historiography of black-white relations gives rise to a number of reflections about historical criticism and revision. One is a doubt that the tasks of criticism and revision are ever completed so long as the consequences of events and developments under study remain unresolved. Sometimes they are never fully resolved. Another reflection, suggested by the first, is that if knowledge of the past

[14] William H. Chafe, "The End of One Struggle, the Beginning of Another," in *The Civil Rights Movement in America,* ed. Charles W. Eagles (Jackson, 1986), 127–48, esp. 130; William Julius Wilson, *The Inner City, the Underclass, and Public Policy* (Chicago, 1988); also a searching critique of Wilson by Christopher Jencks, "Deadly Neighbors: How the Underclass Has Been Misunderstood," *New Republic,* June 13, 1988, pp. 23–32; Chafe, "End of One Struggle," 145.

[15] For an assessment of recent scholarship on the inner city and a selected bibliography, see Martha A. Gephart and Robert W. Pearson, "Contemporary Research on the Urban Underclass," Social Science Research Council, *Items,* 40 (June 1988), 1–10.

helps our understanding of the present, the opposite may also be true. I say this, I hope, with due respect for the integrity of the past, its inviolability, and with full consciousness of the received wisdom about the dangers of "presentism." For all that, I persist in the belief that writings of any historian about the subject under discussion would have been impoverished by indifference or blindness to the ironic and totally unanticipated outcome of the events of the past he recorded. Along with the findings of new research in the subject, events of the present and future are likely to continue to require more of the never-completed revisions in the history of the subject.

This subject, like virtually all aspects of American race relations, has often prompted strong moral impulses. Perhaps we are sufficiently alerted to threats to the integrity of history from church and state, from economic and political interests, and from ideas and ideologies. But I wonder if we have been sufficiently alerted to the menace of morals—moral concerns such as the passion for justice, the commitment to decent human relations and the brotherhood of man, and a dedication to noble causes. Those passions inspire many works of history and sometimes whole careers. To an increasing extent, contemporary historians tend to be identified by the good causes to which they are most dedicated. Before proceeding further, let me say that I am not against morals or justice or decency or noble causes. I am only saying that the integrity of the art over which Clio presides can be threatened by the just as well as the unjust, the righteous as well as the unrighteous, the moral as well as the immoral.

It was confusion over that point that betrayed Count Leo Tolstoy into proposing some of the most remarkable standards for criticism ever published by a serious artist. Works of art, he declared, speaking mainly of literature but including all other arts, to be of the highest order had to meet "the demands of morality." That meant, in a phrase he repeatedly used, that they had to demonstrate "the filial relation to God and the brotherhood of man." Among other things, "art should remove violence" and diminish crime, war, and madness. Tolstoy arrived at those standards after his great works of fiction were written, but he did not spare them on that account and sternly pronounced them "bad art."[16]

According to his own standards of criticism, Tolstoy enjoyed some impressive company in that respect. Applying the standards to the giants of world literature, he cited many who flunked his morality test. Among them William Shakespeare stands out for the woeful deficiencies and moral ambiguities of *King Lear*. In an essay on the teaching of moral values, Jaroslav Pelikan compares Tolstoy's views of that tragedy with those Thomas Jefferson expressed 127 years earlier, quoting the latter as writing in 1771 that "filial duty is more effectively impressed on the mind of a son or daughter by reading *King Lear* than by all the dry volumes of ethics and divinity that ever were written."[17]

Before bursting into applause for Jefferson's superior literary taste, however, we should remember that he was in this instance, at least, using much the same standards as Tolstoy—moral standards. In his letter of 1771 he defined as "useful" literature any that "contributes to fix in the principles and practices of virtue." How *King Oedipus* of Sophocles as monitor of filial piety might have been rated according to the standards of either Jefferson or Tolstoy is worth pondering. Applying his own standards, Tolstoy rated *Uncle Tom's Cabin* far above *Lear* and declared it to be one of the "models of a higher art, which arises from the love of God and of our neighbour."[18]

Should the standards of criticism that set *Uncle Tom* above *King Lear* be applied to classical works of history, the conse-

---

[16] Leo Tolstoy, *What Is Art?* in *The Complete Works of Count Tolstoy*, ed. and trans. Leo Wiener (Boston, 1904–1905), XXII, 297–98, 314, 319, 322, 342, 343.

[17] G. Wilson Knight, *Shakespeare and Tolstoy* (London, 1934); George Gibian, *Tolstoj and Shakespeare* (The Hague, 1957); Jaroslav Pelikan, "King Lear or Uncle Tom's Cabin? Alternative Methodologies for Teaching Values," in *The Teaching of Values in Higher Education: A Seminar* (Washington, 1986), 9–10.

[18] Thomas Jefferson to Robert Skipworth, Aug. 3, 1771, Thomas Jefferson, *Writings: Autobiography, a Summary View of the Rights of British America, Notes on the State of Virginia, Public Papers, Addresses, Messages, and Replies, Miscellany, Letters*, ed. Merrill D. Peterson (New York, 1984), 740–45; Tolstoy, *What Is Art?* 300.

quences for library stacks, required reading lists, and great books courses would be chaotic. And yet there is no lack of contemporary examples of such misapplied standards in historical criticism. It is not unusual to find reviews pronouncing works good because they promote good works—worthy causes, movements for justice, equality, the brotherhood of man, the sisterhood of women.

To give Jefferson his due, he remarked dryly in that same letter that, "considering history as a moral exercise, her lessons would be too infrequent" and too little "attended with such circumstances as to excite in any high degree this sympathetic emotion of virtue." On the whole he thought tragedy, comedy, and epic poetry more useful for that purpose.[19] Those reflections make his defense of *King Lear* all the more interesting, since that play filled the stage with clowns, fools, villains, and howling madmen. They were actors with roles and devious schemes differing little from the sort he said historians regularly recorded.

Historians recording the course of race relations in the American democracy have long been confronted with demands that they teach moral lessons, excite the "sympathetic emotion of virtue," and use history for those purposes. Justice for the oppressed and punishment for the oppressor were demands echoed through decades of moral recrimination, four years of our bloodiest war, and the subsequent century that it took to resolve its issues even partially. Given the circumstances, some corruption of history by morals was unavoidable. No one could remain entirely insensitive to the moral issue, and few were entirely successful in keeping it from influencing what they wrote. I know that I was not always as careful as I might have been in that respect. The critics were right in calling me to terms when I failed. Most of them would agree with me, I believe, that such failings should be kept to a minimum.

[19] Jefferson to Skipworth, Aug. 3, 1771, Jefferson, *Writings*, ed. Peterson, 741–42.

VI

SCIENCE *AND* ART

A profession with tendencies to split periodically into
two antagonistic camps presents those who practice it with difficulties. That has been the plight of the history profession for the
last century or more. Its members commonly deal with the problem in one of three ways: ally themselves exclusively with one or
the other camp or keep one foot planted in each of them. In the
university those of the first two persuasions seat themselves comfortably or defiantly on one or the other side of the imaginary line
dividing the Faculty of Arts and Sciences, while those of the
third persuasion shift uneasily back and forth across the aisle.
Honorary societies such as the American Philosophical Society divide the historians they elect quite illogically between the class
called Humanities and the one called Social Sciences according to
whether they are known primarily for work in periods before or
after some arbitrary date such as the year 1700. Taking a no-
nonsense approach, the American Academy and Institute of Arts
and Letters dumps all of its handful of historians in with the Literature Department, which at least has the merit of denying them
honors as sculptors, architects, painters, or musicians.

Unhappy with these ways of classifying history, I have whenever possible rejected them all and experimented with other pos-

sibilities. Why, indeed, should history submit to either/or classifications of any sort? Pointing to the great seniority of our elderly craft over younger disciplines of the academy, I have suggested that the latter might have more to learn from history than history has to learn from them. To be sure, over the centuries historians have gained insights through passing affinities with many disciplines, from theology to biology, without losing their own identity in the process. They stand to gain similarly from the social sciences—without becoming one with them. *Or* without forfeiting their much older humanistic affinity and original literary tradition.

Assuming this mediating posture, I have sought a flexibility that would enable me to encourage both students with a literary bent and those with scientific inclinations to pursue their calling in history. I hoped also that I might discreetly use the role of mediator to redress the balance should either the literary or the scientific preference gain excessive influence. During the years when the pieces in this section were written it seemed to me that the scales were tipping rather heavily toward scientific pretensions. It will be seen from the predominant tone of the sketches that follow and the historians chosen to illustrate my theme that I was leaning for corrected balance to the humanistic and traditional side. The mildness of the tone may not prepare the reader for the outrage and indignation with which some opponents greeted my suggestions, but the reaction will suggest the passion with which such convictions are held. A sample of this sort of response is provided in the foreword to the piece immediately following.

18

A Short History
of American History

When the first volume of The Oxford History of the United States appeared, the New York Times Book Review invited this contribution from the general editor of the series. I used it in part, without presuming to speak for the authors or commit them to a point of view, to say that I thought there was still a place for the old as well as the new history, a need for narrative history written for the general reader, and a use of the art of the craft to report its findings, however scientific they might be. These conciliatory gestures were, however, greeted with a long letter to the editor from a West Coast historian who denounced my views as "Reaganism of the New Right: a demand for a return to simpler times and simpler tales, for a world no longer mired in complexity and opacity. . . . This critique represents the worst in the recent wave of anti-intellectual Luddism." I quote this in the hope it might help explain my concern for restoring mental balance in the profession.

AMERICAN HISTORY WAS FIRST WRITTEN BY EXPLORERS and the earliest settlers. They wrote in the old tradition or were inspired by it, as were historians of the next three centuries and more. It was essentially a literary tradition, that of an avocation or a "calling," and its practitioners were as individual and autonomous as poets or playwrights. They might think of themselves as learned or wise but not as scientists or professionals. They took pride in their prose and in the clarity and drama of their narrative and descriptive writing, and most of it was narrative. All of them addressed an unspecialized general public and took pains to please their readers and write on subjects of common interest in language the public understood.

As time passed, the early chroniclers of discovery and those of a theological bent gave way to patricians and later to self-made scholars and free-lance writers. Successful amateur historians have never been lacking. Decidedly the most successful of all in terms of readership were the 19th-century patricians, William Prescott, George Bancroft and Francis Parkman, contemporaries of Thomas Carlyle and Thomas Macaulay, who outsold even them. For a time history was the best-selling branch of literature, and the outstanding historians were men of enormous prestige. These giants were succeeded by self-made scholars, still amateurs and patricians, such as Henry Adams, James Ford Rhodes, Theodore Roosevelt and John Bach McMaster. They did not win as many readers as their predecessors, but they were the acknowledged authorities on American history in the late 19th century and thoroughly dominated the field.

It was this formidable group, its prestige and the amateur tradition it represented, plus the weight of the ages supporting the tradition, that comparatively unknown scholars such as J. Franklin Jameson and Herbert Baxter Adams confronted with their claims of professional status in the 1880s. The fledgling professionals acknowledged the awkwardness of the situation in various ways. For one thing, in the early decades they almost invariably chose an amateur instead of a professional as the annually elected president of their professional association. Not all of those so honored seemed duly impressed. One of them, Theodore Roosevelt, complained that "the conscientious, industrious, painstaking little pedants" did not understand "their own limitations" or appreciate the need "for great writers, great thinkers."

Other successful amateurs, with an eye to comparative sales and readers, came to share disdain for the "pedants." In all fairness, the professional did not aspire to compete for public attention, and the public reciprocated with indifference. The pro did not so much lose the public as abandon it. Professionals wrote for each other, to "make a contribution," to fill gaps in knowledge, to advance "science." The modesty of their aims is reflected in the call of one of their leaders in the 1890s for "the spread of thoroughly good second-class work." No strictly professional historian in this country, according to Professor John Higham, "published a major book prior to the twentieth century." Continued deference to the amateurs as late as the 1940s is suggested by the vote of a body of professional leaders choosing the six greatest American historians no longer living: All the front-runners were of the old school save one, Frederick Jackson Turner, who published only one book apart from collected essays during his lifetime.

The scorn of the patrician amateurs and the apathy of the reading public, however, were not the main sources of embarrassment for professional historians. Having rejected literary standards and philosophic themes, they stoutly asserted their dedication to the cause of science. But here again they ran into trouble. What hurt most was the mounting challenge to the scientific status of history from the social sciences and from fellow scholars whom historians considered close allies. Arrogance and unfairness marred the attack, for historians had anticipated some methods of the social scientists, and the latter were not all that secure in their own pretensions. The attack nevertheless contributed to the decline in morale, confidence and vigor that afflicted the second generation of professional historians.

New life was breathed into the dispirited ranks by the rise and eventual dominance of the progressive school of historians before and between the two world wars. Much of the attention and many of the recruits attracted by the new school may be accounted for by its alliance with a popular movement of reform. Others were attracted by the banner of revolt the Western and Southern progressives raised against the dominance of conservative historians of New England. Frederick Jackson Turner, Charles A. Beard, Carl Becker and Vernon L. Parrington were eloquent spokesmen who gained the ear of a lay public. They celebrated an advancing partnership of science, democracy and progress and made of history an exciting struggle for the realization of democratic ideals. When hope for those ideals faded with the rise of dictators, the progressive influence fell into decline. History lost the support of a popular movement but began to rid itself of a disproportionate present-and-future-mindedness inherent in progressivism.

It was not really until after World War II that the guild gained the self-confidence it had so far lacked. Part of the credit goes to rapidly expanding college enrollments and the consequent increase in the number of historians to teach them. No other country could boast nearly so large a historical profession. Emboldened by numbers, historians overcame some old feelings of inferiority, resolved self-doubts, rather arbitrarily settled internal disputes over theory and demanded, and often regained, the respect of fellow scholars of other disciplines. If the founders had declared their independence from literature and philosophy, the new generation of professionals proclaimed that history was neither science nor art but autonomous—sui generis. These historians published prolifically, and a few began to attract a reading public to rival the amateurs', especially those whose books shared the current public mood of nationalism and pride in the American past. The more prominent of these, Allan Nevins and Samuel Eliot Morison, for example, always retained much of the old tradition of the storyteller.

The emerging sense of confidence began to crumble in the 1960's under pressures from outside and inside the guild. Student patronage shrank and with it the available jobs for historians. Public interest turned from the past (especially a celebrated past) to a troubled present. Within the ranks of the craft itself, a rift opened between the "old" historians and a set of New Historians marching under an old banner dating back to the founders: scientific history. The new ones bore names more familiar to other historians than to the public—David S. Landes, Samuel P. Hayes, Allan Bogue and Stephan Thernstrom, for example.

This time "science" meant more than a rhetorical commitment to objectivity and austerity. It meant extensive innovations in method, technique, training, subject matter, sources, style and intelligibility, and in the readers addressed. The New Historians were analytical rather than narrative, used statistical rather than "literary" and "traditional" sources and concentrated on circumstance and "behavior" rather than on events, actions and policy. Modeled on the social sciences (at a time, oddly, when those disciplines themselves were in a state of disarray and self-doubt), the New History adopted their fields of investigation as well as their strategies of research. They wrote about the masses and the powerless more than elites and the powerful. They turned from the public to the private sector: to the family, the nursery, the bedroom, the deathbed and their psychological secrets; to demography and long-term shifts in population, marriage, birth rates and sex roles; to popular culture; to the history of prisons, hospitals, villages, cities and churches; to voting behavior as prompted by ethnic and religious, rather than public, issues.

The New History undoubtedly started a rejuvenation of professional scholarship. Computers and sophisticated mathematical techniques not only revolutionized economic history but spread methods of quantification through many other fields. The findings raised new questions and hypotheses, undermined old assumptions, demanded fresh research and opened up unexplored subjects. Only a small number of historians became practicing converts, but nearly all historians felt challenged and influenced, and some felt threatened. It was clear that many New History innovations were here to stay and had to be coped with. For a time it seemed that their champions might become the new power elite of the profession.

Old heads, who had watched waves of innovation rise and fall over the generations, waited for familiar signs. Making converts and attacking the establishment are always more exciting than practicing what is preached and preaching to the already converted. Enthusiasm and arrogance subsided as avalanches of computer printouts and data-bank inflation overwhelmed their users. Quantifiers themselves acknowledged the limitations, blunders and dangers of their methods. Computers abhor ambiguity. Doubts also arose about the fragmentation of the profession into highly specialized fields, each with its own journal and organization and sometimes a special language. Were all the subdisciplines for different ethnic groups and sexes, urban and rural history, psychological and social history, demographic and ecological history—on and on—really that necessary? History was once called a habitation of many mansions, but it has been more recently described as scattered suburbs, trailer camps and a deteriorating central city.

Most deplored by those who cling to a basic tradition of the craft is an indifference toward the layman, the assumption that history has findings and secrets too arcane for the unspecialized general reader. The enduring faith, on the other hand, holds that it is the duty and privilege of historians, unlike scholars of other disciplines, to present the results of the guild's researches, or at least their significance, to the layman in readable, unspecialized prose he can understand and enjoy. The amateurs still flourish (though in the freelance rather than the patrician style), but they are not much help here. They often cannot read, much less "do," some of the New History and would be baffled by much of the rest. The New Historians, with notable exceptions, have written mainly for each other, and some of them chiefly for those in their own subdiscipline. The task of passing on to the public their findings (as well as those of the "old" historians, who have continued quite active) falls to the pro. But it must be the professional who is able and happy to revive some very old traditions of the craft, including those of the storyteller.

Fortunately, narrative history has enjoyed something of a recent renaissance among professionals, even among New Historians themselves, as Lawrence Stone has pointed out. Undaunted by disparagement of traditional "literary" and "storytelling" fogies, professionals such as Jonathan D. Spence, David M. Potter, Peter Gay and France's Emmanuel Le Roy Ladurie have championed and practiced narrative and descriptive history of a high order. The heritage of Parkman and Morison is by no means extinct.

The need for periodic syntheses such as the multivolume Oxford History of the United States will continue. The professionals who write these volumes must have a command of the old as well as the new history. They should also keep in mind that the lay reader has a legitimate interest in the actions as well as the behavior of peoples of the past, in their aspirations as well as their circumstances, in things that cannot be quantified even more than those that can. The public's interest can be captured for the more important discoveries of the New History if their significance is made clear. People of a democratic tradition can surely be interested in the historic plight of the powerless, but they have a natural and abiding concern for power and those who have wielded it and to what effect—a concern that historians should never have neglected anyway. If they can now revive the art of the craft, historians can also reclaim a general public.

19

History
and the
Third Culture

For this paper the occasion was a conference on history and the social sciences held in London in 1967 to bring East European historians into a discussion then preoccupying Western members of the profession. It was well attended by representatives from the Warsaw Pact countries. They had little to say for the record, but assured me in private that they shared my views about quantifiers and history, but for reasons I did not have foremost in mind: That these types always turned up with evidence that things were not so bad before the revolution.

A REGULAR FEATURE OF THE ANNUAL MEETING of the American Historical Association during the thirty-odd years of my membership has been a session on the social sciences and history. I am assured by older heads as well as by the record that the tradition goes back at least thirty years before that. I have taken part in such sessions myself. The predominant tone of the papers has been hortatory and the responses of the audience ranged from humble resignation to eager approval. It is true that from time to time a dissenter would say that things had gone too far, that the newcomers were too aggressive or presumptuous, and that history after all was an art and not a science. More often, however, the reaction to the annual exhortations was self-congratulatory. At last we had turned a corner, faced up to modern trends, and shaken off the lethargy of tradition. Hereafter things would be different.

Actually, things remained very much the same, in spite of exhortations and manifestos, and have continued much the same over the years. One limited exception to the rule is a development that has occurred largely since the Second World War. The generation of historians who began to publish then had completed their formal training with the sense that they had been ill-prepared by their masters. The craft as it was taught them seemed, as one of them put it, 'an intellectually invertebrate affair,' wholly lacking in sound canons of criticism, beset by contradictory concepts, and afflicted with an appalling heterogeneity of interpretations. Since no remedy for the shortcomings was apparent within the profession, some of the disenchanted turned to the social sciences for guidance and inspiration, for new clues to needed principles of order for their calling. A few vocal historians made these intentions and hopes disproportionately conspicuous in the profession. Fewer still was the number who extensively applied those methods, concepts, and findings of the social sciences in the history they wrote.

With their attention focussed on the bulletins, resolutions, and manifestos issuing from conferences of social scientists and historians, rather than on the history actually written, some observers have gathered what I believe is a rather exaggerated impression of the impact of social sciences on history in recent years. So strong is this impression among some as to raise the question whether history has not indeed been absorbed by the social sciences and virtually lost its identity as a discipline. In a recent statement George H. Nadel, editor of *History and Theory*, writes in announcing a conference on History and Social Science: "The opening up of new lines of historical inquiry and the development of new techniques of research (many of them borrowed from the social sciences) have gone so far that it is doubtful whether the notion of "history" as a discipline has any core meaning at all, so various are the meanings which can be imputed to it."

My response to this estimate is borrowed from Mark Twain, who once complained that the press reports of his death were exaggerated. Far from being revolutionized by new techniques, transformed beyond recognition, or swallowed up by the social sciences, much the greater part of history as written in the United States has remained obstinately, almost imperviously traditional. It could be read by historians of the past three generations with scarcely a tremor of surprise over methods and techniques. Like their predecessors and masters, contemporary historians write narrative, largely non-analytical works. They set great store by working from manuscript sources, verifying the facts, and marshalling the evidence. Their publications are praised or blamed in the professional journals according to the old-fashioned canons and values: thoroughness of research, objectivity of view, and clarity of logic, together with lucidity and grace of the writing. Contemporary craftsmen are even more addicted than those of earlier generations to over-specialization and narrowness of subject matter. Like their predecessors, they work with monumental patience through mountains of material for unimpressive conclusions. They aspire, as they modestly say, to "make a contribution." Like earlier craftsmen, they are subject to occupational shortcomings of long standing: their premises are often unexamined, their hypotheses ill defined, their concepts vague, their interpretations confused. The storms of philosophical discourse concerning their basic assumptions and principles go on over their heads, and the innovations of scientific technique in sister disciplines go largely unheeded. The profession is in many ways a living fossil from the pre-scientific age. At its worst, traditional history writing can be a mechanical, almost mindless act, and unfortunately it often is just that. At its best it can still produce work of intellectual distinction that can stand comparison with some of the finer works of earlier periods. But, apart from a few exceptions, in their adherence to traditional ways and values, the best are like the worst, the young like the old.

What then of the restless and innovative historians who have turned to the social sciences in their disenchantment with tradition? How far have they gone with their rebellion? How much have they broken with tradition? The answer is, not really very much and within certain restrictive limits. This is not to dismiss their experiments and explorations as unimportant. I think they are quite important, but I also think the limits they have set are as significant as the innovations they have made.

The evidence of innovation sparkles in their pages, but unobtrusively and for the most part unself-consciously. It appears variously in the form of new questions asked as well as new answers to old questions from the social sciences. It might be an acknowledgment of the neglected relevance of child-training, of status and generational conflict, or of social mobility. It is sometimes manifest in a new awareness of the sociology of knowledge and of the learned professions. It can be detected here in an enhanced sophistication about sampling and statistics and there in an added caution about implicit quantification. More rarely it takes the form of limited experiments with new techniques such as content analysis, career-line analysis, and model-building. Much depends on the individual historian's preferred affinities with particular disciplines, and given his humanstic predilections he naturally feels a greater affinity with the cultural anthropologist than with the physical anthropologist, with the psychoanalyst than with the rat psychologist, and so on with types of sociology, political science, and economics.

In proclaiming their affinities and acknowledging their obligations to the various social science disciplines, however, these historians invariably set certain limits and qualifications to their inter-disciplinary affiliations. "I doubt that history is a social science," writes R. R. Palmer, "but do believe that it should make use of concepts drawn from social science or any other useful source. In most histories, however, these general ideas will ap-

pear unobtrusively, to give meaning and relevancy to the particular."[1] Observing the strenuous efforts of analytical philosophers
to impose scientific models on historical explanation over the last
twenty-five years, J. H. Hexter confesses that he finds "no per-
ceptible modification of the object of their attentions, the writing
of history, which seems to absorb the onslaught and resume its
initial non-scientific shape rather like a foam-rubber pillow."[2]
David M. Potter, who has made extensive overtures to the behavioural sciences and effective use of their findings, believes
nevertheless that "history has not been, and cannot and should
not be, regarded as one of the cluster which makes up the behavioural group." He doubts that history can "even operate in close
relationship with them" or that they will ever make "very congenial academic teammates," in spite of his conviction that they
should collaborate. What keeps them apart essentially is not a
disparity in subject matter but a difference in theatres of operation. For behavioural scientists the most critical theatres are the
nursery, the bathroom, and the bedroom. Grateful for any insights gained from these quarters, the historian is nevertheless inhibited by his more elderly and dignified muse from prying into
such private areas and leaves them to the younger and more uninhibited disciplines with licence and proclivity for snooping.[3]
Richard Hofstadter is also grateful for insights from the social
sciences, for bringing the historian "into working relationship
with certain aspects of the modern intellectual climate," for "a
fresh store of ideas with which to disturb the excessively settled
routines of his thought," and for "their addition to the speculative richness of history." He does not believe, however, that "what
historians do is in any very satisfactory sense of the term scientific." What they do might best be described, he thinks, "as a
sort of literary anthropology." Their aim is "a kind of portraiture

[1] R. R. Palmer, "Generalizations about Revolution: A Case Study," in
Louis Gottschalk, *Generalization in the Writings of History* (Chicago, 1963),
66.

[2] J. H. Hexter, "The Rhetoric of History," *History and Theory*, VI
(1967), 12.

[3] David M. Potter, *People of Plenty: Economic Abundance and American
Character* (Chicago, 1954), xv, xxi, 65.

of the life of nations and individuals, classes and groups of men."[4] In spite of a keen interest in the social sciences, especially cultural anthropology and psychoanalysis, H. Stuart Hughes believes that "history will continue in its original literary tradition." What historians do is "to draw up imprecise 'explanation sketches' rather than to employ the narrow and more rigorous methods of social science." This is "not necessarily 'unscientific,'" but "should the social scientists insist that historians abandon this loose type of procedure, I do not think that the result would be better history. It would simply be a narrower kind of historical writing lacking the range and flexibility of the historian's craft as it has traditionally been practiced." Hughes thinks that "the study of history offers living proof of the complementary nature of art and of science," and asks his fellow historians to "take pride in the mediating character of their own discipline."[5]

What these gentlemen are proposing is not a marriage but a mediation, a genial compromise. Their association with the social sciences has by no means infected them with an inferiority complex. They are fully conscious of the seniority of their muse and the honour and antiquity of their tradition. They are aware of the extreme youth and inexperience of the junior disciplines and struggle against the impulse to be patronizing. They are talking here of an *entente cordiale*, not an *Anschluss*. They would never think of bowing to the laws and customs of these alien disciplines, and they obviously intend to be fastidiously eclectic in borrowing alien concepts and methods. In Professor Hughes's words, they should "pick and choose." These gestures should never be taken, as they apparently have been by some, as an abandonment of professional identity or an abasement of traditional pride.

In their adjustment to the social sciences, which someone has called the "Third Culture," historians have in mind the long

[4] Richard Hofstadter, "History and the Social Sciences," in Fritz Stern (ed.), *Varieties of History: From Voltaire to the Present* (New York, 1956), 361–4.

[5] H. Stuart Hughes, "The Historian and the Social Scientist," *American Historical Review*, October, 1960, 31–3; *History as Art and Science* (New York, 1964), 3.

history of relations between their guild and other disciplines within their own humanistic culture. They were for centuries at great pains to adjust to the preoccupations and strange ideas of theologians and metaphysicians, for example, without themselves becoming theologians or metaphysicians or wholly subscribing to their laws and methods. More recently they have survived the ordeal of exposure and invasion from the Second Culture, the natural sciences, which came upon historians with the overbearing prestige and arrogance of world conquerors. We still bear the scars of that encounter, and the compromises of recent memory we seemed compelled to make with the "laws" of biology and physics are still a source of some historiographic embarrassment.

With these traumatic experiences fresh in mind, history is now confronted with the necessity of another accommodation, an adjustment to the Third Culture. It has not overwhelmed us with the power and prestige of, say, twelfth-century theology or nineteenth-century biology. It does not as yet, indeed, possess any such power and prestige. But its cohorts are endowed with the vigour and confidence of youth and have friends in powerful places—the foundations, for example. It is not surprising that historians are a bit wary and defensive and at times show withdrawal symptoms. Taking their cue from past experience, the bolder and more flexible diplomats of the guild urge a policy that combines accommodation with resistance. They propose in effect that we learn the language and techniques of the aliens, that we consult with them amiably on problems of mutual concern, that we press upon them the doctrine of free trade in ideas, and that we benefit from such exchanges wherever we can. But they would draw the line at adopting the new religion or subscribing to the new mystique.

On the whole this liberal policy of accommodation, though it still meets with resolute opposition from the last-ditch, no-compromise traditionalists, is gaining ground within the guild. It has already proved its worth in the civilizing effect it has had upon some of the new people. They have shown a gratifying improvement in manners and even on occasion a proper deference to a senior guild. It is true that they still habitually approach history with the urge to teach rather than learn, as instructors rather than pupils, with answers rather than questions. But there are already promising exceptions. The younger school of analysts, for example, will confess in unguarded moments that they are really concerned to do much the same thing as historians in trying to free men from the burden of the past by helping them to understand it, and that their formidable paraphernalia of Freudian and post-Freudian apparatus is in large part presenting us with their defences. Anthropologists, who never fully lost touch with traditional culture, tend to mellow with time and to age gracefully. Even some of the sociologists, in the presence of historians, abandon or modify their special language and speak in the common vernacular, especially when they realize with embarrassment that we know what they are talking about. It becomes increasingly apparent that we may be able to live with these people, to learn from them, and perhaps in time to teach them some of the arcane ironies and darker enigmas of an ancient craft.

In the meantime historians should be warned that their policy of accommodation and watchful waiting is not infallible, and that in fact it has already been put under dire stress and strain by the powerful eruption of the cult of quantification. Here we are dealing with something more like an ideology than a church. It has infiltrated the priesthood of virtually all social science Sanhedrins and threatens to take over some of them completely, so that the compromises historians had worked out with the older establishments of these denominations are now in jeopardy. The quantifiers certainly include men of moderation and balance, but the zeal and heedless assurance of the more vocal spokesmen of the cult have sometimes strained the limits of polite intercourse. Their aggressive posture and their occasional philistinism have thrown some of our more conservative historians into a state of shock.

In his presidential address to the American Historical Association, Carl Bridenbaugh, who is still worried about "the dehumanizing methods of social sciences" in general, warned the faithful never to "worship at the shrine of that Bitch-goddess,

QUANTIFICATION."[6] Edward C. Kirkland, a distinguished economic historian of the traditional school, interpreted the recent book of a self-styled "Cliometrician" as "a new manifesto which, if I get the message, threatens: 'Retool, rethink, reform, or be plowed under.' New are the assumption of infallibility, the all-or-nothing tone, the disdain for words and style, by inference a means of making error plausible. Every page . . . has a statistic but never a trace (beware the implicit quantification!) of humour about either themselves or those who differ from them."[7] Among the younger and presumably more flexible craftsmen, Arthur M. Schlesinger, Jr., puts quantifiers on notice that their "mystique . . . leads its acolytes to accept as significant only those questions to which the quantitative magic can provide answers. As a humanist, I am bound to reply that almost all important questions are important precisely because they are *not* susceptible to quantitative answers."[8]

Even those historians who have taken the lead in conciliatory accommodation of the social sciences tend to draw the line against the more doctrinaire quantifiers. H. Stuart Hughes, one of the statesmen of compromise, calls the mathematical model-builders "starry eyed platonists." He deplores the "condescension for mere 'fact-gatherers'" among mathematically oriented economists, believes they "fly in the face of more than two millennia of historical practice," and thinks "they have put a faith in the overarching construction of the human mind that is almost religious in its intensity."[9]

Let me confess first of all that I share many of these misgivings. As much as any of my colleagues I fear abstraction and unequivocal conclusions about equivocal and inscrutable problems. Like them I renounce the postulate that man's purpose and

[6] Carl Bridenbaugh, "The Great Mutation," *American Historical Review*, January 1963, 326.

[7] Edward C. Kirkland, review of R. W. Fogel, *Railroads and Economic Growth*, in *American Historical Review*, July 1967, 1494.

[8] Arthur M. Schlesinger, Jr., "The Humanist Looks at Empirical Social Research," *American Sociological Review*, December 1962, 770.

[9] Hughes, "The Historian and the Social Scientist," *loc. cit.*, 35; for other reservations see J. H. Hexter, "Some American Observations," *Journal of Contemporary History*, January 1967.

conscious will may not be the cause of his action, and that man's actions are not as legitimate a subject for study as his "behaviour." I think there is a certain amount of anti-intellectualism as well as a delusive pretence of finality implicit in exclusively statistical statements. I deplore an obsession with gadgetry, and I regard the vulgar disdain for style as barbarous. For all that, I feel impelled to remind my fellow historians that their humanistic aversions will not make quantification go away. It is here to stay, and we must find more effective means of coping with it. Rhetorical indignation and the neo-Luddite posture of our conservatives are not effective responses. Smashing computers is not quite the answer.

I say this for a number of reasons, some but not all of which are peculiarly felt in my own country. One is a well-known American weakness for numbers. I shall illustrate this implicit anthropological quantification unscientifically by a story in the *New York Times* about the unveiling of an abstract sculpture by Picasso in Chicago. With unerring instinct for news essentials, the *Times* first reported (16 August 1967) that 12,000 square feet of blue percale were used to veil the 50-foot sculpture of 163 tons of steel on a plaza 345 by 220 feet—and only then turned to esthetic details and qualities. In America statistics command attention, if not something like reverence. All too often a lively discussion in my graduate seminar has been brought to a dead stop by anyone who waves a graph, a column of figures, or a stack of computer print-out—though they may entirely beg the question.

Another reason, not I believe peculiar to America, is the continued emphasis on political history in the guild, and the unquestionable susceptibility of certain types of political hypotheses and generalizations, quite common in the trade, to rigorous test by the quantifier's techniques. Unless we are prepared to let the political scientists, who are increasingly giving their subject a historical dimension, have the final word in a field of study sacred to the concerns of historians for centuries, we must look to our techniques. If we can't lick 'em, we must join 'em. The same goes for the field of economic history, with certain reservations about joining the "Cliometricians." Those concerned with the contemporary or recent history of industrial, industrializing, and post-industrial countries are especially vulnerable to the quantifiers' criticism, for these historians are dealing with mass societies that march to the drum of numbers and counters. They are preeminently numbers-minded, not only in their getting and spending, but in their fighting and voting. Their historian is obliged to master their language.

To prove that a thing *can* be done is no adequate demonstration that it *should* be done. But it should be clear by now that the traditional defence that it *can't* be done—if this only means a lack of the data, the techniques, the machinery, or the funds—simply no longer holds water. The data archives, or "banks" (a characteristic turn of phrase) are impressive. The Inter-University Consortium for Political Research in Michigan, with some sixty member universities in Canada, Great Britain, Europe, and the United States, has built up among other things a vast collection of election statistics, census data, and legislative voting records in considerable historical depth. The American political historian now ignores at his peril the existence in "machine-readable form" (usually on magnetic tape) basic election statistics for both major and minor parties, by county, for the offices of governor, senator, congressman, and president from 1824 to the present; United States census information from 1820 to the present, and nearing completion in "computer-usable form," congressional roll-call voting data from the Continental Congress to the present. In addition to numerous other "banks" in the United States there are data archives in London, Amsterdam, Cologne, Bad Godesberg, and Bergen, to mention only a few. In 1966 there was founded in London a European Federation of Social Science Data.[10] If this is further ugly evidence of "Americanization," it has its European champions.

The techniques of data manipulation developed by the social sciences for their purposes are often adaptable to those of history, and seminaries of eager proselytizers invite historians to "retool" (another favourite phrase) at summer sessions, expenses

[10] Ralph L. Bisco, "Social Science Data Archives: A Review of Developments," *American Political Science Review*, 1966, 93–109.

paid. As for the "hardware," each successive generation of computers grows more fabulously ingenious and intricate, and professional programmers are ready to oblige. And as for the funds available, the mere mention of the word "computer" in an application elevates the historian to scientific citizenship, makes him eligible for National Science Foundation grants, and quadruples his normal humanities-class stipend.

Let me hasten to add that for the great majority of serious, valid, and important historical endeavours, these banks, sophisticated techniques, and terrifying machines have little or no relevance. And where they are relevant and useful, the techniques applicable in most instances are quite simple and unsophisticated. When R. R. Palmer showed that the percentage of émigrés from the American Revolution was much larger than that from the French Revolution and that, unlike the French, they did not return home, he was quantifying effectively with nothing more sophisticated than addition and subtraction. Some kinds of historians have legitimate suspicions of quantification. Historians on the political left tend to lean towards the methodological right in this respect and to shun quantification. It is true, as Lawrence Stone admits, that "the quantification of the past two decades has been used by right-wing revisionists to take the ideological steam out of historical debate and to prove that things were not so bad after all *before the revolution.*" He maintains, nevertheless, that much of this revisionism has stood up under criticism.[11] Be that as it may, the gentlemen of the left have reason to complain that counting heads does not get at the essence of revolutionary situations or the dynamics of insurrectionary minorities. A scientific opinion poll of Negro sentiment has revealed that Negro Americans with few exceptions are reasonably content, moderate, and non-violent—but large areas of Detroit and other American cities lie in ashes.

But even in areas of history where quantification is legiti-

[11] Lawrence Stone, review of Barrington Moore, Jr., *Social Origins of Dictatorship and Democracy,* in *New York Review of Books,* 24 August 1967; in Moore's book see 509–23; see also Irwin Unger, "The 'New Left' and American History," *American Historical Review,* July 1967, 1241.

mately applied (and there *are* several), and where the most refined and sophisticated techniques are legitimately employed and
all resources in "hardware" and expertise are marshalled, the results can still be plagued with human fallacies and problems that
are quite familiar to traditional historians. For quantification does
not eliminate error and can be the means of entrenching it more
deeply and securely. It does not ensure accuracy and it can sometimes go further than a felicitous literary style in making error
plausible. No technique or machine has yet been devised to eliminate the need for intuition and imagination and no gadget invented to serve as a substitute for thought. The gathering, pro-
cessing, manipulating, and machining of data can be used as
effectively as the endless taking of notes and verifying of facts
for postponing or escaping hard intellectual work in interpreting
and writing history. The older and wiser heads among the quantifiers know this and say so, but the zealots in our midst will tell
you that all but a few of the books should be stored in ware-
houses and the library space thus salvaged converted to computer
centres and electronic information retrievers.

It is mainly our young who need to be protected. I find
among them a mood of incipient panic, a mounting fear of technological displacement, and a disposition among a few to rush
into the camp of the zealots. They should be authoritatively assured that there is plenty of history to be written, and that much
the larger part of it will continue to be written without much reference to these innovations. But that is not enough. It is too late
for the older of us to retool or adapt our work very much to the
new techniques even if we acquire them. And it is not necessary
for many of the young to master them, though all should know
their possibilities. But a small cadre should definitely be armed
with all the weapons, trained in all the techniques, and schooled
in the ideology of the invaders. Only in that way will they be
able effectively to cope with the philistines among us, to be on
guard against their sophistries, see through their pretensions, and
turn to the uses of our craft such tricks and notions of these people as meet our standards and serve our needs.

I take great stock in this strategy. For one thing historians have already infiltrated the highest councils of the quantifiers themselves, some of them men of sound mind and balanced judgment with allegiance to our guild and its standards who may be depended upon to restrain the zealots.[12] For another thing, in America at least, and in some other countries as well, it was not the social scientists but the historians of the latter part of the last century and the earlier years of this who were the pioneers and innovators of quantification. Most of their students tended to drift away from their example and failed to exploit or refine their innovations. But the precedent is there and historians have a tradition, always a comfort to them, on which to fall back.

Happily a comparable situation exists in reverse within the heritage of the Third Culture. Without exception, to my knowledge, all the social sciences find in their legitimate lineage nineteenth-century masters and founding fathers whose work was deeply concerned with historical problems and informed by historical learning. One thinks of the classical economists as well as Marx, of Tocqueville, Bluntschli, Bryce and many others in the study of politics, of Spencer and Weber in sociology, of Freud in psychology. Their students drifted away from these historical moorings and turned to exclusive concern with the present and with small, neat topics adapted to methodological preoccupations. In recent years, however, social scientists in all departments have been reviving their interest in history, shifting from microscopic to macroscopic focus, from short-range to long-range analysis, and adding a historical dimension to the problems of economics, politics, sociology, and psychology.[13]

In view of the directions in which the two are moving, history towards the social sciences and the social sciences towards history, there would appear to be ample meeting ground and the promise of closer relations. I would hope that the social scientists will approach history with questions as well as with answers,

[12] See, for example, William O. Aydelotte, "Quantification in History," *American Historcial Review,* April 1966.

[13] Compare, for example, Robert A. Dahl, "The Behavioral Approach," *American Political Science Review,* 1961, 771; and an unpublished paper of August 1967 by Samuel H. Beer, "Political Science and History," to appear in Volume VII of *History and Theory.*

with the desire to learn as well as to teach, as allies with common interests and not as imperialists seeking territorial aggrandisement. If they do, then the prospects of mutual commerce, cultural interchange, and peaceful co-existence with the Third Culture would seem propitious.

20

Francis Parkman
(1823-1893)

IT IS WELL THAT FRANCIS PARKMAN came along when he did, or historians might not have gained so early a footing, if any footing at all, in The Library of America, which is presenting the country's foremost authors in a series of new editions. Parkman worked in the 19th century, between the time when historians moved out of the pulpit and the time when they took up permanent residence in the university. American historians had virtually missed the interlude of polite society in the 18th-century salon that endowed European historians with literary reputations. So even in the next century, the Americans were craftsmen with an avocation, not yet scholars and pedagogues with a profession. Historians thought of themselves in Parkman's time as men of letters, or rather gentlemen of letters, dedicated to the pursuit of an art as well as scholarship. As historians they were quite conscious of having Clio as an authentic muse of their own, but they were ready to serve other muses too.

While he was an undergraduate at Harvard, Parkman had firmly decided to write a history of North America. But he wrote a book of travel and adventure, one forgotten novel and some literary criticism before he began his grand historical opus, *France and England in North America.* Herman Melville was the author of a genial, if rather patronizing, review of his first book, which became famous as *The Oregon Trail* but which Parkman's publisher called *The California and Oregon Trail* to take advantage of gold fever when he brought it out in 1849. Melville reproved the young man for choosing a pretentious title and for treating the Indians contemptuously but cordially welcomed him into the literary fold. There he felt as welcome for his offerings of historical narrative as other members did for their poems, novels and essays. His welcome was no less warm for his impeccable credentials as a patrician among Boston Brahmins, but his standing as a man of letters had to be earned by the skill of his pen and the depth of his researches. Like fellow historians of the Romantic school, Parkman believed that the re-creation of the past demanded imaginative and literary art, and he was determined to be literary. He looked to such writers as Sir Walter Scott, James Fenimore Cooper and Lord Byron more than to historians for inspiration in his narrative style.

To measure up to such models and give scope to ambitions they inspired, the historian's subject had to be of a grand scale, with a stage large enough to accommodate vast events—the conquest of continents, the clash of cultures or struggles of mighty consequence between future and past or progress and reaction, perhaps even between right and wrong. Scenery for this stage should include nature in sublime and exotic forms and, if possible, some picturesque ruins. History as drama, especially moral drama, required a cast of characters that supplied not only villains but authentic heroes.

Parkman found his subject for *France and England in North America* in the forests of Canada and his native land but especially in France—France, with her absolute monarch and her ties with Rome, and her iron-willed explorers, chivalric warriors, indomitable priests and wily monks, all in splendid procession through nations and tribes of red savages, under gothic arches of virgin forests, down endless chains of lakes and unexplored rivers. (It is difficult to write about Parkman without reflecting his rhetoric.) No lack of heroes and heroic themes here. Between

1865 and 1892, Parkman published the seven parts of his classic history under separate titles. "Each work," he wrote, "is designed to be a unit in itself, independently of the rest; but the whole, taken as a series, will form a connected history of France in the New World."

I have said Parkman found his subject. Rather, his subject found him—seized, possessed and obsessed him wholly. "I was haunted with wilderness images day and night," he wrote. To the challenge of a heroic subject he gave a heroic response, for that is the only way this puritan's labors can be described. No historian, no writer I know, worked against greater odds. For forty years or more of his working life he was tormented by ailments of body and mind. These included semiblindness, arthritis, heart trouble, indigestion, pains of head and ear, mental confusion and relentless insomnia. "Four successive nights absolutely without sleep," he once wrote his doctor. The doctors scarred his neck with nitric acid and blistered his spine with red-hot irons, and he suffered on in silence. He lost his only son, his wife and temporarily his mind, he feared, within one year. For some years he could do no brain work whatever. For long periods he could read but one hour a day, in one-minute intervals, and for many years he could work only five minutes at a time and no more than two hours a day.

He worked against what he always called "the enemy"—his many adversities. If we choose to call them his neuroses, that makes them no less painful and crippling. His health was never fully restored, and yet his dedication never wavered. The great volumes of *France and England in North America* poured out through the 1860s', 70's and 80's until the vast work was completed the year before his death in 1893. He said he loathed research, and yet he did staggering amounts of it, scrupulously thorough, mainly without assistance, and he always relished new discoveries. Parkman was capable of irony and subtlety, even in the characterization of his most heroic figure, La Salle, the French explorer and colonizer of the Mississippi Valley. He could also manage humor and ambiguity. It was his style that put the greatest distance between this Romantic puritan and our time, a distance greater than that between us and Edward Gibbon, who wrote in the 18th century. Take this passage, for example, from Parkman's *Pioneers of France in the New World*:

> The French dominion is a memory of the past; and when we evoke its departed shades, they rise upon us from their graves in strange, romantic guise. Again their ghostly campfires seem to burn, and the fitful light is cast around on lord and vassal and black-robed priest, mingled with wild forms of savage warriors, knit in close fellowship on the same stern errand. A boundless vision grown upon us; an untamed continent; vast wastes of forest verdure; mountains silent in primeval sleep; river, lake, and glimmering pool; wilderness oceans mingling with the sky. . . . Plumed helmets gleamed in the shade of its forests, priestly vestments in its dens and fastnesses of ancient barbarism. Men steeped in antique learning, pale with the close breath of the cloister, here spent the noon and evening of their lives, ruled savage hordes with a mild, parental sway, and stood serene before the direst shapes of death. Men of courtly nature, heirs to the polish of a far-reaching ancestry, here, with their dauntless hardihood, put to shame the boldest sons of toil.

Before he wrote *Montcalm and Wolfe*, his masterpiece, Parkman had toned down his heroic prose and pruned some of his trite imagery, but he retained many attitudes and biases that nettle modern sensibilities and defy current fashions: for example, his sharp distinction between "civilization" and "savagery," instructive contrasts between Protestantism and Roman Catholicism, which he calls the Mother Church ("now a virgin, now a harlot"), and his stereotypes of national character. Worst of all was his portrayal of the Indian (with exceptions, to be sure) as a forest beast, "man, wolf, and devil, all in one," one of a race irrevocably and rightly doomed. Furthermore, on issues of his own time Parkman's views find little favor now. He detested the proletariat as cordially as he did the plutocracy, pronounced universal suffrage a failure, would deny the ballot to women and spurned mass democracy.

And so Parkman's books gathered dust on the shelves, and

he was put out of mind. Even historians, save for his devoted apostle Samuel Eliot Morison and a few others, ceased to read him. Great events, grand themes, heroic enterprises are not subjects favored by modern historians. With a few notable exceptions, they have said a long farewell to greatness, not only in their subjects but for themselves as well, and settled for something rather more mundane. Heroes have become the specialty of psychoanalysts. Narrative history itself has fallen under suspicion, and so have any professionals who might claim a "reading public" in the old sense. The notion that history could employ any art or be identified as "literature" finds few defenders.

After long neglect, however, Parkman is back in print, and I believe he will find readers again, perhaps more of them than the monographs of modern historians will find after another century has passed *them* by. If the man Parkman seemed sometimes touched with madness, he was also touched with greatness. So were his writings, and surely his subject was. I, for one, agree with David Levin, the editor of this Library of America edition, that Francis Parkman has earned a place in the New England Renaissance of the last century and deserves to be remembered along with such contemporaries as Hawthorne and Melville.

21

Henry Adams
(1838-1918)

ALTHOUGH THE LIBRARY OF AMERICA was planned to consist of literary classics, it has already found space for the masterpieces of two historians. The first of these was Francis Parkman's *France and England in North America.* There could have been little debate about Henry Adams's work on the age of Jefferson and Madison qualifying for a place beside Parkman as a classic or any question about its author being considered literary. But Adams (1838–1918), though only 15 years younger, was more than a literary generation removed from Parkman (1823–93), the great romantic.

Wit and irony were more the Adams style than awe and wonder. He loved paradox, and his mood shifted readily from derision to pity, from compassion to contempt. He was analytical rather than celebratory and liked to think of himself as a scientist. Henry Adams did his work during the transition from traditional to scientific history, and the change from history as an avocation of gentlemen to history as a profession of pedagogues. His allegiances remained divided. He trained historians at Harvard, but was never trained himself. He remained a man of letters and strove to become a man of science. The tensions between allegiances are among the sources of his appeal to modern readers.

Other sources of interest are the period he chose to write about and his personal and hereditary relation to his subject. The period was the first 16 years of the 19th century, and it happened to fall between the Administrations of John Adams, his great-grandfather, and John Quincy Adams, his grandfather. He was therefore an Adams writing on Jefferson, a scion of Federalists on their Republican foes, an heir to the failures of two Adams Administrations on the failures of two Jeffersonian Administrations and a New England Yankee on Virginia Southerners—with the passions of a civil war interventing. Adams the historian was acutely conscious of his audience. (His great-grandfather is not mentioned by name until after 555 pages of the original edition.) No filial piety or ancestral vindication here—at least none needlessly exposed.

Intrinsic interests of the period itself are of great appeal. It was then that Russia and America stood simultaneously on the periphery of Napoleon's turbulent empire, and both were impelled into new directions. It was this that inspired Tocqueville's prophecy that these two nations would one day share mastery of the world. Henry Adams's biographer, Ernest Samuels, has remarked that while Adams was as thoroughly American as his contemporary Tolstoy was Russian, the pages of the historian and those of the novelist, both dealing with the Napoleonic era, sounded the same themes: the insignificance of heroes, the power of mechanical determinism and the absence of free will in the historical process. And to both writers "history was a vast irony, a web of paradoxes."

It was Adams's not unwelcome duty to introduce his cast of Jeffersonian dreamers onto a European stage dominated by such colossal figures as Napoleon, Talleyrand, Pitt and Wellington: Bonaparte, "like Milton's Satan on his throne of state," and at his side "a figure even more sinister and almost as enigmatical"—Talleyrand. Into this company came Jefferson's emissaries with their faith in America's destiny, American exceptionalism and New World immunity from Old World wickedness. Like the Americans who were introduced to European society a century later in the novels of Adams's friend Henry James, their innocence was in for rude shocks and shattering experience.

Adams on Jefferson: our most philosophical historian on our most philosophical President; one aristocrat on another, all in the name of democracy. The portrait could not lack interest, however distorted. "According to the admitted standards of greatness, Jefferson was a great man," but. . . . Countless qualifications and elaborations followed. One trouble, admitted Adams, was that while other American statesmen "might be described in a parenthesis. . . . Jefferson could be painted only touch by touch, with a fine pencil," stroke upon stroke. As stroke followed touch and contradiction succeeded paradox, the portrait grew more enigmatic. With his "excessively refined" tastes and the instincts of "a liberal European nobleman," the Virginia *philosophe* knew that "to feed upon Homer and Horace were pleasures more to his mind than any to be found in a public assembly." Yet this paragon of elegant tastes regularly appeared in public clad in faded corduroy overalls and also made a political issue of ignoring protocol at his White House table by seating foreign dignitaries pell-mell.

Patronizing amusement gave way to impatience and animus as Adams observed that this "sunny and sanguine" philosopher-prince "generalized without careful analysis," was "a martyr to the disease of omniscience" and seemed "prepared to risk the fate of mankind" to prove a theory. Among his theories was one that "war was a blunder, an unnecessary risk" that had "made the Old World a hell, and frustrated the hopes of humanity." Now he proved ready to risk the honor and security of his country to avoid bloodshed "as though eternal peace were at hand, in a world torn by wars and convulsions and drowned in blood." As disasters and disgraces mounted in consequence, the philosopher-historian sometimes stooped to satire and mock heroics, but while the philosopher-statesman is made to appear quixotic, he comes off, like Don Quixote, with a modicum of respect and affection mixed with the ridicule. "Poor dear old Jefferson!" Adams once exclaimed in a private letter.

Most of all, Henry Adams savored the multiple ironies of his tale and obviously relished the telling. He loved such vignettes as the one from Jefferson's first inaugural where "the assembled senators looked up at three men who profoundly disliked and distrusted each other": Jefferson in the center, Vice President Aaron Burr on the right, and Chief Justice John Marshall on the left. The last, an immovable rock of Federalism, "had no superior, perhaps no equal" and only one weakness— "he detested Thomas Jefferson." He was, of course, not the only one. Three months after the inauguration, Theodore Dwight delivered an oration in New Haven in which he declared "the great object of Jacobinism" and of Thomas Jefferson's Government of "blockheads and knaves" was "to destroy every trace of civilization in the world, and to force mankind back into a savage state. . . . Can the imagination paint anything more dreadful on this side of hell?"

Yet Jefferson's first Administration was a sensational success and a personal triumph, enough to turn the head of any President and more than enough, in Adams's view, to turn this President's. He fulfilled all his hopes; annihilated opposition and won re-election by a landslide in which even Massachusetts and Connecticut joined. It was obvious that the people were more pleased with the new President "than they ever had been with the old"—that is, with John Adams. But for Henry Adams the cream of the jest was that Jefferson's success came at the cost of principle, that the more he betrayed Jeffersonian Republicanism and adopted Adams's Federalism the more successes he enjoyed. And in the historian's view, "it was hard to see how any President could have been more Federalist than Jefferson himself."

Adams cited as evidence Jefferson's enlargement of the national debt, support and energetic use of the Navy, extension of the national bank and the huge increase in the powers of the national Government. No instance of the expanded Government powers was nearly so great or so popular as the Louisiana Purchase, which vastly more than doubled the national domain. By this act, as Adams put it, "Jefferson bought a foreign colony without its consent and against its will, annexed it to the United

States by an act which he said made blank paper of the Constitution; and then he who had found his predecessors too monarchical . . . made himself monarch of the new territory, and wielded over it, against its protests, the powers of its old kings." There could hardly have been a more regal exercise of Federalist doctrine, and yet it "sounded the death-knell of Federalism altogether" by stealing the old party's thunder.

Ironies of the Louisiana Purchase do not end at the three-mile limit. They collected at the heart of the Napoleonic empire, and Adams squeezed the last precious drop out of them. "The sale of Louisiana," he wrote, "was the turning point in Napoleon's career; no true Frenchman forgave it." But why should the mightiest emperor in the world at the height of his power sell for a song the largest and potentially richest colony of his domain? The reason was that the French colonial system centered not on Louisiana but on Haiti, which Louisiana was meant to feed and fortify. But French control of the rich colony was lost in a slave rebellion led by Toussaint L'Ouverture, that "miserable Negro," as Bonaparte called him. So it was that the Jeffersonians owed the vast colony, to be used in part for the expansion of slavery, "to the desperate courage of five hundred thousand Haytian negroes who would not be enslaved." Count Tolstoy would have relished Adams's account of both Napoleon's frustration and the triumph of Jeffersonian democracy.

In Jefferson's second Administration the ambiguities multiplied, and the cutting edge of the ironies was this time turned against him. This time he was enforcing Republican principles by Federalist means. Abhorring war, he resorted to stopping trade by embargo rather than fight Britain for seizing American ships. As it turned out, the embargo proved more expensive in money and more destructive of personal liberties, party principle and political support than war would have been. The President's popularity vanished and his reputation dissolved in ruins. "I felt the foundations of the government shaken under my feet by the New England townships," wrote Jefferson. And yet New England actually suffered less than other regions, both because of smuggling and through the monopoly of American markets the embargo conferred on New England manufactures. The real burden fell on the South, and most heavily on the President's home state of Virginia. He left office "as strongly and almost as generally disliked as the least popular President." The historian undoubtedly had in mind John Adams when *he* left office.

James Madison inherited the failure of Jefferson's embargo and continued to suffer the consequences. Adams treated Madison with even less patience and sympathy than he had Jefferson, and underrated him even more. It is of course true that Madison was the less attractive figure of the two and that he was miscast for the role he had to play in leading the country to war. For that was what the peace policy came to—war with a powerful Britain, war without the preparation Madison urged on Congress, a bungled war with many humiliations. These included the burning of the White House and the Capitol by the British, the flight of President and Cabinet to the Virginia woods and the threat of New England's secession. Toward the end President Madison was described to a member of Jefferson's Cabinet as "miserably shattered and woe-be-gone. In short, he looked heart-broken." Peace came without the gaining of a single war aim, but not before a series of notable American military victories in the final months gave the bungled war a blaze of glory and the illusion of a triumph. The final irony was that the apparent loser of the war was to emerge as a world power destined to eclipse its European rivals.

Had Henry Adams not cultivated so many other arts and fields of learning he would not have been so richly gifted as a historian. These volumes of history were preceded in the Library of America by another volume of Adams's writing that included two novels he published anonymously; an autobiography, printed privately and published posthumously; and two long poems, one of which appeared after his death. These in addition to his *Mont Saint Michel and Chartres* on the Middle Ages. Yet Adams knew that he was staking his claim to the enduring interest of posterity on his work on the Administrations of Jefferson and Madison. To listen to him one might think he wrote it off as a failure. He liked to say he did not know ten people who had read it. It is a mistake, however, to listen to Adams on Adams without full knowledge of his habit of self-deprecation. He by no means considered it a failure, even though he said some foolish things about it and about history writing generally.

But how can we now, in an age of new history and new methods, still pronounce this long narrative traditional history, written a century ago and out of print for several decades, a great classic? It is, to be sure, mainly concerned with political, military and diplomatic developments and the elites who directed them—or thought they did. It is one thing, however, to say these subjects do not include all worthwhile history—and quite another to say they are not worth including. In fact, national leadership and government may tell us more about a country than any other aspect of its history. And when the pen is in the hand of a master of English prose, a master whose very name opened for the first time to an American historian the secret archives of Paris, London, Madrid and Seville, it is more understandable how he could have produced a history yet to be replaced.

Before we risk becoming patronizing over the antique merits of an old master or apologetic about his shortcomings, it would be well to read the first six and the last four chapters of this magisterial work, all of which are devoted to kinds of history other than the traditional—social, economic, technological and intellectual included. They do not include any algebraic equations or regression analyses. Nor do they speak up for current fashions, fads, ideologies or worthy causes, for the promotion of which much history now seems to be written. But long after the causes are won, or forgotten, Adams's history will be read, admired and remembered.

22

In Memoriam

Richard Hofstadter
(1916–1970)

The following is a tribute read at a memorial service for Richard Hofstadter held in New York shortly after his death.

I SPEAK IN THE PRESENCE OF THOSE WHO knew and loved Richard Hofstadter best and therefore with the knowledge that nothing I can say will fully express their sense of loss and grief. I will not even be able to put my own feelings into words, much less the feelings of those of you who have known him better and longer, even less those of his family. He was too much a part of our own lives, too much a point of reference in our thoughts, too deeply fixed in our hearts, and the pain of his loss is too raw and too recent to be expressed, much less healed, by words.

My own friendship with Dick goes back to a chance meeting in Washington at the end of the Second World War. It developed over the years and has continued for a quarter of a century until his death. It never seemed to be handicapped by the considerable differences in our backgrounds and points of view, and I am as certain as I am of anything that it was never interrupted or threatened by sharp disagreements over our common field of scholarship, even those publicly expressed. It was the very assurance of this that made our friendship possible and enriched its quality. One of his finest traits was his talent not only for giving but for receiving friendship and love.

Like others of his friends, I learned to understand and appreciate his unusual qualities of mind and spirit. They were not always readily apparent. What might first appear to be a chronic melancholia really masked a mischievous wit and a marvelous gift for spotting the absurd. They are the talents out of which great satirists and caricaturists are made. His friends say that the history profession robbed the stage of one of its most gifted mimes. He could imitate anything—domestic animals, public figures, private acquaintances—nothing seemed beyond his range.

As a historian he devoted much of his attention to the odd, the warped, the zanies, and the crazies of American life—left, right, and middle. Once on a quiet summer evening he remarked that the bobwhite across the field (or was it a whippoorwill?) was just like one of his "one-idea men." Dick seemed to have a solid understanding, if not a private affection, for his one-idea men. He combined this with a mastery of the common touch that was essential to a historian destined, as he once said, "to look at a society like ours from its nether end."

An intensely private man, he stubbornly resisted public appearances, large conventions, and elaborate conferences. At any conference he did attend he was likely to be the one with the most important things to say and at the same time the one to say the least. He was mercifully spared the public roles in the history profession to which he would have been destined.

He was also spared the pitfalls of dogma and theory and fad by his native skepticism and his abundant good sense. The originator of many new theories and methods of historical analysis, he never became a crusader for any of them or a prisoner of any of them. Critical of many aspects of American life, he never joined the fashionable cult of anti-Americanism. A devoted teacher and friend of students, he never joined the youth cult in juvenophilia.

The foremost historian of anti-intellectualism, he rejected the notion that alienation was the only honorable stance of the intellectual.

Whatever the ultimate verdict on his historical scholarship may be, it was already apparent during his life that he had become a figure of pivotal significance in the history of American history. More clearly than any other historian he marked the transition from the Progressive to the post-Progressive era of historiography. As symbolically as any he signified the shift of perspective from the province to the metropolis. And more fully and magnificently than any he exemplified the break from the tradition that bound the professional historian to a restricted period or region and a specialized reading public.

Any one of these rebellions would have filled a normal career, and it is no wonder that the three of them together determined much of the shape and content of his voluminous writings. The rebellion from his Progressive forebears and the struggle for generational identity began early, continued throughout his life, and left us some of the richest historiographical criticism in our literature. His effort to redress the historical perspective long weighted on the side of rural, provincial, Protestant, fundamentalist America has left us a perceptive revision of American political and social history. His adventurous experiments with social science concepts and theories have inspired fruitful techniques and new viewpoints.

To fellow craftsmen, perhaps his revolt against the tradition of specialization was at once the most impressive and the most controversial. No such defiance of tradition could escape challenge, and critics were not lacking. But the rebel went his way undeterred. He followed his first book, which was on the nineteenth century, with a second deeply engaged with the seventeenth and eighteenth centuries, followed by extensive excursions through the twentieth. Next to his last book took off from the eighteenth century, and his last published was inspired, as much of his history was, by preoccupations with the present.

It seems almost unkind to speak of Richard Hofstadter as a fulfilled historian—when he was cut down so cruelly in his prime, deeply engaged in what appeared to be his most ambitious and promising work. Yet in quantity as well as quality, in grace of style as well as in subtlety of scholarship, in scope of subject as well as in variety of method, the richness and abundance of his creative work proclaim a valorous fulfillment, a great victory of the spirit, a moral triumph that is rare.

Through it all those who knew him best could but marvel at the quiet passion and dedication he threw into his work. There was nothing grim or routine or desperate about it. Rather there was an undertone of gaiety and confidence, very often a spirit of play, serious, but still play. But there was always the same unrelenting self-discipline.

He was not always an easy man to vacation with. The beaches tended to be strewn with bibliographical disputation, and languorous tropical mornings tended to be disturbed by the clatter of a typewriter. He gave us all an inferiority complex—which we felt we thoroughly deserved.

Work was indeed a kind of religion with Dick—not pious, not proselytizing, not prideful, but still something transcending the flesh and something distinctly of the spirit. The single aspect of the youth rebellion that troubled him most was the apparent defection from the discipline of creative work.

The only complaint about himself that escaped his lips during his final ordeal with cancer came when he was compelled to pack up his unfinished manuscript, knowing, or half-knowing, he might never return to it. That complaint took the form of one round oath. And it was not about his own fate, but the fate of his work.

In a later and more desperately physical phase of his ordeal, his wife involuntarily exclaimed at some superhuman exertion he was making. "I never had a problem about will," he replied. It was the flesh that failed him, and the flesh alone.

Toward the end of *The Republic*, Plato attempts to sum up the ideal aims of the discipline of education. In doing so he puts the following words, according to a recent version, into the mouth of Socrates:

The wise man will give all his powers, all his days, to making the state in his soul more just, more temperate, and more wise, and give the highest place to whatever will make it so. And as to the outcome of it all in the opinions others form of him, and the rewards and honors they offer him, he will keep the same measure before his eyes, and prize only what will make him a better man. In public and private life he will put aside all that might overturn the constitution of his soul.

And that is the way I would like to remember my friend Dick Hofstadter.

David Morris Potter
(1910–1971)

A more formal obituary, prepared for the Year Book of the American Philosophical Society, the following tribute to an old friend omits such personal references to our relationship as characterized the preceding piece on Richard Hofstadter. Yet my friendship with David Potter was older and longer and at times closer. That began in college days at Emory, was kept alive by visits, deepened after we both became historians, and continued until his death, only a few months after that of Hofstadter. Both men were at the height of their powers.

IN 1969 SIR DENIS BROGAN OF CAMBRIDGE UNIVERSITY described David Morris Potter as "one of the truly great interpreters of American history." This may have come as a surprise to those outside his discipline, for Potter never sought or won a very wide reading public. It would not surprise his fellow historians in America, however, for they were in the process of electing him president of their two major professional organizations, the American Historical Association and the Organization of American Historians. He held both of these offices at the time of his death on February 18, 1971. It was part of the poignancy of his sudden loss from cancer that he lived neither to complete these offices nor to finish his major life work on the background of the Civil War. We are assured, however, that it is so near completion that it will be possible to publish later and that another volume of his essays will also appear posthumously.[1]

David Potter was born in Augusta, Georgia, December 6, 1910, grew up there, and took his bachelor's degree at Emory University in 1932. During and immediately after his graduate training at Yale he taught at the University of Mississippi for two years and at Rice Institute for four years. His native region left its mark upon him in many recognizable traits which he wore lightly but never denied. He also interested himself professionally in Southern history, but made his major interest and earned his reputation in national history. In 1942 he joined the Yale History Department, where he was to remain for twenty years. During that period he also served as Harmsworth Professor of American History at Oxford University, 1947–1948, as editor of the *Yale Review,* 1949–1951, and for several years headed the Department of American Studies. In 1961 he resigned to accept the Coe Professorship of American History at Stanford University, which he held for the remaining ten years of his life. He was elected a member of the American Philosophical Society in 1965.

The main influence on the historian in his student days seems to have been that of Ulrich Bonnell Phillips, the leading authority on American slavery. Phillips also came from Georgia and was still teaching at Yale when Potter arrived for graduate work, though he died two years later. That the apprentice was apostle of no man and follower of no "school" was apparent immediately on the publication of his first book *Lincoln and His Party in the Secession Crisis* in 1942. A revision of his doctoral dissertation, this substantial work was obviously, as Denis Brogan has said, "a very remarkable performance." Only thirty-two at the

---

[1] The work was completed and edited by Don E. Fehrenbacher: David M. Potter, *The 'Impending' Crisis, 1848–1861* (New York, 1976); The other book, also edited by Fehrenbacher: David M. Potter, *History and American Society: Essays of David M. Potter* (New York, 1973).

time of its publication, the young author demonstrated a ripeness of learning, a mastery of craftsmanship, and a maturity of mind far beyond his years.

In the same book Potter exhibited many of the gifts and distinguishing attitudes that characterize all his work. Among these are a low-keyed but elegant style, a scrupulous disdain of eloquence, rhetorical tricks and moral stridency, and a profound suspicion of all "lessons" and assumptions of teleology in history. Especially notable was his wariness of hindsight among historians, the fallacy of explaining the present by the past, the assumption that "what happened" had to happen, and the habit of making historical figures culpable for acting as if things might have turned out differently. To understand fully what did happen, Potter maintained that the historian must also explore the possibilities and plausible alternatives as they presented themselves to historical actors. Thus plausibilities and possibilities—even fantasies—as well as actualities were subjects essential to historical investigation.

Potter brought to bear this searching skepticism and insight upon the hoary and hairy problems of the Secession Crisis of 1860–1861. One of the most often debated, frequently investigated, and hotly disputed subjects up to that time, the old crisis along with the threadbare evidence and the worn documents took on new life and fresh meaning in the hands of the young historian. He not only disclosed new meaning in the old evidence, but brought in abundant new evidence of his own finding. Under his scrutiny old certainties and "inevitabilities" dissolved, new uncertainties and doubts arose, conventional assumptions and polemical postures proved untenable. In short, an old problem became a new problem, or rather many new problems.

Much of Potter's revisionary reassessment of the Secession Crisis followed from his determined rejection of "hindsight." Denying the forbidden knowledge to his historical protagonists and their contemporaries as well as to himself had the effect of restoring many blurred and neglected realities of 1860–1861. Lincoln was not the President he was to become. The crisis was not a "war crisis," for war was not expected. The "mandate" the Republicans received in 1860 was narrowly limited and un-defined. The party itself was badly divided and leaderless. The North tragically misunderstood the temper of the South, the South that of the North, and neither grasped the consequences of its own mood nor their common proximity to the brink. The great actors of both sides moved in an impenetrable fog of peace, without any script, with lines improvised and often nonsensical. Though the wish for compromise predominated in the North, the compromisers knew neither what the North would be willing to offer nor what the South would be willing to accept. "And the war came"—unwanted, unexpected, and unprepared for.

Potter's revision has held up under criticism for thirty years and remains a lasting contribution to American history. But students have rightly seen it as more than that. For it is also a profound statement on the nature of history, on the way it should be written and read and interpreted. These insights pervaded his subsequent work and guided his teaching, his historical criticism, and his writings on historiography. Although he continued his research and teaching in the field of sectional conflict and civil war, it was the problems of historiography, particularly as related to the social sciences, that became the subject of his next book.

People of Plenty: Economic Abundance and the American Character, published in 1954, grew out of a series of lectures Potter gave at the University of Chicago in 1950. It was the kind of subject for which his vast store of learning and diversity of intellectual interests uniquely equipped him. Analyses of previous generalizations about national character produced brilliant chapters on the shortcomings of both historians and social scientists in this field. Wholly hospitable to insights from the social scientists, he believed that interdisciplinary influences should not be all one way—that the social scientists had much to learn from historians, as well as vice versa. Not content with negative criticism, he offered and tested his own hypothesis that "the unusual plenty of available goods or other usable wealth which has prevailed in America" had had important effects in shaping national culture and national character.

There has rarely if ever been a more fruitful conjunction of the historical mind and the social science disciplines than in *People of Plenty*. After an analysis of the nature of American abundance through the nation's history, there follow astute chapters on the way in which abundance has shaped and influenced mobility and status in this country and remade the social structure, how the same influence gave the concept of "democracy" a distinctive meaning in America, and how it has led to miscalculations of the "American mission" in matters of foreign policy. One chapter reassesses the frontier thesis as "only one phase or one manifestation of the factor of abundance." Another treats national advertising in the formation of personality and its role in the transition from a producer-oriented to a consumer-oriented society. And finally, returning to basic influences on the molding of national character, Potter takes up the impact of abundance on the rearing of the American child. In the course of these lectures he had invaded the fields and exploited the methods of anthropologists, economists, political scientists, sociologists, and psychologists. In doing so he had demonstrated to the hilt that if "behavioral scientists may use the culture to explain human behavior, they must rely upon history to explain the culture." He had also supplied a model and inspired a school of interdisciplinary studies.

As important and seminal as these excursions and explorations proved to be, they constituted a diversion rather than a change of course or a fundamental shift of interest on the part of the historian. As he wrote in 1968, over his long span of academic experience he had "spent a great deal of time teaching about the South and pondering its history, its problems, its evils, its anachronisms, its graces, and its agonizing situation." One consequence of these concerns was a considerable body of essays and papers published in various places, many of which were collected and published in 1968 under the title, *The South and Sectional Conflict*. They fall into three categories, "The Nature of Southernism," "Three Historical Forays," and "The Crisis of the Union."

While admitting that "the South now shares increasingly in

a national way of doing things" that has reduced the level of regional distinctiveness, he conceives it to be the task of Southern historians to "focus their analysis at points where the conditions of the Southern region differ from those of other regions and should concentrate their attention upon historical developments which are relevant to these differences." With his characteristic combination of fairness, generosity, and astute criticism, he reviews attempts of other historians to fathom the "enigma" of Southern distinctiveness. He then persuasively argues, though never develops fully, his own theory that the persistence of folk culture among whites and blacks of the South is the root of regional distinctiveness. Perhaps in no other of his writings are his remarkable powers of historical analysis and criticism displayed more impressively than in his essay "The Historian's Use of Nationalism and Vice Versa." Here he demonstrates how the modern historian, caught in the ideology of the secular religions of nationalism and liberalism, has allowed them to warp and bias his reading of history. Potter's insights apply generally to the problems of modern history, but are illustrated in the context of the dual loyalties of the South during the sectional crisis in American history.

Those who knew David Potter best and most appreciated the rare qualities of his wisdom realized that he did not always apply the same measure of sagacity to the management of his own affairs. Too often he bent his energies to tasks that might have better been left to colleagues of lesser talents. He lavished an excessive amount of his time on teaching, academic chores, and generous help to his students. His last years were tragically darkened by the illness and suicide of his wife. His major work on the coming of the Civil War went forward, but at a slower pace than it otherwise would. Until it is published, the full measure of his stature and the greatness of his powers will not be generally appreciated.

Provenance
of the Contents

All but two of the essays in this volume have been previously published. The only editorial changes have been minor ones made in order to eliminate anachronisms, such as reference to a book as "forthcoming" that has already appeared, or duplications such as a quotation that has been previously used. Should the item have been published in more than one form or under a different title, this will be indicated along with citation of the original publication.

1. "The Future of the Past." *American Historical Review*, 75 (1970), 711–26.
2. "Clio With Soul." *Journal of American History*, 56 (1969), 5–20. This also appeared under the title "American History (White Man's Version) Needs an Infusion of Soul," *New York Times Magazine*, April 20, 1969, pp. 32–33, 108–14.
3. "The Future of Southern History." In *The Future of History: Essays in the Vanderbilt University Centennial Symposium*. Edited by Charles Dalzell. Nashville, 1977. Pp. 135–49.
4. "The Age of Reinterpretation." *American Historical Review*, 66 (1960), 1–19; later published with some revisions under the same title as a pamphlet by the American Historical Association in its Service Center for Teachers of History, Publication Number 35 (1968). It is used here as revised in the second form cited.
5. "The Aging of America," *American Historical Review*, 82 (1977), 583–94. A somewhat shorter version entitled "The Graying of America: Reflections upon Our Most Enduring Myth As We Put the Bicentennial Behind Us, and Move On," appeared in the *New York Times*, December 29, 1976. The version cited first is used here.

6. "The Fall of the American Adam." *American Academy of Arts and Sciences Bulletin*, 35 (November, 1981), 24–34. A slightly shorter version under the same title appeared in *The New Republic*, December 2, 1981, pp. 13–16. The first of the two is reprinted here.

7. "The Comparability of American History." In *The Comparative Approach to American History*. Edited by C. Vann Woodward. New York, 1968. Pp. 3–17.

8. "Emancipations and Reconstructions: A Comparative Study." Paper presented at the XIII International Congress of Historical Sciences, Moscow, and published by Navka Publishing House, 1970. In revised form under the title "The Price of Freedom," it appeared in *What Was Freedom's Price?* edited by David G. Sansing. Jackson, Mississippi, 1978. Pp. 93–113. The second version is used here under the original title.

9. "The Lash and the Knout." *The New York Review of Books*, November 16, 1987.

10. "Reconstruction: A Counterfactual Playback." Although this article has not been previously published, some of the comparisons made in it have been used elsewhere.

11. "Why the Southern Renaissance?" *Virginia Quarterly Review*, 51 (1975), 222–39.

12. "History in Robert Penn Warren's Fiction." Heretofore unpublished, this paper was read at a conference on Warren's work with scholars from the Soviet Union and the United States at Yale University in 1987.

13. "Fictional History and Historical Fiction." A review essay on William Safire's novel, *Freedom* in *The New York Review of Books*, November 16, 1987. Pp. 38–43.

14. "Mary Chesnut in Search of Her Genre." *The Yale Review*, (1984) 199–209.

15. "The Antislavery Myth." *The American Scholar*, 31 (1962), 316–27.

16. "Southerners Versus the Southern Establishment." The 1987 Elson Lecture for the Atlanta Historical Society, *Atlanta History*, 31 (1987), 6–16.

17. "*Strange Career* Critics: Long May They Persevere." *Journal of American History*, 75 (1988), pp. 857–68. A response invited by the editor of the *Journal* to criticism appearing in the same issue.

18. "A Short History of American History." *New York Times Book Review*, August 8, 1982.

19. "History and the Third Culture." *Journal of Contemporary History*, 3 (April, 1968), 23–35.

20. "Francis Parkman." This paper was given on May 17, 1983, at the Smithsonian Institution in the Frank Nelson Doubleday Lecture Series. Slightly expanded, it appeared in the *New York Times Book Review*, July 3, 1983. The original version is used here.

21. "Henry Adams." A review essay on The Library of America edition of his *History of the United States of America During the Administrations of Thomas Jefferson and James Madison*, in the *New York Times Book Review*, July 6, 1986, under a longer title.

22. *"In Memoriam"*

"Richard Hofstadter (1916–1970)." *The New York Review of Books*, December 3, 1970.

"David M. Potter (1910–1971)." *Year Book of the American Philosophical Society* (1971), pp. 139–43.

Index

DATE DUE